S0-EJJ-256

Principles of Soil Conservation and Water Management

Principles of Soil Conservation and Water Management

H.R. ARAKERI
ROY DONAHUE

ROWMAN & ALLANHELD
PUBLISHERS

ROWMAN & ALLANHELD

Published in the United States of America in 1984
by Rowman & Allanheld, Publishers
(A division of Littlefield, Adams & Company)
81 Adams Drive, Totowa, New Jersey 07512
by arrangement with Oxford & IBH Publishing Co.,
66 Janpath, New Delhi 110001

Library of Congress Cataloging in Publication Data

Arakeri, H.R. (Hanumappa Ramappa), 1919-1983
Principles of soil conservation and water management.

Includes bibliographical references.
1. Soil conservation. 2. Water conservation.
I. Donahue, Roy Luther, 1908- . II. Title.
S623.A65 1984 631.4 83-27044
ISBN 0-8576-7350-2

PRINTED IN INDIA

Introduction

Khana wrote in circa 600 A.D.

> Ridges made of earth should at first be constructed for the purpose of dividing the fields and for conserving water in the fields, and then the seeds are to be sown.

The ridges mentioned by Khana are now known as bunds or terraces. On sloping cropland, bunds are needed more than ever to conserve soil and water because soils are farmed more intensively.

A viable alternative to high bunds, however, are being researched by the International Crops Research Institute for the Semi-arid Tropics, with headquarters near Hyderabad, Andhra Pradesh, India.* These alternatives include wide, raised beds, known by the name of "broad-bed-and-furrow" system. The research is being conducted on Vertisols (Black Cotton Soils) and on Alfisols (Red Loams).

Because research on soil conservation and water management is continuing in India and throughout the world, this book can never be the ultimate truth on all phases of the subject. Whereas the principles of soil genesis, taxonomy, and physical and chemical properties will not change over time; it is anticipated that recommended practices of soil conservation and water management to be modified in time by ongoing research.

H.R. Arakeri
Roy Donahue

*Annual reports for the year 1979 and thereafter for the International Crops Research Institute for the Semi-arid Tropics, Patancheru Post Office, Andhra Pradesh, 502 324 India.

Contents

CHAPTER 1

Soil-Water-Production

1:1 INTRODUCTION

Soil nourishes life through the medium of water. All life on earth requires essential elements that come from soil. These chemical elements move from soil to plants as ions and molecules in a water solution. Plants are eaten by animals and people and hence the same soil elements provide essential nourishment—also through water as a solvent. Even fishes and other aquatic life feed on plants nourished by soil nutrients dissolved in water. Soil and water are thus the bases of plant and animal production and therefore of civilization itself.

Supplemental essentials for productive plant growth are oxygen and carbon dioxide from air, and heat and light from the sun.

The kinds of soil and water existing in an area and the skill with which they are managed will determine whether people in that region have production and prosperity or destruction and adversity. The ideal ambient terrestrial environment for maximum productivity consists of a rich loam soil high in organic matter lying on a gentle slope, with temperatures favorable for plant growth, and maintained constantly moist (but not wet) by adequate rainfall or irrigation water of suitable quality. However, most soils of the world are less than ideal for optimum plant production because they are too shallow, clayey, sandy, stony, sloping, cold, and/or too dry, and with inadequate rainfall or inferior irrigation water. Present land use pattern in the world is as given in Table 1.1.

Nevertheless, scientific and appropriate research and management can achieve a high level of productivity and a stable and prosperous civilization with less-than-ideal temperatures, soils, and water.

1:2 DOCUMENTED SUCCESS

On adverse soils, scientists around the world are successfully selecting, breed-

Table 1.1. Land use pattern in the world (1978)

Land use	Area in hectares (1000)
Total area	13,390,315
Land area	13,073,597
Arable land	1,326,320
Land under permanent crops	87,909
Permanent meadows and pastures	3,150,862
Forests and Woodland	4,056,673
Other land	4,451,833
Irrigated land	200,913

Source: FAO, "1979 Production Yearbook". Vol: 33, FAO, Rome, Italy 1980.

ing, and testing higher yielding and better quality food crops that are adapted to adverse climates, pests, and soils. Documented examples of such successes follow:

Rice cultivars have been developed that are lodge-resistant; insensitive to length of day; capable of tolerating colder climates; producing high yields with low levels of soil nitrogen, phosphorus, potassium, sulfur, iron, and zinc; high soil concentrations of soluble iron, aluminum, manganese, salinity, acidity, alkalinity, and sodicity; resistance to drought and to many nematodes, insects and diseases; and resistance to being eaten by rodents.[1, 2, 3, 4, 5, 6, 7, 8]

Wheat cultivars have been improved by selection and breeding to yield satisfactorily on Oxisols low in phosphorus and high in soluble aluminum; to resist lodging; and to withstand stresses of drought, low temperatures, many insect pests, and resistant to the three types of wheat rust.[9, 10, 11]

Corn cultivars selected and bred for contrasting soils in various climatic zones of tropical lowlands, tropical highlands, and temperate regions; drought tolerance; fewer days to maturity; several altitudes and latitudes; many mean growing season temperatures; variable grain color; resistance to specific insects and diseases; and for improved quality of the protein of the kernel.[9]

Triticale, a hybrid created by crossing wheat and rye, outyields wheat on Oxisols and Ultisols in Brazil, Kenya, Ethiopia, Tanzania, Pakistan, Nepal, and India.[9]

Pigeonpea grain yields on Vertisols and Alfisols in south central India were *not* increased by 20 or 200 kg/ha of nitrogen (N) fertilizer. Furthermore, the N fertilizer *decreased* natural rhizobial nodulation by 48 percent. In another experiment in India, pigeonpea yields were higher when planted on north-south rows than on east-west rows.[12] Corn in India gave similar results.[13]

Tapioca (cassava) yields on Oxisols and Ultisols (soil pH 4 to 5) in Colombia, South America were more than doubled with an application of 300 kg/ha of P_2O_5 fertilizer. Minor responses were also obtained with lime, nitrogen, potassium, and zinc. The tapioca plant has a unique tolerance for as much as 80 percent soil saturation of aluminum. This concentration of soil aluminum is toxic to most plants.[14]

Similar successes are being repeated in nearly every country in the world. However, people are multiplying faster than food, feed, and fiber to sustain them at a minimum human level. The only logical answer is to educate and train more soil scientists, more plant breeders, and those in related disciplines and to inspire them with a world view and a dedication to help people to increase productivity by a more efficient management of soils, water, and plants.

Increased efforts are called for to develop and transfer appropriate agricultural technology for use by millions of farmers all over the world. The World Bank in its policy paper published in 1981 noted that, "Carefully implemented agricultural research can be an important contributor to the achievement of key development objectives." It is further stated that, "A desirable investment target for research for many countries with poorly developed agricultural research systems could be an annual expenditure (recurring and capital) equivalent to about 2 percent of agricultural gross domestic product (GDP)." At present, the investment in developing countries on agricultural research is much below this level.

1: 3 SOILS, WATER, AND PLANTS

Soils, water, and plants are the world's greatest natural resources; without them there would be no animals nor people. Managed for *long-term* productivity, there can be abundance for everyone; managed for *immediate* profits (like the stock markets of the world); soils will become impoverished and erode, waters will disappear as in a desert, and plants will wither and die.

Proper management of soils, water and plants has sometimes been defined as, "use without abuse—in perpetuity." Efficient management of soils, water, and plants starts with scientific knowledge of the essential elements for plant growth and in what form they are absorbed. Plants are the necessary link between soil, water, air, and sunlight and the food, feed, and fiber crucial for well-being and survival of people.

Green plants require only 16 of the 88 elements occurring in nature, although some scientists believe they need four more (sodium, cobalt, silicon, and vanadium). These essential elements and the chemical ionic or molecular forms in which they are absorbed by plant roots, leaves, and by some kinds of stems are as follows:

From air and water, plants absorb hydrogen (H^+ and HOH), oxygen (O_2, OH^-, CO_3^{2-}, SO_4^{2-}).

The primary nutrients from soils and fertilizers are nitrogen (NH_4^+ and NO_3^-), phosphorus ($H_2PO_4^-$ and HPO_4^{2-}), and potassium (K^+).

The secondary nutrients absorbed by plants from soils and fertilizers are magnesium (Mg^{2+}), calcium (Ca^{2+}), and sulfur (SO_4^{2-}).

The micronutrients absorbed by plants from soils and fertilizers are chlorine (Cl^-), copper (Cu^{2+}), boron [$H_2BO_3^-$ and $B(OH)_4^-$], iron (Fe^{2+} and Fe^{3+}), manganese (Mn^{2+}), molybdenum (MoO_4^{2-}), and zinc (Zn^{2+}).

Since plants are the "pipeline" through which animals and people obtain nourishment from the soil, it is necessary to know if the elements essential for plants are identical to those needed by animals and people. The answer is "minus 2 plus 6." Animals and people *do not need* boron and molybdenum, as do plants, but *do need* sodium, iodine, selenium, vanadium, chromium, and cobalt which are not essential for plants. Although not required, plants absorb many nutrients which they do not need, including the six essential for animals and man. The conclusion is that many animals and some people are able to thrive by eating *only* plants.

Plants use these 16 elements and heat and light to manufacture foods, starting with hexose sugar, as illustrated by this simplified diagram of photosynthesis:

$$\underset{\text{From air}}{6\,CO_2} + \underset{\text{From soil}}{12\,H_2O} \xrightarrow[\text{Chlorophyll in plant}]{\text{Light heat energy from sun}} \underset{\text{Hexose sugar}}{C_6H_{12}O_6} + \underset{\text{Oxygen}}{6\,O_2}$$

Simple hexose sugars are then transformed to sucrose ($C_{12}H_{22}O_{11}$), more complex sugars, starch, cellulose, and pectin. Likewise, amino acids, fatty acids, glycerol [$C_3H_5(OH)_3$], true fats (triglycerides), waxes, and phospholipids either are produced directly or are synthesized from products of photosynthesis. About 90 percent of all dry matter of green plants is manufactured during photosynthesis.

The plant obtains its carbon from the carbon dioxide of the air, oxygen from atmospheric and soil air, and hydrogen from soil water. The other 13 essential nutrients are absorbed in ionic form primarily through plant roots growing in the soil. Nutrient uptake includes three mechanisms: mass flow, diffusion, and root interception.

1) *Mass flow.* The movement toward roots of plant nutrients dissolved in the soil water. Essential elements in the soil solution around the plant roots are absorbed as cations and anions.

2) *Diffusion.* The movement of nutrient ions from the soil solution into root cells by *passive* or *active* absorption without mass flow of water. In *passive*

absorption, each nutrient cation or anion moves independently from an area of high concentration of that nutrient to an area of low concentration of the same nutrient. In *active* absorption, ions move into cells against a concentration gradient using energy from respiration.

3) *Root interception.* The extension (growth) of plant roots into new soil areas where untapped supplies of nutrients are available. Roots then absorb nutrients as in mass flow and/or diffusion.

For the proper nutrition and growth of corn, for example, the relative amounts of selected nutrients absorbed by the three mechanisms of nutrient uptake are as follows:[15]

Nitrogen, sulfur—mostly mass flow.
Phosphorus, potassium—mostly diffusion
Calcium, magnesium, sulfur, molybdenum—mass flow and root interception.

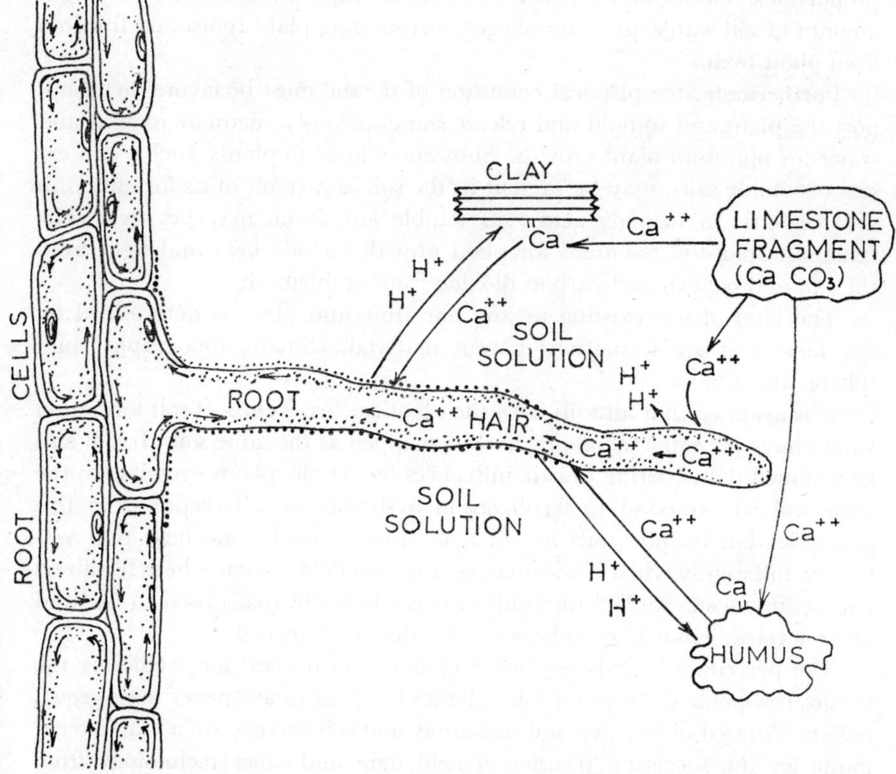

Fig. 1.1. Schematic drawing showing how a root hair absorbs nutrients from clay and humus surfaces and from the soil solution.

Plant root hairs absorb nutrients from clay and humus particles and from the soil solution by releasing hydrogen cations for equivalent amounts of other cations (Ca^{2+}, Mg^{2+}, K^{2+}, NH_4^+) and carbonate (HCO_3^-) anions for equivalents of the nutrient anions NO_3^-, $H_2PO_4^-$, and SO_4^{2-} (Fig 1.1).

As plant roots absorb nutrients from clay and humus particles, the nutrients are replaced from slowly-soluble minerals and from decomposing organic matter. Plants are capable of absorbing nutrients even against a concentration gradient. This means that, for example, calcium may be in higher concentration inside the root cells than in the soil solution. The additional energy necessary to do this comes from respiration.

1: 4 SOILS, PLANTS, AND FERTILIZERS

The soil supplies 13 of the 16 elements required for the nutrition of higher plants. These essential elements must be available continuously in balanced proportions. Plants also require mechanical support, sunshine, the right amount of soil water, plentiful oxygen surrounding plant roots, and freedom from plant toxins.

Furthermore, the physical condition of the soil must be favorable to support the plant and to hold and release simultaneously adequate oxygen and water for optimum plant growth. Substances toxic to plants, such as an excess of soluble salts, may be present in the soil as a result of its formation in arid regions. In strongly acid soils soluble aluminum may be toxic. The remaining non-soil essentials for plant growth include heat and light from the sun and oxygen and carbon dioxide from ambient air.

The kind of soil existing at any one time and place is determined by five factors of soil formation: parent material, climate, topography, biosphere, and time.

It is assumed that all soils with the identical five factors of soil formation would have the same taxonomy and be mapped as the same soil. It can also be assumed that, barring drastic influences by people, plants growing on the same soil will respond to fertilizers in a similar way. Exceptions to this generalization include soils in old fence rows; soils in one field that was treated differently when it was managed as two fields; areas where fertilizers and/or lime were applied unevenly; areas where old roads used to be; and areas leveled, eroded, or otherwise drastically disturbed.

The preceding logic is the best technique yet devised for predicting the fertilizer response of crops on soils where such plants have never been grown before. Phrased differently, soil taxonomy and soil surveys are a viable technique for the successful transfer of field data and other technology from known soil-plant response and predicting the response on similar soils where the same plant had never been grown.

The latest United States system of soil taxonomy, adaptable worldwide, was started in 1951, became official in 1965, and was published in one document in 1975.[16]

Throughout the years of development of the system, the soil scientists used this question to guide them: "Do these soil groupings permit us to make more precise predictions of soil behavior?" Soil behavior includes plant response to unamended soil and to the application of fertilizers and soil amendments. Soil taxonomy is also closely correlated with mechanization systems, as documented by an in-depth study in equatorial Africa.[17]

The United States system of soil taxonomy comprises 10 soil orders, 47 suborders, 185 great groups (225 worldwide), 970 subgroups, 4,500 soil families, and 10,500 soil series. Phases include texture of the surface soil, slope, stoniness, and degree of erosion (see Chapter 3).

Soil taxonomy is the scientific basis for differentiation among soils on soil maps. The use of soil maps permits a more precise transfer of technology, including plant response to fertilizer and lime. The 10 soil orders and their extent in the world are detailed in Table 1.2.

Table 1.2. Areas of soil orders of the world and their percentages of total land area

	World		
Soil order	Square miles	Square kilometers	Percentage of total land area
Alfisols	6,630,200	17,138,200	13.19
Aridisols	9,433,600	24,384,000	18.76
Entisols	4,162,400	10,759,200	8.28
Histosols	452,500	1,169,600	0.90
Inceptisols	4,464,000	11,538,400	8.88
Mollisols	4,310,900	11,143,200	8.57
Oxisols	4,277,900	11,057,600	8.51
Spodosols	2,150,000	5,557,600	4.28
Ultisols	2,794,100	7,222,400	5.56
Vertisols	905,300	2,340,000	1.80
Miscellaneous	10,697,100	27,650,000	21.27
Totals	50,278,000	129,960,200	100.00

Source: Soil Conservation Service. Soil map of the world, 1971, scale—1: 50,000,000.

1: 5 BALANCING NUTRITION THROUGH FERTILIZATION

Because all plant and animal life is dependent on food produced by plants through photosynthesis, *balanced* nutrition through fertilization of plants is of universal, crucial concern.

The term ***balanced nutrition through fertilization*** is easy to define but difficult to practice. It means the continuous availability to plants of all 16 essential elements, with none in excess and none deficient. Balanced nutrition of plants in relation to animals can also mean applying fertilizers to increase the nutritional value of the forage or feed. For example, phosphorus fertilizer added to alfalfa may increase the percentage of phosphorus in the forage to 0.3 percent phosphorus, an acceptable level for dairy cows. Oat grain, however, may contain 0.3 percent phosphorus on many soils without the addition of phosphorus fertilizer. Stated in another way, the oat plant is capable of concentrating more phosphorus in the seed than can alfalfa in its leaves and stems when cut for hay (Fig. 1.2).

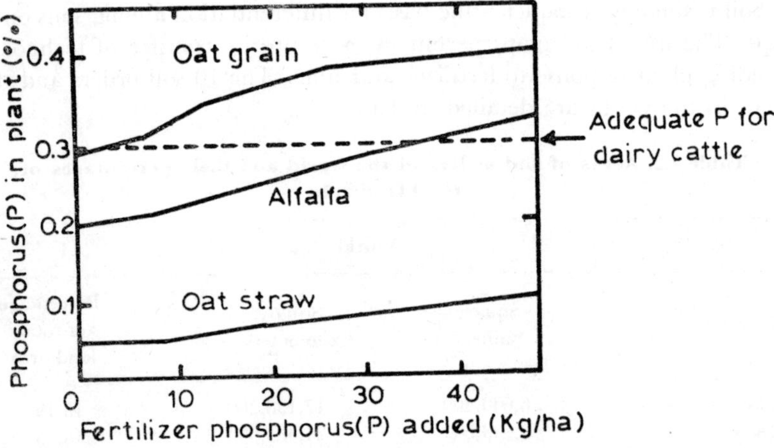

Fig. 1.2. "Balanced nutrition through fertilization" could mean increasing the percentage of phosphorus (P) in forage/fodder/grain by fertilizers to achieve adequate phosphorus (0.3% P) intake when fed to dairy cattle. Under these experimental conditions, oat grain had adequate phosphorus with no phosphorus fertilizer, but alfalfa was adequate only after an application of 30 kg/ha of phosphorus (P). (*Courtesy:* U.S. Plant, Soil, and Nutrition Laboratory, Ithaca, N.Y.).

Success in balancing plant nutrition by fertilization and liming throughout the world is being achieved by the following recommendations based on soil tests correlated with field plot response on soils of known taxonomy (see Chapter 7).[18, 19]

1: 6 FOOD FROM FERTILIZERS

The Food and Agricultural Organization of the United Nations reports that world food production per person in recent years has varied from about a 1.75 percent increase per year for all developed countries to 0.3 percent for all developing countries, averaging 0.8 percent worldwide.[20] The food production increase and population increase must be adequate and in balance to provide enough food for everyone. What are the facts?

In the developed countries the population increase has averaged 1 percent, compared with a food increase of 1.75 percent. *Result:* Surplus food. Population growth in the developing countries has averaged 2.4 percent, eight times the food increase of 0.3 percent. *Result:* The developing countries must obtain surplus food from the developed countries or starve. On a world basis, the population growth has averaged 2 percent and the food production increase, about 1 percent. *Result:* Worldwide effort must try to decrease population growth and aim to double the rate of increase of food production during the next 25 years.

A decrease in population growth seems next to impossible, but an increase in food production is possible by increasing the total hectares of arable land and/or increasing yields per hectare primarily with an increase in use of fertilizer.

An estimate was made of the hectares available in the world for cultivation of food crops that *are not now cultivated.* This means forested and grassed areas where precipitation is adequate for crop production, as well as arid areas with a potential for irrigation (Table 1.3).

Table 1.3. Hectares of soils in the world suitable for cultivation but are not now cultivated, by regions

Region	Million hectares
South America	608
Africa	567
North America	243
Asia	122
Australia and New Zealand	122
U.S.S.R.	122
Europe	40
Total	1,824

There are about one billion hectares in the tropics where the population is increasing faster than food production.[21]

It *cannot* be assumed that these potentially arable soils are ideal for crop production without expensive inputs. Most of them will require very expensive land clearing, road building, wild animal control, disease and insect control, weed control, irrigation water, soil amendments, and chemical fertilizers. Sometimes the success of new land developments depends on the health and happiness of resettled farm families.

Most professional people who have studied the "more hectares or more yield per hectare" option have concluded the following:

1) The option is specific to each sovereign country or part of the country.

2) The greatest need for more food is in the densely populated countries where most of the arable land is already being used for food production. The principal exception is most of South America where many countries have more hectares of soils to clear and cultivate. However, South America has more than 10 percent of its land surface classified in the soil order of Oxisols, the least fertile of all 10 world soil orders.

3) Increasing yield per hectare in most countries is the more feasible of the two alternatives because it is cheaper, and the greatest need is in countries where population pressure is greatest and there is almost no new land to clear.

Whether the option is for more hectares or greater yields per hectare (or both), more lime on strongly acid soils, more acidifying and sodium-replacing salts on sodic soils, more organic mulches, and especially more chemical fertilizers will be necessary to enhance yields of food crops.

For immediate results, chemical fertilizers are the best single agricultural input for increasing crop yields per hectare. In developing countries the increase in use of fertilizer has exceeded 10 percent a year and is expected to continue at this rate in the future. With good management, about 4.5 kg (10 lb) of food grains can be expected for each kilogram (pound) of fertilizer used. *Enlightened people estimate that half of the increase in yield of food crops in developing countries can be attributed to the use of fertilizers.*[22]

1: 7 SUMMARY

Survival and well-being of animals and people depend on plants growing on a productive soil with adequate water. However, scientists have selected and bred food plants to tolerate stresses of fertility, water, temperature, and pests. A hungry world needs an acceleration of this research to assure adequate food for the increasing billions.

For growth and reproduction, plants require 16 elements; animals and people need 14 of the same 16 plus six more. Since plants absorb elements which they do not need, including the six needed exclusively by animals and people, many species and individuals of the animal kingdom live exclusively on plants. Proper fertilization can balance plant nutrition and composition, and accelerate growth; the result can be higher yields as well as more and more nutritious food and feed for people and their animals.

More food and feed for more people and livestock can be produced by greater yields per hectare and/or the use of more land. Both techniques are being used with success but at an accelerating cost. The ultimate options include more research on soil, water, and plant production, more education of people to use new technologies, and family planning to reduce population growth.

CITED REFERENCES

1. F.N. Ponnamperuma. "Specific Soil Chemical Characteristics for Rice Production in Asia." IRRI Research Paper Series No. 2, 1976. International Rice Research Institute (IRRI), Manila, Philippines.

2. I. Watanabe, K.K. Lee, B.V. Alimagno, M. Sato, D.C. del Rosario, and M.R. de Guzman. "Biological Nitrogen Fixation in Paddy Field Studied by *in situ* Acetylene-Reduction Assays." IRRI Research Paper Series No. 3, 1977. IRRI, Manila, Philippines.

3. F.N. Ponnamperuma. "Physicochemical Properties of Submerged Soils in Relation to Fertility." IRRI Research Paper Series No. 5, 1977. IRRI, Manila, Philippines.

4. F.N. Ponnamperuma. "Screening Rice for Tolerance to Mineral Stresses." IRRI Research Paper Series No. 6, 1977. IRRI, Manila, Philippines.

5. F.N. Ponnamperuma. "Behavior of Minor Elements in Paddy Soils." IRRI Research Paper Series No. 8, 1977. IRRI, Manila, Philippines.

6. K. Alluri and I.W. Buddenhagen. "Evaluation of Rice Cultivars for Their Response to Limiting Nutrients." *In* International Rice Research Newsletter, 3/77, June, 1977, page 2. IRRI, Manila, Philippines.

7. International Rice Research Institute. "Annual Report for 1978." Manila, Philippines. 1979, 478 pages.

8. IRRI Reporter 3/80. "IRRI Germplasm Bank-Treasure of Mankind." IRRI, Manila, Philippines. Sept., 1980, 4 pages.

9. "CIMMYT Review, 1979." Centro Internacional de Mejoramiento de Maizy Trigo. ("International Center for Improvement of Corn and Wheat.")

10. Calvin O. Qualset, John D. Prato, and Herbert E. Vogt. "Breeding Success With Spring Wheat Germplasm." *In* California Agriculture 31, No. 9, Summer 1977, pages 26, 27.

11. Tropical Soils Research Program. Annual Report for 1975. Soil Science Department, North Carolina State University, Raleigh, North Carolina, Nov., 1976, pages 40-65. (Supported by Contract USAID/ta-c-1236, U. S. Agency for International Development.)

12. "ICRSAT Annual Report, 1976-1977." International Crops Research Institute for the Semi-Arid Tropics. Hyderabad, Andhra Pradesh, India, pages 87, 168, 169.

13. G.H. Dungan, U.S. Sisodia, and G.D. Singh. "The Benefit of Sowing Maize for Fodder in North and South Lines." Allahabad Farmer, Allahabad, India, 1955.

14. "CIAT Annual Report, 1978." Centro Internacional de Agricultura Tropical (International Center of Tropical Agriculture), Cali, Colombia, South America, pages A-78, A-79.

15. Roy L. Donahue, Raymond W. Miller, and John C. Shickluna. Soils: An Introduction to Soils and Plant Growth, 5th Edition, Prentice-Hall, Inc., Englewood Cliffs, New Jersey, 1983, pp. 208-213.

16. Soil Survey Staff, "Soil Taxonomy: A Basic System of Soil Classification for Making and Interpreting Soil Surveys," USDA—Soil Conservation Service, Agriculture Handbook No. 436, Dec., 1975.

17. C.K. Kline, D.A.G. Green, Roy L. Donahue, and B.A. Stout. "Agricultural Mechanization in Equatorial Africa." Research Report No. 6, Institute of International Agriculture, College of Agriculture and Natural Resources, Michigan State University, Contract USAID/Afr.—459, Dec., 1969.

18. H.D. Bhaumik, H. Sankarasubramoney, V.K. Leley, and Roy L. Donahue. "Soils, Soil Testing, and the Efficient Use of Fertilizers." A Terminal Report of the Team on Soils and Fertilizers, the Intensive Agricultural Districts Programme, as of July 1, 1966. The Ford Foundation, New Delhi, India, 35 pages.

19. Gilbert R. Muhr, N.P. Datta, H. Sankarasubramoney, V.K. Leley, and Roy L. Donahue, "Soil Testing in India." 2nd Edition. United States Agency for International Development Mission to India, New Delhi, India, 120 pages, 1965.

20. "Population, Food Supply, and Agricultural Development." *In* "The State of Food and Agriculture, 1974," Chapter 3, Food and Agriculture Organization of the United Nations, Rome, Italy, 1975.

21. United Nations' World Food Conference, "The World Food Problem—Proposals for National and International Actions," published for the World Food Conference, Rome, Italy, 1974.

22. John A. Hannah. "Fertilizer—A Key to Solution of World Food Problem." Fertilizer News, Fertiliser Assn. of India, New Delhi, India, Jan., 1978, pages 14-17.

ADDITIONAL REFERENCES

Andrew, C.S., and E.J. Kamprath, eds. "Mineral Nutrition of Legumes in Tropical and Subtropical Soils." Commonwealth Scientific and Industrial Research Organization, Melbourne, Australia, 1978, 415 pages.

Arakeri, H.R., G.V. Chalam, P. Satyanarayana, and R.L. Donahue. "Soil Management in India." 2nd Edition, 1962, 609 pages.

Bornemisza, E. and A. Alvarado, eds. "Soil Management in Tropical

America." Proceedings of a Seminar held at CIAT, Cali, Colombia, Feb. 10-14, 1974, 565 pages.

Donahue, R.L., R.H. Follett, and R.W. Tulloch. "Our Soils and Their Management." The Interstate, Printers and Publishers, Inc., Danville, Illinois. 5th Edition, 1983, 622 pages.

Donahue, R.L., R.W. Miller, and J.C. Shickluna. Soils: An Introduction to Soils and Plant Growth. Prentice-Hall, Inc., Englewood Cliffs, New Jersey, 5th Edition, 1983, 667 pages.

Follett, R.H., L.S. Murphy, and R.L. Donahue. Fertilizers and Soil Amendments. Prentice-Hall, Inc., Englewood Cliffs, New Jersey, 1981, 557 pages.

Kellogg, C.E. "Agricultural Development: Soil, Food, People, Work." Soil Science Society of America, 1975, 233 pages.

Moormann, F.R., and N. van Breemen. "Rice: Soil, Water, Land." IRRI, Manila, Philippines, 1978, 185 pages.

Raychaudhuri, S.P., et al. "Soils of India." Indian Council of Agricultural Research, New Delhi, India, 1963, 496 pages.

Swindale, L.D., ed. "Soil-Resource Data for Agricultural Development." Hawaii Agr. Experiment Station, College of Tropical Agriculture, University of Hawaii, Honolulu, Hawaii, 1978, 306 pages.

Tamhane, R.V., D.D. Motiramani, Y.P. Bali, and R.L. Donahue. Soils: Their Chemistry and Fertility in Tropical Asia. Prentice-Hall of India (Private) Ltd., New Delhi, India, 1964, 475 pages.

Thorne, D.W. and M.D. Thorne. Soil, Water and Crop Production. Avi Publishing Company, Inc., Westport, Connecticut, 1979, 353 pages.

Thorp, J. "Geography of the Soils of China." The National Geological Survey of China, Institute of Geology of the National Academy of Peiping and the China Foundation for the Promotion of Education and Culture, Nanking, China, 1936, 552 pages.

Tisdale, S.L. and W.L. Nelson. Soil Fertility and Fertilizers. Macmillan Publishing Co., Inc., New York, 1975, 694 pages.

Troeh, F.R., J.A. Hobbs, and R.L. Donahue. Soil and Water Conservation. Prentice-Hall, Inc., Englewood Cliffs, New Jersey, 1980, 718 pages.

U.S. Government Printing Office. "The World Food Problem." Vol. I—"Summary," 127 pages; Vol. II—"Report of the Panel on the World Food Supply," 722 pages; Vol. III—"Report of the Panel on the World Food Supply" 332 pages, 1967, Washington, D.C.

Wright, M.J., ed. "Plant Adaptation to Mineral Stress in Problem Soils." Proceeding of a Workshop held at the National Agricultural Library, Beltsville, Maryland, Nov. 22, 23, 1976. Pub., 1977, 420 pages.

CHAPTER 2

Soil Genesis

"The geological deposit, the glacial till, the sandy deposits of sand plains, the lake-laid or marine clays, sands, silts, and gravels, the residual earth resulting from rock decay constitute soil materials or parent materials of soils." Curtis F. Marbut, 1923 (1863-1935).

"A mature soil is one that has assumed the profile features characteristic of the predominant soils on the smooth uplands within the general climatic and botanic region in which it is found." Curtis F. Marbut, 1926 (1863-1935).

"Soil, in its traditional meaning, is the natural medium for the growth of land plants, whether or not it has discernible soil horizons. . .soil has a thickness that is determined by the depth of rooting of plants." Soil Taxonomy, 1975.

2:1 INTRODUCTION

Genesis means origin. This chapter explains how soils develop from parent materials. Most soils develop from weathered minerals in rocks, with small amounts of organic matter; others originate mostly from plant and animal residues. Some soils originate from weathered minerals directly above the bedrock from which they came. However, most soils come from the weathered mineral parent materials after such materials have been moved by one or more of nature's transport agencies: water, wind, moving ice, and/or gravity. Soils from plant and animal residues form in wet places without movement.

Soils from mineral materials are developed by the dynamic forces of climate and the action of plants and animals (biosphere), as modified by topography (lay-of-the-land) over time (in years). Temperature and precipitation delimit the kinds of plants and animals that *can* thrive and their rate of decomposition in a particular soil environment. But the relative availability of plant nutrients in rocks and soils and relative soil wetness also control rate of plant and animal growth and the rate of decomposition of their residues. For example, high temperatures and high rainfall favor rapid plant growth as well as a rapid rate of decomposition. But *high* temperatures and *very high* rainfall are conducive to rapid growth but *slow* decomposition and high organic accumulation. Conversely, low temperatures and low precipitation favor slow growth but slower decomposition and therefore organic matter accumulation. In fact in any combination of temperatures and precipitation, organic matter may accumulate under conditions of continuous soil wetness. Histosols (peat and muck soils) may form in any climate but are more common on continuously wet soils in humid, cool climates.[1]

To summarize: At any one time and place, the soil is the result of the interacting natural forces, climate and biosphere operating over time on the passive factors of parent materials and their topography. Stated in another way, soil genesis is the result of these five factors: climate, biosphere, parent material, topography, and time.

These five factors have interacted for centuries to generate a soil, a three-dimensional body at the surface of the earth capable of supporting plants.

But a soil is more than the dead and stable residues of physical, chemical, and biological weathering of minerals and organic accumulations. Components of the soil also include synthesized clay minerals and other minerals and billions of plant roots and soil microbes, both living and dead, interacting in a dynamic equilibrium.

2: 2 GENESIS OF PARENT MATERIALS

Parent materials of *mineral soils* are weathered minerals in rocks. Parent materials of *organic soils* (called cumulose materials) are mostly plant residues preserved by low oxygen because of excessive wetness, as in a shallow lake.

Weathering of minerals consists of physical, chemical, and biological processes of disintegration and decomposition.[2]

2: 2.1 Physical Weathering

Physical weathering includes the slow process of disruption by disintegration of minerals because of expansion and contraction of water as it freezes into ice; the expansion of minerals as they heat and cool; abrasion of minerals as they move against each other in flowing water, high winds, moving glaciers, and rolling and sliding downhill in response to gravity. Because of a reduction in the size of minerals, physical weathering results in larger total surfaces, thereby hastening the genesis of parent materials by accelerating further physical, chemical, and biological weathering.

2: 2.2 Chemical Weathering

Chemical weathering is a surface phenomenon and is often quite rapid. Under the same environment the rate of weathering depends upon the relative solubility of the minerals. For the most common rock minerals this rate, from high to low solubility, is:

Olivine—an iron-magnesium silicate
$(Mg, Fe)_2 SiO_4$
Augite—an iron-magnesium silicate
$Ca (Mg, Fe, Al) (Al, Si_2O_6)$
Hornblende—an iron-magnesium silicate—a complex
Ca, Na, Mg, Ti, Al silicate
Biotite—an iron-magnesium silicate
$K (Mg, Fe)_3 AlSi_3O_{10}(OH)_2$
Orthoclase—a potassium-aluminum silicate
$KAlSi_3O_8$
Muscovite—a potassium silicate
$KAl_3Si_3O_{10}(OH)_2$
Quartz—a silicate
SiO_2

The four most soluble rock-forming minerals are iron-magnesium silicates. Why, then, do they have different solubilities? The answer lies in the fact that their crystal structure and composition of other elements are different.

In summary, quartz (silicon dioxide), one of the most common soil minerals, is most resistant to weathering. For this reason, sand grains, mostly quartz, will "forever" remain sand grains in an environment conducive to chemical weathering (warm, humid). Sand weathers mostly physically due to wide fluctuations in temperature.

The kinds of chemical weathering include solution, hydrolysis, hydration, carbonation, oxidation, and reduction.

Solution is the change of a mineral from a solid to a liquid state. For example, halite (NaCl, common table salt) dissolves readily in water to form ions of sodium and chlorine, as illustrated:

NaCl	+	HOH	⟶	Na^+	+	Cl^-	+	HOH
(halite)		(water)		(sodium ions)		(chloride ions)		(water molecules)

Hydrolysis is a chemical weathering process in which a mineral combines with water to form an acid and a base. The hydrolysis of the common mineral orthoclase is a good example that frequently occurs in soils.

$KAlSi_3O_8$	+	HOH	$\longrightarrow$	$HAlSi_3O_8$	+	KOH
(orthoclase mineral) (slowly soluble)		(water)		(acid silicate clay) (more soluble)		(potassium hydroxide) (very soluble)

Hydration is the combining of water molecules within the structural lattice of a mineral to form a different mineral. A common example in soils is the hydration of hematite to limonite, as follows:

$2\ Fe_2O_3$	+	$3\ HOH$	$\longrightarrow$	$2\ Fe_2O_3 \cdot 3\ H_2O$
(hematite, red, firm)		(water)		(limonite, yellow) (softer, more easily decomposed)

Carbonation is a common process in nature whereby carbon dioxide gas in the air combines with water to form carbonic acid, which further reacts with carbonates to produce more soluble bicarbonates. An example follows in two steps.

CO_2	+	HOH	$\longrightarrow$	H_2CO_3
(carbon dioxide gas in air)		(water)		(carbonic acid)

H_2CO_3	+	$CaCO_3$	$\longrightarrow$	$Ca(HCO_3)_2$
(carbonic acid)		(calcite mineral) (slowly soluble)		(calcium bicarbonate) (very soluble)

Oxidation in mineral weathering is the combining of a chemical with oxygen or the loss of one or more electrons from an ion or an atom. Two common examples are the oxidation of the minerals, sulfur and zinc.

S	+	$1\frac{1}{2}\ O_2$	+	H_2O	$\longrightarrow$	H_2SO_4
(mineral sulfur) (slowly soluble)		(oxygen)		(water)		(sulfuric acid) (biologically oxidized by *Thiobacillus* bacteria) (very soluble)

Zn	+	O_2	$\longrightarrow$	ZnO_2
(mineral zinc) (slowly soluble)		(oxygen)		(zinc oxide) (chemical oxidation) (readily soluble)

Reduction is a chemical process of removing oxygen from a mineral; e.g., when hematite is reduced to metallic iron. Reduction also means a decrease in positive valence or an increase in negative valence. In other words, reduction is the addition of electrons to an atom or ion. An example of reduction is the change of ferric iron (Fe^{3+}) to ferrous iron (Fe^{2+}) due to low soil oxygen because of excessive wetness.

2: 2.3 Biological Weathering

Biological weathering processes in the genesis of parent materials comprise the action of all living things in the soil that disintegrate and decompose minerals and organic matter into simpler products. Principal agents of biological weathering are people, digging animals, earthworms, and these microorganisms: Algae, fungi and bacteria.

People hasten the weathering of soil minerals physically by tillage and other earth-moving operations and chemically by applying lime and fertilizers. Animals such as rats and mice dig burrows and thereby cause soil minerals to become smaller by abrasion. The increase of carbon dioxide on and in the soil from animal respiration and the decomposition of their manures hastens mineral weathering by carbonation.

Earthworms ingest (eat) large amounts of organic matter along with fine clay soil minerals. Their excreted casts are ideal environments for faster chemical and microbiological weathering of minerals.

Algae are green and manufacture food by photosynthesis. Several species of algae are capable of colonizing and corroding moist and barren minerals. Upon their death, bacteria and fungi "feed" on the corroded mineral products and the residues from algal decay.[3]

Decaying organic residues release a large quantity of carbon dioxide. This changes to carbonic acid and is capable of degrading minerals by a solubilization process known as carbonation.

Fungi have no chlorophyll and therefore do not use light to manufacture food. They subsist on available readily oxidizable carbon in organic matter. However, certain fungal species form a symbiotic relationship with some algal species to produce lichens. Lichen colonies are especially effective in disintegrating and decomposing iron-bearing minerals.[3]

Bacteria most concerned with mineral breakdown in the genesis of soils from parent materials are classified as chemautotrophs. Members of this group obtain their carbon from carbon dioxide and their energy from the oxidation of such mineral substances as nitrogen, iron, or sulfur. Examples are[3]:

Nitrosomonas bacteria

$$NH_4^+ + 1\tfrac{1}{2}\,O_2 \longrightarrow NO_2^- + 2\,H^+ + H_2O$$

(ammonium) (oxygen) (nitrite) (hydrogen) (water)

Nitrobacter bacteria

$$NO_2^- + \tfrac{1}{2}\,O_2 \longrightarrow NO_3^-$$

(nitrite) (oxygen) (nitrate)

Thiobacillus ferro-oxidans bacteria

$$\underset{\text{(ferrous iron)}}{4\,Fe^{2+}} + \underset{\text{(oxygen)}}{O_2} + \underset{\text{(hydrogen)}}{4\,H^+} \longrightarrow \underset{\text{(ferric iron)}}{4Fe^{3+}} + \underset{\text{(water)}}{2\,H_2O}$$

Thiobacillus thio-oxidans bacteria

$$\underset{\text{(mineral sulfur)}}{S} + \underset{\text{(oxygen)}}{1\tfrac{1}{2}\,O_2} + \underset{\text{(water)}}{H_2O} \longrightarrow \underset{\text{(sulfuric acid)}}{H_2SO_4}$$

2: 2.4 Residual Parent Materials

Residual parent material is parent material formed from weathered minerals overlying bedrock. Neither water, wind, ice, nor gravity have moved the mineral fragments as they have disintegrated and decomposed as a result of weathering of bedrock to make parent materials. The logical conclusions are that residual parent materials were formed only on relatively level topography where winds were never severe and where glaciers never existed.

The origin of the parent materials may be from minerals weathered from igneous, sedimentary, or metamorphic rocks.

Igneous (origin: *fire*) rocks consist of an aggregate of silicate minerals formed by cooling and solidification of magma (molten rock). When solidified slowly and deeply within the earth, they are called *plutonic* rocks (such as granite); when flowed (lava) or blown (volcanic ash) from a volcano, they are known as *volcanic* rocks. Both plutonic and volcanic rocks are characterized by a massive (noncrystalline) structure.

Sedimentary (origin: settling; to sit) rocks are rocks formed from sediment by mechanical or chemical means or from organic residues. Conglomerate, sandstone, and shale are examples of sedimentary rocks formed by mechanical settling in water. Rock salt (halite) and gypsum are formed by chemical precipitation. Limestone may be formed by chemical precipitation or by organisms. Sedimentary rocks are usually layered in structure, with layers parallel to the surface of the earth. Sedimentary rocks are the immediately underlying bedrock, for about 75 percent of the land area of the world.

Metamorphic (origin: changed form) rocks are igneous or sedimentary rocks whose texture and/or chemical composition has been changed by heat, pressure, and/or chemically active fluids after original formation. Examples are marble from metamorphosed limestone, quartzite from metamorphosed sandstone, and schist from metamorphosed granite. Metamorphic rocks are characterized by a banded structure which is at right angles to the earth's original pressure planes.

These rocks may weather into parent material slower or faster than the original rock. For example, marble and quartzite are harder and weather more slowly than the limestone or sandstone, respectively, from which they came; whereas, schist, being softer, weathers faster than granite.

2: 2.5 Transported Parent Materials

Only a small percentage of the parent materials of the world have developed from the bedrock beneath them. Most parent materials have formed from weathered rock minerals that have been moved to another location by water, wind, moving ice, and/or gravity. Observed at any one time, a specific parent material *could* have been: (1) weathered from minerals in underlying rock, and then (2) transported by water and, years later, blown by wind, moved by glacial ice, and finally rolled down a hill in response to the pull of gravity. Then this parent material *could* develop into a soil if it stayed at rest for several hundred years.

The agencies of transport and the geologic names of the parent materials transported are shown in Table 2.1.[4]

Table 2.1. Transported parent materials: agency of transport and geologic name of parent material transported

	Agency of transport	Geologic name of parent material transported
Water	Flowing Water	Alluvium
	Lakes	Lacustrine
	Oceans	Marine
Wind	Strong winds of any age	Eolian (aeolian) (usually sandy)
	Moderate winds immediately after last glacier	Loess (usually silty)
Moving Ice	Glaciers	Moraine
		Till plain (ground moraine)
		Outwash plain
Gravity	Forces in center of earth causing down-slope movement	*Colluvies* (colluvial)

2: 2.6 Cumulose Parent Materials

Cumulose parent materials could be called residual because they have formed in place; in another sense, they are not residual because they did not develop from underlying bedrock.

Parent materials of organic soils (cumulose materials) are mostly plant residues preserved by excessive soil wetness. Organic parent materials may form in any climate from arctic to tropical and from arid to humid. However, they occur most abundantly in very poorly drained and cool humid areas.

There are at least five kinds of organic parent materials sold on world markets as peats, as follows:

1) *Moss peat*—mostly sphagnum moss and hypnum moss, only slightly decomposed.

2) *Reed-sedge peat*—from reeds, sedges, marsh grasses, and cattails, only slightly decomposed.

3) *Peat humus*—originating from hypnum moss or reed-sedge peat in a state of advanced decomposition.

4) *Muck soil*—consists of highly decomposed plant residues of no recognizable origin, mixed with washed-in mineral soil and/or underlying mineral parent material.

5) *Sedimentary peat*—originating from highly decomposed algae, plankton, water lilies, and pond weeds.[5]

2: 2.7 Soil Genesis—A Living Synthesis

Simultaneously with disintegration and decomposition of minerals, *new* minerals are synthesized. These include the soil clay minerals, montmorillonite, kaolinite, and illite which form from the physico-chemical breakdown products of rock minerals. In addition, other minerals are formed by various organisms. As of 1981, 31 such minerals had been identified. Twenty-five are synthesized by animals, 11 by protoctists, eight by monerans, seven by vascular plants, and four by fungi.[6]

2: 3 FACTORS OF SOIL GENESIS (FORMATION)

At any one time and place on the land mass of the earth, there are five factors at work making soil from parent material. The resultant soil will be determined by the interrelationships among these factors: climate, biosphere, parent material, topography and time.

A soil is generated when the ACTIVE factors of *climate* and *biosphere* interact with PASSIVE *parent material* and modified by PASSIVE *topography* over NEUTRAL *time.*

Jenny[7] proposes to show the interrelationship among the factors in this way:

*S*oil = *f*unction of (*c*limate, *b*iosphere, *r*elief (topography), *p*arent material, *t*ime)

Joffe[8] suggests the term *active factors* apply to climate and biosphere and *passive factors* to parent materials, relief (topography), and time. The authors of this book agree with Joffe with the exception of the designation of time as a neutral factor.

Depending on the character and interaction of the five factors, soil genesis may be hastened or retarded. Well-distributed rainfall, for example, hastens soil profile development; whereas, an arid climate retards it. Trees hasten and grasses retard the development of horizons. A permeable loam will develop horizons faster than either a sand or a clay soil. Likewise, soils develop faster on smooth than on hilly topography. And regardless of the other four factors of soil genesis, several hundred years are normally required for a soil profile to develop (Table 2.2).

Table 2.2. Factors that hasten or retard soil genesis

Factors that hasten soil genesis	Factors that retard soil genesis
Climate	
Moderate to high, well-distributed, precipitation; high relative humidity; moderate to high temperature.	Arid to semiarid, poorly distributed, precipitation; low relative humidity; low temperatures.
Biosphere	
Trees; high population of bacteria, actinomycetes, and fungi; low population of earthworms, termites, other burrowing creatures; no fires, clearing, cultivation, liming, or fertilizing.	Grasses; few microbes, many burrowing creatures; many fires and much cultivation, liming, and fertilizing.
Parent Material	
Moderately permeable, medium textured (such as a loam); well-drained; rich in soluble salts; rich in weatherable minerals.	Slow-to-weather minerals such as quartz; parent materials high in calcium or sodium carbonate. Very permeable sands or slowly permeable clays; poorly drained (any texture); low in soluble salts and low in easily-weatherable minerals.
Topography	
Smooth to gently undulating relief.	Hilly and rolling topography; also depressed areas receiving water and erosion sediments from surrounding slopes.
Time	
Old land surfaces such as unglaciated areas with no volcanic action and no water or wind erosion.	Young land surfaces such as recent alluvium or volcanic ash.

2: 3.1 Climate and Soil Genesis

Climate is average weather. The word *climate* is of Greek origin and refers to the angle of the sun's rays striking the earth. In fact, this angle of incidence of the rays of the sun determines the seasons and thus the amount of light and heat received on earth. Differential heating causes local variation in the earth's temperature which causes air mass movement and influences precipitation.

Climate is a dominant active factor in the formation of soil from parent material. Of the components of climate, precipitation and temperature are paramount. For example, for every 10°C increase in temperature all chemical reactions are doubled.

Precipitation and temperature determine the rate of weathering of minerals in rocks and the rate of soil formation. They also govern the rate of leaching of ions, molecules, and soluble compounds and the translocation (eluviation) of colloidal clay and humus and its deposition (illuviation) in a lower soil horizon.[9]

In the transformation of alkaline parent material into a soil, first the chlorides and sulfates are leached. Some chlorides and sulfates move laterally with surface runoff to surface waters and some move downward into the incipient soil profile. Calcium sulfate then is solubilized and is precipitated in the lower profile, followed by calcium carbonate usually above the calcium sulfate deposit.

Over greater time and more leaching, the calcium sulfate and calcium carbonate are moved in solution into waters of deep percolation, to emerge in springs and streams.

From the beginning of soil formation, new soil silicate clays are crystallized such as illite and montmorillonite. These clays have a net negative charge and are therefore capable of adsorbing cations such as hydrogen, calcium, magnesium, potassium, sodium, and ammonium.

With increased time and further leaching, hydrogen ions generated from decomposition of organic matter replace the basic ions. The soil is now acid. Under acid conditions high rainfall, high temperature, and with further time, illite and montmorillonite weather to kaolinite and iron and aluminum sesquioxide clays.

Precipitation and temperature are dominant factors in the formation of clays throughout the world. The clays containing silica (the silicate clays) are formed under conditions of limited leaching. Such clays include montmorillonite, illite, vermiculite, chlorite, and kaolinite. On old, well-drained land surfaces in the humid tropics, sesquioxide clays are formed. Amorphous clays can be formed rather quickly in any climate from recent volcanic ash[10] (Table 2.3).

An attempt has been made to relate the influence of climate and other

Table 2.3. Principal clays of the world: their composition and climate in which they are usually formed

Clay	Composition	Climate in which clay is formed
Montmorillonite	O, Si, Al	Arid to humid; any temperature; limited leaching
Illite	O, Si, Al, K	Subhumid; cool; with mica
Vermiculite	O, Si, Al, Mg	Subhumid to humid; any temperature; with mica
Chlorite	O, Si, Al, Mg, K, Fe	Any climate; marine sediments
Kaolinite	O, Al, Si	Subhumid to humid; warm to hot; well-drained; old land surfaces
Sesquioxides	O, Al, Fe	Humid; tropical; well-drained; old land surfaces
Amorphous	O, Al, Si	Humid; warm to hot; recent volcanic ash

dominant environmental factors on the genesis of the ten soil orders in the United States System of Soil Taxonomy. Because of the interaction of climate, parent material, biosphere, topography, and time, the correlation of climate, formation of clay minerals, and soil genesis is less than perfect.[11] (Table 2.4).

Table 2.4. The ten soil orders and the climate and other dominant factors in their genesis

Soil order	Dominant factors in soil genesis	
	Climate	Other factors
Alfisols	Humid to semiarid, any temperature	Incipient illuvial clay in B horizon
Aridisols	Arid, any temperature	Any parent material
Entisols	Any climate	Recent parent materials
Histosols	Any climate but mostly humid, cool	Poorly drained sites or prolonged and heavy rainfall on other sites
Inceptisols	Any climate	No illuvial clay in B horizon
Mollisols	Semiarid, cool to warm	Calcareous parent material
Oxisols	Humid, tropical	Well-drained parent material on old land surfaces
Spodosols	Humid, cool to warm	Sandy, acid parent material
Ultisols	Humid, warm	Well-drained parent material
Vertisols	Semiarid, warm	Calcareous clay parent material

For example, Entisols may occur in any climate on young (recent) parent materials; whereas, Aridisols are best correlated with a dry climate but with *any* temperature.

Histosols develop in any climate provided surface water is abundant over the year. By contrast, Oxisols develop *only* in a tropical climate on old well-drained land surfaces. Ultisols are most common in humid subtropical climates on well-drained parent materials. Both Mollisols and Vertisols develop on calcareous parent materials, but a greater percentage of clay exists in Vertisols and a cool season seems to be essential for Mollisols development. Spodosols occur in humid and cool-to-warm climates but only on sandy, acid parent material. Alfisols and Inceptisols do not seem to be as closely correlated with climate or parent materials.

2: 3.2 Biosphere and Soil Genesis

Biosphere is a word derived from the Greek, *bios*, life. It is defined as the environment of living organisms penetrating and interacting with the lithosphere (rock minerals and soil), hydrosphere (water), and atmosphere (air). Included in living organisms are plants and animals from low-growing grasses to giant trees and from microscopic microbes to greedy goats.

The natural vegetation throughout the world is determined principally by precipitation and secondarily by soils and parent materials. This general relationship is as follows:

Superhumid—trees
Humid—trees, some grasses on high-lime clay soils
Semiarid—grasses, some trees on sandier soils
Arid—grasses

Figure 2.1 gives the principal plant formations of the world.

Soils developing under a forest vegetation are sharply contrasting in appearance from those under a grass vegetation. This contrast is especially noticeable in the tension zone between a humid and a semiarid climate. In this zone where temperature and precipitation are identical, soil profiles on similar well-drained parent materials under trees and grasses exhibit these contrasting characteristics:

Typical Forested Profile	*Typical Grassed Profile*
1. More total horizons	1. Fewer horizons
2. Undecomposed surface litter	2. Humified surface
3. First mineral horizon leached and light-colored	3. First mineral horizon humified and dark in color
4. Illuviated (accumulated) clay in B horizon	4. Humified B horizon with less illuviated clay

The billions of microbes of the biosphere include bacteria, actinomycetes,

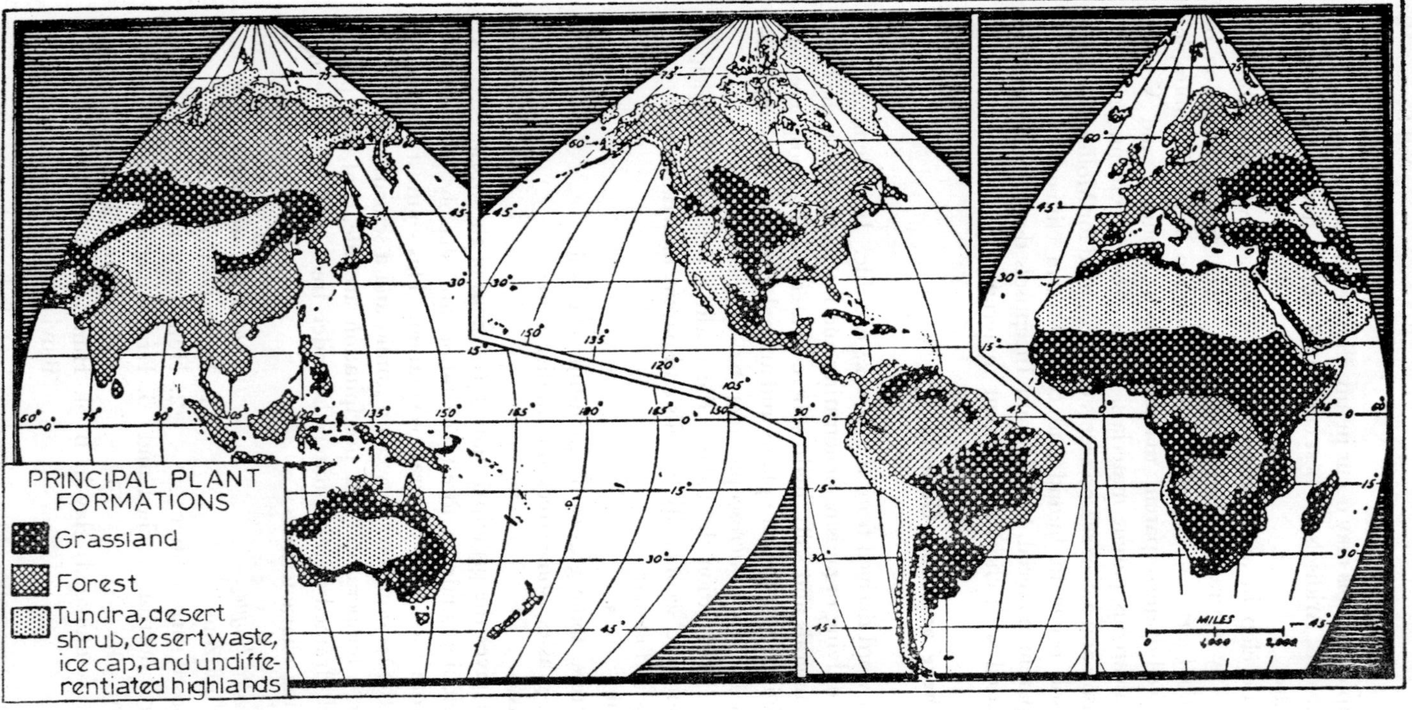

Fig. 2.1. The four great plant formations of the earth's land surface are forest, grassland, desert shrub, and tundra. Grasslands are believed to include about one-fourth of the area occupied by these types of vegetation and about one-fifth of the earth's land surface. These four formations reflect chiefly climate. As a rule, humid lands are woodlands and dry lands are desert shrub or waste; the grasslands lie between these climatic extremes in zones of intermediate moisture supply. There are, however, many important exceptions to this generalization. (*Source:* Grass : The Yearbook of Agriculture, 1948. U.S. Department of Agriculture, page 46.)

fungi, algae, and protozoa. None of these can be seen without a microscope. In general, the more productive the soil the greater the numbers of microbes. This positive correlation has both a cause and effect relationship. Microbes require adequate nutrients, organic matter, water, and air in the soil to reproduce. Also the microbes increase the productivity of the soil environment by disintegration and decomposition of rock and soil minerals and organic residues.

Of special interest in the influence of biosphere on soil genesis from parent materials is the action of lichens. Lichens consist of an algal and a fungal symbiont (an alga and a fungus in symbiotic relationship). Lichens colonize barren surfaces and corrode and "weather" minerals for their own nutrition. Carbon dioxide from respiration is released by the lichens, which changes to carbonic acid and solubilizes the rock and soil minerals. Also the symbiotic alga fixes atmospheric nitrogen. Upon death of the alga, the biologically fixed nitrogen is used by the alga and fungus for their growth and reproduction. When the lichens die and decay, higher plants are able to grow in an environment richer in nutrients and in available water because of the added organic matter, nitrogen, and nutrients solubilized from minerals.

The biosphere of the soil also includes many members of the animal kingdom, comprising termites, ants, earthworms, birds, rats, mice, monkeys, goats, sheep, cattle and people. Termites and ants burrow into the soil and thereby mix the first few feet. The immediate result is crop destruction but the long-term effect is to increase soil productivity by aerating and by bringing to the surface many nutrients which have been leached below the root zone (rhizosphere).

Earthworms occur on moist and fine textured soils rich in fresh and palatable organic matter. They plow, aerate, and hasten the cycle of organic decomposition and mineral weathering.

Except for bank swallows, most birds do not burrow into the soil. However, where birds and bats concentrate in large numbers, such as in rookeries, their droppings retard soil horizon development by enriching the soil. *Guano* is bird or bat manure collected from rookeries and sold as a fertilizer.

Rats and mice near an assured food supply dig burrows in the soil. The long-time effect is to retard soil profile development by stirring the soil and parent material and by enrichment of the soil because of more available nutrients.

By their overgrazing, goats, sheep, and cattle deplete protective vegetation which causes erosion. This retards soil genesis and decreases soil productivity.

Of all biotic factors, people have probably the greatest influence on soil and its genesis. Practices that cause excessive soil disturbance are clearing and plowing to plant crops, burning to discourage trees and encourage grasses, and overstocking the range. All of these practices decrease soil productivity and retard soil development.[12] Fertilizing and liming retard soil profile development but increase soil productivity. In humid regions, these practices make the soil environment more favorable for grasses than for trees.[13]

2: 3.3 Parent Materials and Soil Genesis

At any one time and place, the observed passive parent material may have originated from the weathering of underlying rock (see Section 2: 2.5) or transported by water, wind, ice, or gravity (see Table 2.1). Regardless of its origin, the parent material at its present location is being influenced by the active factors of climate and biosphere, the passive factor of topography, and the neutral factor of time.[14]

When the parent material is actually transformed into a soil is often difficult to determine. However, there is common agreement that when soil horizons are recognized by soil scientists, a soil has been generated (soil genesis). The time required for soil horizons to develop from parent material vary from about 50 years for a sandy loam in a warm and humid climate on well-drained and moderately level topography to perhaps a million years for a sand soil in an arid climate. An incipient soil developed in 45 years from volcanic ash in humid, tropical Indonesia after the eruption of the Krakatoa volcano in 1883.[2] For comparison, some residual soils in central Canada have developed from granite rock in 10,000 years and from limestone in central United States in about 2,000 years.[15] In contrast, desert sands subject to constant wind erosion do not develop soil horizons and will therefore always remain as parent material.

In any climate, recognizable horizons will develop *faster* in a sandy loam to loam soil, high in easily-weathered minerals, on well-drained, moderate slopes. By contrast, in any climate, soil horizons develop *slower* when the parent material is a sand, poor in easily-weathered minerals, very high in clay, very high in calcium, very fertile, poorly drained, lying on steep slopes, or constantly mixed by animals or people.

2: 3.4 Topography and Soil Genesis

Topography refers to relief, lay-of-the-land, or the levelness or sloping character of the land surface.

Soil genesis is faster when the parent material is well-drained and fairly level. Here a large percentage of the precipitation moves through the parent material, leaching soluble salts and moving downward fine clay and humified organic matter. These actions hasten soil profile differentiation and therefore soil genesis (soil formation).

On the same gentle slopes, if the parent material is too high in clay or has a hardpan to reduce the downward movement of water, soil genesis will be slower. If the land surface is depressed and the downward flow of water is ponded, peat and muck soils (Histosols) may form.

Parent materials on steep slopes hasten overland flow of rainfall and resultant erosion. When surface soils erode as fast or faster than soil profile development, the parent material may *never* develop soil horizons and therefore forever remain parent material.

Southern- and westerly-facing slopes in the northern hemisphere receive more direct rays of the sun and are constantly warmer and drier than northerly- or easterly-facing slopes. Warmer and drier soils will have vegetation more typical of areas receiving less rainfall and lying farther south. On warmer and drier slopes, the horizons will develop slower and be thinner than on other aspects (slope-facings). In the tension zone between trees and grasses, more grasses will occur on the warmer and drier southern and western aspects. In the southern hemisphere (south of the equator) conditions are reversed, i.e., northern and eastern slopes are warmer and drier than other slopes.[10]

2: 3.5 Time and Soil Genesis

There is no general agreement on how much weathering or translocation of materials from a freshly deposited parent material is necessary before the parent material can be called a soil. Some of the criteria for such determinations are as follows:

1) When horizon development can be observed in the field or measured by laboratory techniques. For example, when many of the soluble salts have leached from the A horizon and have either concentrated in the B horizon or have leached from the profile into underground or surface waters.

2) When iron, aluminum, clay and/or humus have eluviated (leached) from the A horizon and illuviated (concentrated) in the B horizon. This deposition usually begins along soil cracks and around soil peds (natural soil aggregates).[5]

2: 4 SUMMARY

Most upland soils developed from weathered mineral geological deposits with small amounts of plant and animal residues. Other soils in depressions consist principally of organic residues preserved by excessive wetness. By far the largest percentage of the soils of the world have developed on geological parent materials that have been moved one or more times by water, wind, glaciers, and/or gravity.

No one can be certain when a particular geological deposit changes from parent material to a soil. Some scientists believe that as soon as parent material supports plants it is a soil. Another group is of the opinion that before parent material can be called a soil it must have discernible horizons. However, everyone agrees that there are five factors interacting to produce a soil. These are: Active climate and biosphere, passive parent material and topography, and neutral time.

Parent materials originate from the weathering of minerals in rock. This weathering is a combination of physical, chemical, and biological processes. Rocks are classified as igneous, sedimentary, and metamorphic.

Soils are more than residues from mineral weathering with an admixture of organic matter. From the weathered residues of primary minerals, secondary clay minerals are synthesized. The principal clay minerals formed are montmorillonite, illite, vermiculite, chlorite, kaolinite, sesquioxides, and amorphous. Sesquioxides may be crystalline or noncrystalline and amorphous minerals are noncrystalline.

Soil genesis is faster under conditions of high temperature, high and year-long rainfall, moderately permeable loam parent material, and nearly level topography.

CITED REFERENCES

1. Sopher, C.D. and J.V. Baird. Soils and Soil Management. Reston Pub. Co., Reston, Virginia. 1978, pages 13-35.

2. Leet, L.D. and S. Judson. Physical Geology. Prentice-Hall, Inc., 3rd Edition, 1965, pages 72-90.

3. Alexander, M. Introduction to Soil Microbiology. 2nd Edition, John Wiley & Sons, New York, 1977, pages 34, 85, 371, 375.

4. Donahue, R.L., R.W. Miller, and J.C. Shickluna. Soils: An Introduction to Soils and Plant Growth. Prentice-Hall, Inc., 5th Edition, 1983, pages 16-36.

5. Donahue, R.L., R.H. Follett, and Rodney W. Tulloch. Our Soils and Their Management. Interstate Printers and Publishers, Danville, Illinois, 5th Edition, 1983, pages 7-11.

6. Lowenstam, H.A. "Minerals Formed by Organisms." Science, Vol. 211, 13 March, 1981, pages 1126-1131.

7. Jenny, H. Factors of Soil Formation. McGraw-Hill Book Co., Inc., New York, 1941.

8. Joffe, J.S. Pedology. Rutgers University Press, New Brunswick, New Jersey, 1949.

9. Kellogg, C.E. "Climate and Soil". *In* "Climate and Man," Yearbook of Agriculture, U.S. Department of Agriculture, Washington, D.C., 1941, pages 265-291.

10. Berger, K.C. Introductory Soils. The Macmillan Co., New York, 1965, pages 98, 99, 103.

11. Buol, S.W., Hole, F.D., and R.J. McCracken. Soil Genesis and Classification. Iowa State University Press, Ames, Iowa, 1973, pages 84-86.

12. Whyte, R.O. "The Grassland and Fodder Resources of India." Scientific Monograph No. 22, $\frac{\text{ICAR 10.22}}{2000}$ Indian Council of Agricultural Research, New Delhi, 1957, pages 77-87.

13. USDA. "Grass: The Yearbook of Agriculture, 1948." United States Department of Agriculture, Washington, D.C., pages 45-66.

14. Ahn, P.M. West African Soils. Oxford University Press, London, England, 1970, Vol. 1, pages 43-86.

15. Thorp, J. "The Nature of the Pedological Record in the Quaternary." Soil Science, Vol. 99, No. 1, 1965.

ADDITIONAL REFERENCES

American Geological Institute. "Dictionary of Geological Terms." Anchor Press/Doubleday, Garden City, New York, 1976, 472 pages.

Arakeri, H.R., G.V. Chalam, S. Satyanarayana and R.L. Donahue. Soil Management in India. Asia Publishing House, Bombay, New Delhi, London. 2nd Edition, 1962, 584 pages.

Bates, Robert L. and Julia A. Jackson, Editors. "Glossary of Geology." American Geological Institute, Falls Church, Virginia, 2nd Edition, 1980, 751 pages.

Brady, N.C. The Nature and Properties of Soils. 8th Edition, Macmillan Pub. Co., Inc., New York, 1974, 639 pages.

Lutgens, F.K. and E.J. Tarbuck. "The Atmosphere: An Introduction to Meteorology. Prentice-Hall, Inc., Englewood Cliffs, New Jersey, 1979, 413 pages.

Raychaudhuri, S.P. Land and Soil. National Book Trust, New Delhi, India, 1966, 75 pages.

Raychaudhuri, S.P., et al. Soils of India. Indian Council of Agricultural Research. New Delhi, India, 1963, 496 pages.

Swindale, L.D., ed. Soil-Resource Data for Agricultural Development. Hawaii Agricultural Experiment Station, Univ. of Hawaii, Honolulu, Hawaii, 1978, 306 pages.

Tamhane, R.V., D.P. Motiramani, and Y.P. Bali, in collaboration with R.L. Donahue. Soils: Their Chemistry and Fertility in Tropical Asia. Prentice-Hall of India, Pvt., Limited, New Delhi, India, 1964, 475 pages.

Thompson, L.M. and F.R. Troeh. Soils and Soil Fertility. McGraw-Hill Book Co., New York, 1978, 516 pages.

USDA. "Climate and Man: Yearbook of Agriculture, 1941." U.S. Dept. of Agriculture, 1942, 1248 pages.

USDA. "Soil: The Yearbook of Agriculture, 1957." U.S. Dept. of Agriculture, Wash. D.C., 1958, 784 pages.

USDA. "Soil Taxonomy: A Basic System of Soil Classification for Making and Interpreting Soil Surveys". U.S. Dept. of Agriculture, Agr. Handbook 436, 1975, 754 pages.

USDA. "Trees: The Yearbook of Agriculture, 1949." U.S. Dept. of Agriculture, Wash. D.C., 1950, 944 pages.

USDA. "Water: The Yearbook of Agriculture, 1955." U.S. Dept. of Agriculture, 1956, 751 pages.

Young, A. Tropical Soils and Soil Survey. Cambridge University Press, Cambridge, 1980, 468 pages.

CHAPTER 3

Soil Taxonomy and Soil Survey

3: 1 INTRODUCTION

The word *taxonomy* is derived from the Greek, *taxis,* meaning arrangement or order. Soil taxonomy is therefore an orderly arrangement of soils in the field for the purpose of more effectively studying their properties, with the ultimate aim of increasing plant productivity and enhancing the human environment.

As predictable, there are many systems of soil taxonomy throughout the world. Explained in this chapter will be the soil taxonomy systems currently in use by the United States, the U.S.S.R., France, Canada, and Australia. Also discussed will be the U.S. Soil Map of the World and the Soil Map of the World published by continents by the Food and Agriculture Organization (FAO) of the United Nations in collaboration with the United Nations Educational, Scientific, and Cultural Organization (UNESCO).

Soils do not recognize country boundaries; for this reason, international cooperation is essential for the optimum understanding and maximum utilization of this essential world resource. International cooperation on the science of soils, including soil taxonomy, is deterred by language barriers.

Three soil scientists deserve the primary credit for originating world soil taxonomy and for bridging the language barrier. V.V. Dokuchaev (1846-1903), a Russian, is credited with the first publications on soil taxonomy. Glinka (1867-1929) translated some of Dokuchaev's works from Russian to German, adding some of his own ideas in the translation. Marbut (1863-1935) then translated into English Glinka's German language edition. In this way, the original studies of Dokuchaev on soil taxonomy became available to the Germans via Glinka's translation and to the English-speaking world through the translation by Marbut. However, it should be explained here that both Glinka and Marbut were renowned soil taxonomists in their own right and each added to world knowledge by their respective translations (Glinka, 1914, 1927; Marbut, 1927).

Although the origin of soil taxonomy is credited to Dokuchaev, Glinka, and Marbut, many other scientists also made significant contributions. Among the ancient were Aristotle (384-322 B.C.), Theophrastus (372-287 B.C.), Cato the Elder (234-149 B.C.), Varro (116-27 B.C.), Virgil (70-19 B.C.), Columella (about 45 A.D.), and Pliny the Elder (23-79 A.D.). Later scientists who made a contribution to soil and plant science and to soil taxonomy were Jan Batiste Van Helmont (1577-1644), J.R. Glauber (1604-1668), John Mayow (1643-1679), Jethro Tull (1674-1741), Arthur Young (1741-1820), Justus von Leibig (1803-1873), Jean Batiste Boussingault (1802-1882), E.W. Hilgard, 1906 (1833-1916), and V.R. Williams (1863-1939).

Contemporary scientists who advanced soil taxonomy are C.E. Kellogg, 1938, 1961; G.D. Smith, 1964; M. Baldwin, 1938; H. Jenny, 1941; M.G. Cline, 1949; F.D. Hole, 1963, 1973; O.W. Bidwell, 1963; W.M. Johnson, 1978; R.W. Simonson, 1964; J. Thorp, 1936, 1938, 1949; S.W. Buol, 1973; and R.J. McCracken, 1973.

3: 2 UNITED STATES SYSTEM OF SOIL TAXONOMY

3: 2.1 Introduction

From the time the term *soil series* was proposed by Whitney in 1909, the United States soil scientists have been refining their system of soil taxonomy. Major steps in this process have included the system proposed by Baldwin, Kellogg, and Thorp in 1938; Marbut's Atlas of American Agriculture, Soils of the United States, 1935; and the Seventh Approximation in 1960 and the 1964 Supplement (Soil Survey Staff, 1960 and 1964). In 1965 the U.S. System of Soil Taxonomy was slightly modified and officially adopted in the United States; however, the complete system was not published until 1975 (Soil Survey Staff, 1975).

The present system of soil taxonomy in the United States is open-ended and adaptable to all soils of the world; as more is learned, the system can be modified. Its six categories are: order, suborder, great group, subgroup, family, and series. Terms essential to soil mapping and practical use of soils include soil phase and soil type. Soil phases include surface soil texture, horizon thickness, percentage of slope, degree of stoniness, degree of saltiness, and degree of erosion. Soil type, a textural phase of a soil series, consists of the series name plus the texture of the surface soil; e.g., Miami silt loam. A mapping unit is a phase of a series and includes the soil series name plus one or more of the phases. For example:

NrB_2 is a mapping unit in the Coastal Plains of the southern United States and stands for Norfolk sandy loam, 1 to 6 percent slopes, eroded.

In the United States, there are 10 soil orders in the U.S. system of soil taxonomy, divided into 47 suborders, 185 great groups, 970 subgroups,

4,500 soil families, and about 10,500 series. Each of these categories will be discussed.

3: 2.2 Soil Orders

Nine of the 10 soil orders in the United States System of Soil Taxonomy are mineral soils differentiated primarily on the basis of the presence or absence of specific diagnostic horizons. The tenth soil order, Histosols, are organic soils.

The 10 soil orders are listed alphabetically in Table 3.1 along with their formative element, derivation of formative element, percentage of world

Table 3.1. Soil orders of the United States system of soil taxonomy: names, formative element of names, percentage of land area of the world, and diagnostic characteristics (Soil Survey Staff, 1975)

Soil order	Formative element	Derivation of of formative element	Percentage of land area of world	Principal diagnostic characteristics
Alfisols	alf	Meaningless syllable	13.19	Mineral soils; relatively low in organic matter; relatively high in base saturation; an illuvial horizon of silicate clays; moisture adequate to mature a crop.
Entisols	ent	Meaningless syllable	8.28	Mineral soils; pedogenic horizons weakly developed or absent; no deep, wide soil cracks in most years.
Aridisols	id	Latin, *aridus*, dry	18.76	Mineral soils; relatively low in organic matter; a few pedogenic horizons; inadequate water to mature a crop in most years.
Histosols	ist	Greek, *histos*, tissue	0.90	Organic soils; organic in more than half of upper 80 cm of profile.
Inceptisols	ept	Latin, *inceptum*, beginning	8.88	Mineral soils; relatively low in organic matter or base saturation or both; some pedogenic horizons and some weatherable minerals; no horizon of illuvial clays; water adequate in most years to mature a crop.

Table 3.1 (*Contd.*)

Soil order	Formative element	Derivation of formative element	Percentage of land area of world	Principal diagnostic characteristics
Mollisols	oll	Latin, *mollis*, soft	8.57	Mineral soils; thick, dark colored surface horizons; relatively high in organic matter; relatively high in base saturation in all horizons; no deep, wide soil cracks in most years.
Oxisols	ox	French, *oxide*, oxide	8.51	Mineral soils; no illuvial horizon of silicate clays; no weatherable minerals; clays very inactive.
Spodosols	od	Greek, *spodos*, wood ash	4.28	Mineral soils; an illuvial horizon of amorphous aluminum and organic matter, with or without amorphous iron.
Ultisols	ult	Latin, *ultimus*, last	5.56	Mineral soils; horizons low in base saturation; an illuvial horizon of silicate clays; water adequate in most years to mature a crop.
Vertisols	ert	Latin, *verto*, turn	1.80	Mineral soils very high in clay; deep, wide cracks at some time in most years.

land area, and principal diagnostic characteristics. Of the soil orders, Aridisols are the most extensive and Histosols the least common.

Table 3.2 gives the summary of world soils.

Table 3.2. Summary of world soils

	Percentage	Square kilometres	Square miles
Soils included in the 10 soil orders	78.73	102,310,200	39,580,900
Mountain soils, undifferentiated	19.68	25,578,000	9,895,500
Miscellaneous areas	1.59	2,072,000	801,600
Grand Total	100.00	129,960,200	50,278,000

3: 2.3 Soil Suborders

The 47 soil suborders in the United States System of Soil Taxonomy are separated mostly because of differences in soil horizons or lack of horizons resulting from contrasts in soil moisture, soil temperature, anthropic influence, soil mineralogy, soil texture, and stage of decomposition of organic matter.

Table 3.3 lists the first formative elements used in naming soil suborders, their derivation, and a simplified explanation of the formative elements.

Table 3.3. Soil suborders of the United States system of soil taxonomy: formative element of names and their simplified explanation (Soil Survey Staff, 1975)

First formative element	Derivation of formative element	Explanation (simplified)
1	2	3
alb	Latin, *albus,* white	A soil with a nearly white eluvial horizon near the surface resulting from wetness.
and	Japanese, *ando, an,* black; *do,* soil	A dark colored soil derived from volcanic ash, with appreciable allophane, an amorphous clay mineral composed of a hydrous aluminum silicate.
aqu	Latin, *aqua,* water	A soil that is currently very wet, or was formerly wet and now artificially drained.
ar	Latin, *arare,* to plow	A soil with only fragments of horizons because of artificial (anthropic) disturbance.
arg	Latin, *argilla,* white clay	A soil having an illuvial horizon of silicate clays.
bor	Greek, *boreas,* northern	A cool or cold soil with mean annual soil temperature less than 8° C.
ferr	Latin, *ferrum,* iron	A soil containing appreciable free iron.
fibr	Latin, *fibra,* fiber	A soil consisting mostly of undecomposed plant residue fibers.
fluv	Latin, *fluvius,* river	A soil composed of recent alluvium.
fol	Latin, *folia,* leaf	A soil with leaves, twigs, and branches in all stages of decomposition.
hem	Greek, *hemi,* half	A soil with partly decomposed plant residues.
hum	Latin, *humus,* earth	A soil with appreciable humus.
ochr	Greek, *ochros,* pale	A soil with a surface horizon that is either light in color or low in organic matter, or both.

Table 3.3 (*Contd.*)

1	2	3
orth	Greek, *orthos,* true	A soil decreed by taxonomists to be most representative of a particular suborder; e.g., Orthids have no illuvial B horizon of silicate clays: Orthents are on recently eroded slopes; Orthox have a short dry season or no dry season; and Orthods have a B horizon that contains iron, aluminum, and humus.
plagg	German, *plaggen,* sod	A soil with an artificial (anthropic) surface layer more than 50 cm thick composed of organic debris residual from large applications of animal manures.
psamm	Greek, *psammos,* sand	A soil that is a sand or loamy sand to a depth of 1 meter or more.
rend	Polish, *rendzina,* noise made by plowing dry soil	A shallow dark colored soil less than 50 cm deep overlying limy material testing more than 40% calcium carbonate equivalent.
sapr	Greek, *sapros,* rotten	A soil consisting mostly of highly decomposed plant residues.
torr	Latin, *torridus,* hot and dry	A soil with too little available water to mature a crop without irrigation.
trop	Greek, *tropikos,* of the solstice (when sun is farthest from equator)	A soil that, at a depth of 50 cm, has a difference of less than 5°C between mean summer and mean winter temperatures.
ud	Latin, *udus,* humid	A soil that is moist but not wet; dry for short periods or not at all.
umbr	Latin, *umbra,* shade	A soil with a surface horizon that is dark colored, thick, and acid.
ust	Latin, *ustus,* burnt	A soil that is dry for long periods but moist in the growing season for 90 days or more in most years; droughts are common.
xer	Greek, *xeros,* dry	A soil in midlatitudes that is reliably moist in winter to produce a cool-season crop such as wheat, but too dry in summer for annual crop production.

3: 2.4 Soil Great Groups

Of the 227 known great groups in the world, 185 occur in the United States. Soil great groups are classified primarily on the basis of these characteristics:

1) Similarities in kind, arrangement, and degree of expression of soil horizons.

Table 3.4. Soil great groups of the United States system of soil taxonomy: first formative element of names and their simplified connotation (Soil Survey Staff, 1975)

First formative element	Connotation (simplified explanation)
1	2
acr	Extremely low CEC in clay fraction.
agr	Having an illuvial horizon of clay and humus formed under cultivation.
alb	A nearly white eluvial horizon near the surface, reflecting wetness.
and	Presence of appreciable allophane.
arg	A soil having an illuvial horizon of silicate clays.
bor	A cool or cold soil, mean annual soil temperature $< 8°C$.
calc	A soil that is calcareous throughout and that has an horizon with an appreciable accumulation of lime.
camb	A soil having an altered but not illuvial B horizon.
chrom	Brownish or reddish color.
cry	A soil that is relatively cold even in summer.
dur	A soil having a hardpan cemented with silica.
dys, dystr	Low base saturation.
eu, eutr	High base saturation.
ferr	Presence of appreciable free iron.
frag	Presence of a fragipan.
fragloss	(See *frag* and *gloss.*)
gibbs	Presence of gibbsite in sheets or nodules.
gloss	Presence of gray eluvial tongues in an illuvial horizon of silicate clay.
hal	Wet and somewhat salty.
hapl	The simplest set of horizons.
hum	Presence of appreciable amount of humus.
hydr	Presence of excess water.
luv	A soil having an horizon of illuvial humus.
med	A soil of midlatitudes.
nadur	(See *natr* and *dur.*)
natr	Presence of significant amounts of exchangeable sodium or of magnesium and sodium.
ochr	A surface horizon that is either light in color or low in organic matter, or both.
pale	A soil having horizons that have more than normal development.
pell	A soil that has low chroma.
plac	Presence of a thin (a few mm) pan, cemented by iron or by iron and humus.
plagg	A surface mantle, > 50 cm thick, of materials that have been added by continued manuring.
plinth	Presence of large amounts of plinthite, an iron-rich material that hardens irreversibly on exposure to cycles of wetting and drying.

Table 3.4 (*Contd.*)

1	2	1	2
psamm	Sandy texture, a sand or loamy sand, to a depth of 1 m or more.	ud	Moist but not wet, and dry for short periods or not at all.
quartz	More than 95 percent quartz.	umbr	A thick, acid, dark-colored surface horizon.
rhod	Dark colors due to high iron content, generally dark red.	ust	Dry for long periods but moist in a growing season for 90 days or more in most years; droughts common.
sal	Presence of an horizon with >2 percent salt.		
sider	Presence of appreciable free iron.	verm	Intensively mixed by animals, chiefly worms and their predators.
sphagn	Mostly sphagnum moss.		
sulf	Presence of appreciable shallow sulfides or products of their oxidation.	vitr	Large amounts of glass.
		xer	A soil of midlatitudes that is reliably moist in winter and dry in summer, reflecting Mediterranean climate.
torr	Inadequate moisture to mature a crop without irrigation.		

2) Similarities in soil moisture and soil temperature regimes.
3) Similarities in degree of saturation of bases.

Formative elements of the soil great groups and their connotation are given in Table 3.4 and a complete list of all soil orders, suborders, and great groups in the United States are displayed in Table 3.5.

Table 3.5. Names of all 10 soil orders, 47 suborders, and 185 great groups in the U.S. (225 world-wide) in the United States system of soil taxonomy (Soil Survey Staff, 1975)

Order	Suborder	Great group
Alfisols	Aqualfs	Albaqualfs
		Duraqualfs
		Fragiaqualfs
		Glossaqualfs
		Natraqualfs
		Ochraqualfs
		Plinthaqualfs
		Tropaqualfs
		Umbraqualfs
	Boralfs	Cryoboralfs
		Eutroboralfs
		Fragiboralfs
		Glossoboralfs
		Natriboralfs
		Paleboralfs
	Udalfs	Agrudalfs
		Ferrudalfs
		Fragiudalfs
		Fraglossudalfs
		Glossudalfs
		Hapludalfs
		Natrudalfs
		Paleudalfs
		Rhodudalfs
		Tropudalfs
	Ustalfs	Durustalfs
		Haplustalfs
		Natrustalfs
		Paleustalfs
		Plinthustalfs
		Rhodustalfs
	Xeralfs	Durixeralfs
		Haploxeralfs
		Natrixeralfs
		Palexeralfs
		Plinthoxeralfs
		Rhodoxeralfs
Aridisols	Argids	Durargids
		Haplargids
		Nadurargids
		Natrargids
		Paleargids
	Orthids	Calciorthids
		Camborthids
		Durorthids
		Gypsiorthids
		Paleorthids
		Salorthids
Entisols	Aquents	Cryaquents
		Fluvaquents
		Haplaquents
		Hydraquents
		Psammaquents
		Sulfaquents
		Tropaquents
	Arents	Arents
	Fluvents	Cryofluvents
		Torrifluvents
		Tropofluvents
		Udifluvents
		Ustifluvents
		Xerofluvents
	Orthents	Cryorthents
		Torriorthents
		Troporthents
		Udorthents
		Ustorthents
		Xerorthents
	Psamments	Cryopsamments
		Quartzipsamments
		Torripsamments
		Tropopsamments
		Udipsamments
		Ustipsamments
		Xeropsamments
Histosols	Fibrists	Borofibrists

Table 3.5 (*Contd.*)

Order	Suborder	Great group	Order	Suborder	Great group
		Cryofibrists			Sombritropepts
		Luvifibrists			Ustropepts
		Medifibrists		Umbrepts	Cryumbrepts
		Sphagnofibrists			Fragiumbrepts
		Tropofibrists			Haplumbrepts
	Folists	Borofolists			Xerumbrepts
		Cryofolists	Mollisols	Albolls	Argialbolls
		Tropofolists			Natralbolls
	Hemists	Borohemists		Aquolls	Argiaquolls
		Cryohemists			Calciaquolls
		Luvihemists			Cryaquolls
		Medihemists			Duraquolls
		Sulfihemists			Haplaquolls
		Sulfohemists			Natraquolls
		Tropohemists		Borolls	Argiborolls
	Saprists	Borosaprists			Calciborolls
		Cryosaprists			Cryoborolls
		Medisaprists			Haploborolls
		Troposaprists			Natriborolls
Inceptisols	Andepts	Cryandepts			Paleborolls
		Durandepts			Vermiborolls
		Dystrandepts		Rendolls	Rendolls
		Eutrandepts		Udolls	Argiudolls
		Hydrandepts			Hapludolls
		Placandepts			Paleudolls
		Vitrandepts			Vermudolls
	Aquepts	Andaquepts		Ustolls	Argiustolls
		Cryaquepts			Calciustolls
		Fragiaquepts			Durustolls
		Halaquepts			Haplustolls
		Haplaquepts			Natrustolls
		Humaquepts			Paleustolls
		Placaquepts			Vermustolls
		Plinthaquepts		Xerolls	Argixerolls
		Sulfaquepts			Calcixerolls
		Tropaquepts			Durixerolls
	Ochrepts	Cryochrepts			Haploxerolls
		Durochrepts			Natrixerolls
		Dystrochrepts			Palexerolls
		Eutrochrepts	Oxisols	Aquox	Gibbsiaquox
		Fragiochrepts			Ochraquox
		Ustochrepts			Plinthaquox
		Xerochrepts			Umbraquox
	Plaggepts	Plaggepts		Humox	Acrohumox
	Tropepts	Dystropepts			Gibbsihumox
		Eutropepts			Haplohumox
		Humitropepts			Sombrihumox

Table 3.5 (*Contd.*)

Order	Suborder	Great group	Order	Suborder	Great group
	Orthox	Acrorthox			Fragiaquults
		Eutrorthox			Ochraquults
		Gibbsiorthox			Paleaquults
		Haplorthox			Plinthaquults
		Sombriorthox			Tropaquults
		Umbriorthox			Umbraquults
	Torrox	Torrox		Humults	Haplohumults
	Ustox	Acrustox			Palehumults
		Eutrustox			Plinthohumults
		Sombriustox			Sombrihumults
		Haplustox			Tropohumults
Spodosols	Aquods	Cryaquods		Udults	Fragiudults
		Duraquods			Hapludults
		Fragiaquods			Paleudults
		Haplaquods			Plinthudults
		Placaquods			Rhodudults
		Sideraquods			Tropudults
		Tropaquods		Ustults	Haplustults
	Ferrods	Ferrods			Paleustults
	Humods	Cryohumods			Plinthustults
		Fragihumods			Rhodustults
		Haplohumods		Xerults	Haploxerults
		Placohumods			Palexerults
		Tropohumods	Vertisols	Torrerts	Torrerts
	Orthods	Cryorthods		Uderts	Chromuderts
		Fragiorthods			Pelluderts
		Haplorthods		Usterts	Chromusterts
		Placorthods			Pellusterts
		Troporthods		Xererts	Chromoxererts
Ultisols	Aquults	Albaquults			Pelloxererts

3: 2.5 Soil Subgroups (Soil Survey Staff, 1972)

Great groups are separated into three kinds of subgroups: *typic, intergrade,* and *extragrade.* The name of a subgroup is formed by placing one or more adjectives before the name of the relevant great group. There are more than 1,000 soil subgroups recognized worldwide, of which 970 occur in the United States.

A *typic subgroup* represents the central concept of its great group. A soil in a typic subgroup, however, is not necessarily more extensive than the other kinds of soil in the same great group.

An *intergrade subgroup* has the definitive properties of the great group whose name it carries as a substantive. It also has some of the properties of another taxon or more than one other taxon—an order, a suborder, or a great group. The adjective or adjectives in the intergrade subgroup name are formed from the names of the other taxon or taxa. Formative elements normally are not repeated. Thus, if a soil is an intergrade between two great groups in the same suborder, the first formative element of one great group is used in adjective form to modify the name of the other great group. If a soil is an intergrade to a soil of a different suborder in the same order, the final formative element in the different suborder name is not used as an adjective in the intergrade subgroup name.

The name of any taxon, converted to an adjective, can be used in the name of an intergrade subgroup.

An *extragrade subgroup* has aberrant properties that do not represent intergrades to any known kind of soil. Hard rock, for example, is not considered to be soil. Consequently, a soil with underlying hard rock at a depth of < 50 cm is placed in a *lithic* subgroup. A permanently frozen layer, permafrost, below the soil is the basis for placing a soil in a *pergelic* subgroup. These subgroups, in a sense, are made up of intergrades to "not soil". A soil at the base of a slope may accumulate sediments slowly, producing in time only a very thick dark-colored A1 horizon. Such a soil is placed in a *cumulic* subgroup because there is no known thick soil that consists of only an A1 horizon. The adjectives used in forming the names of extragrade subgroups and their meanings are given in Table 3.6.

Following are examples of how the nomenclature of the taxonomy is applied in forming names from order through subgroup:

Subgroup	*Great group*	*Suborder*	*Order*
Typic Ustorthents...........	Ustorthents..............	Orthents.................	Entisols
Aquic Fragiudalfs...........	Fragiudalfs..............	Udalfs.....................	Alfisols
Typic Fragiaqualfs..........	Fragiaqualfs.............	Aqualfs.....................	Alfisols
Terric Borohemists..........	Borohemists..............	Hemists....................	Histosols
Ustollic Calciorthids........	Calciorthids.............	Orthids....................	Aridisols

3: 2.6 Soil Families of Mineral Soils (Soil Survey Staff 1975)

About 4,500 soil families are recognized in the United States.

A complete family name consists of a subgroup name preceded by a few, usually three, modifiers that narrow the range of properties enough to permit general statements about use and management of the soils. Modifiers in a family name of mineral soils represent the following differentiae, listed according to their sequence in the name.

Particle-size class
Mineralogy class
Calcareous and reaction classes
Soil temperature class
Soil depth class

Table 3.6. Extragrade subgroups of the United States system of soil taxonomy and their meaning (Soil Survey Staff, 1975)

Adjective	Meaning	Adjective	Meaning
abruptic	A large difference in percentage of clay between an eluvial horizon and an illuvial horizon without a significant transitional horizon.	lithic	Hard rock within 50 cm of the surface.
		pergelic	Presence of permafrost.
aeric[1]	Browner and better aerated than typic.	petrocalcic	An indurated horizon of lime accumulation.
anthr	A manmade dark-colored surface horizon.	petroferric	A shallow layer of ironstone.
arenic	Sandy eluvial horizons (sand or loamy sand), mostly between 50 cm and 1 m thick.	pachic	A thick dark surface horizon.
		plinthic[1]	Presence of small amounts of plinthite, an iron-rich material that hardens irreversibly on exposure to cycles of wetting and drying.
cumulic	An overthickened epipedon rich in humus.		
glossic	Tongued eluvial and illuvial horizons.		
		ruptic	Intermittent horizons.
grossarenic	Sandy eluvial horizons (sand or loamy sand) > 1 m thick.	sulfic	Presence of deep sulfides or moderate amounts if shallow, or products of sulfide oxidation.
hydric	Organic soil floating on water if used in name of a Histosol.	superic	Very shallow plinthite.
leptic	Thin soil horizons.	terric	A mineral substratum in an organic soil.
limnic	Organic soil with basal layer of marl, diatoms, or sedimentary peat.	thapto[1]	A buried soil.

[1]Not strictly an extragrade. The name is used to indicate a special departure from the typic subgroup.

Soil slope class
Soil consistence class
Coatings on peds class
Class of permanent cracks

Examples of contrasting mineral soil family names are as follows: clayey, montmorillonitic, euic, thermic; clayey, oxidic, isohyperthermic; coarse-silty, mixed (calcareous), mesic; loamy, mixed, mesic, shallow; loamy-skeletal, mixed (calcareous), mesic; sandy over clayey, mixed, frigid; sandy, mixed, thermic.

Particle-size classes

Particle-size refers to grain-size distribution of the whole soil and is not the same as texture, which refers to the fine-earth fraction. The fine-earth fraction consists of the particles that have a diameter < 2 mm. Particle-size classes are a kind of compromise between engineering and pedologic classifications. In engineering classifications, the limit between sand and silt is a diameter of 74 microns; in pedologic classifications, the limit is a diameter of either 50 or 20 microns. Engineering classifications are based on percentages by weight in the fraction < 74 mm in diameter, and textural classes are based on percentages by weight in the fraction < 2 mm in diameter.

The very fine sand separate (diameter between 0.05 mm and 0.1 mm) is split in engineering classifications. In defining particle-size classes, much the same split is made but in a different manner. A soil that has a texture of fine sand or loamy fine sand normally has an appreciable content of very fine sand, but the very fine sand fraction is mostly coarser than 74 microns. A silty sediment, such as loess, may also have an appreciable component of very fine sand, but most of the very fine sand is finer than 74 microns. So in particle-size classes, the very fine sand is allowed to "float". It is treated as sand if the texture is fine sand, loamy fine sand, or coarser. It is treated as silt if the texture is very fine sand, loamy very fine sand, sandy loam, silt loam, or finer.

Classes of particle-size are used to describe material in the control section. The class named is that of the weighted average of the control section unless two strongly contrasting classes are present. Then both classes are named. In soils that do not have an argillic horizon, the control section normally extends from a depth of 25 cm to 100 cm. In soils that have an argillic horizon, the control section normally is the upper 50 cm of the argillic horizon if the horizon is > 50 cm thick or is the whole argillic horizon if the horizon is < 50 cm thick. If there is rock or permafrost at a more shallow depth, the control section stops at the rock or 25 cm below the top of the permafrost. The same control section is used for classes of mineralogy, but strongly contrasting classes are not used. The mineralogy of the upper part of the control section is named.

No single set of particle-size classes seems appropriate as family differentiae for all kinds of soils. The classes listed in Table 3.7 provide for a choice of either seven or 11 particle-size classes. This choice permits relatively fine distinctions in soils if particle-size is important and permits broader groupings if the particle-size is not susceptible to precise measurement or if using narrowly defined classes produces undesirable groupings. Thus in some families the term "clayey" indicates that there is 35 percent or more clay in defined horizons, but in other families the term "fine" indicates that the clay fraction constitutes 35 through 59 percent of the fine earth of the horizons, and the term "very-fine" indicates 60 percent or more clay. The term "rock fragments" refers to particles 2 mm in diameter or larger and includes all sizes that have horizontal dimensions less than the size of a pedon. It is not the same as the term "coarse fragments," which excludes stones and boulders larger than about 25 cm. The term "fine earth" refers to particles smaller than 2 mm in diameter.

There are three situations in which particle-size class names are not used. In the first situation, the name is redundant. Psamments and Psammaquents, by definition, are sandy, and no particle-size class name is needed or used in the family name.

In the second situation, particle-size is meaningless because, presumably, the soil consists of a mixture of discrete mineral particles and of gels. The concept of either texture or particle size is not applicable to a gel, particularly if the gel cannot be dispersed. Consequently, particle-size class names are not used if the soil is mostly glass or if the exchange complex is dominated by amorphous materials, as is true of Andepts by definition. In families of Andepts and Andaquepts, in most andic subgroups of Inceptisols and in andeptic and andaqueptic subgroups of other orders, and in cindery and ashy families of Entisols and Aridisols, particle-size class names as such are not used for the part of the soil that cannot be dispersed.

In the third situation, the organic-matter content is high and particle-size has only limited relation to the physical and chemical properties of the soils. This seems to be normal in soils that have both a cryic temperature regime and a spodic horizon. Therefore, particle-size class names are not used for the spodic horizons of Cryaquods, Cryohumods, Cryorthods, or Cryic Placohumods.

The terms in Table 3.8 are substituted for particle-size class names for the taxa that have been listed under the second and third situations unless the particle-size modifier is redundant. They reflect a combination of particle-size and mineralogy, and take the place of both.

Mineralogy classes

Mineralogy classes are based on the approximate mineralogical composition of selected size fractions of the same segment of the soil (control

Table 3.7. Modifiers that express particle-size classes in soil family names (Soil Survey Staff, 1975)

Particle-size class	Definition
1	2
1. Fragmental	Stones, cobbles, gravel, and very coarse sand particles; too little fine earth to fill interstices > 1 mm in diameter.
2. Sandy-skeletal	Rock fragments 2 mm or coarser make up 35 percent or more by volume; enough fine earth to fill interstices > 1 mm; the fraction < 2 mm is sandy as defined for particle-size class 5.
3. Loamy-skeletal	Rock fragments make up 35 percent or more by volume; enough fine earth to fill interstices > 1 mm; the fraction < 2 mm is loamy as defined for particle-size class 6.
4. Clayey-skeletal	Rock fragments make up 35 percent or more by volume; enough fine earth to fill interstices > 1 mm; the fraction finer than 2 mm is clayey as defined for particle-size class 7.
5. Sandy	The texture of the fine earth is sand or loamy sand but not loamy very fine sand or very fine sand; rock fragments make up < 35 percent by volume.
6. Loamy	The texture of the fine earth is loamy very fine sand, very fine sand, or finer, but the amount of clay[1] is < 35 percent; rock fragments are < 35 percent by volume.
a. Coarse loamy	By weight, 15 percent or more of the particles are fine sand (diameter 0.25 to 0.1 mm) or coarser, including fragments up to 7.5 cm in diameter; < 18 percent clay in the fine-earth fraction.
b. Fine-loamy	By weight, 15 percent or more of the particles are fine sand (diameter 0.25 to 0.1 mm) or coarser, including fragments up to 7.5 cm in diameter; 18 through 34 percent clay in the fine-earth fraction (< 30 percent in Vertisols).
c. Coarse-silty	By weight, < 15 percent of the particles are fine sand (diameter 0.25 to 0.1 mm) or coarser, including fragments up to 7.5 cm in diameter; < 18 percent clay in the fine-earth fraction.

d. Fine-silty	By weight, <15 percent of the particles are fine sand (diameter 0.25 to 0.1 mm) or coarser, including fragments up to 7.5 cm in diameter; 18 through 34 percent clay in the fine-earth fraction (<30 percent in Vertisols).
7. Clayey	The fine earth contains 35 percent or more clay by weight, and rock fragments are <35 percent by volume.
a. Fine	A clayey particle-size class for soils having 35 through 59 percent clay in the fine-earth fraction (30 through 59 percent for Vertisols).
b. Very-fine	A clayey particle-size class for soils having 60 percent or more clay in the fine-earth fraction.

[1]Carbonates of clay size are not considered to be clay but are treated as silt in all particle-size classes. If the ratio of 15-bar water to clay is 0.6 or more in half or more of the control section, for this purpose the percentage of clay is considered to be 2.5 times the percentage of 15-bar water.

Table 3.8. Modifiers that substitute in some names for other adjectives that connote particle-size and mineralogy classes (Soil Survey Staff, 1975)

Modifier	Meaning
Cindery	Sixty percent or more of the whole soil (by weight[1]) is volcanic ash, cinders, and pumice; 35 percent or more is cinders that have a diameter of 2 mm or more.
Ashy	Sixty percent or more of the whole soil (by weight) is volcanic ash, cinders, and pumice; <35 percent (by volume) is 2 mm in diameter or larger.
Ashy-skeletal	Thirty-five percent or more (by volume) is rock fragments other than cinders; the fine-earth fraction is otherwise ashy.
Medial	Less than 60 percent of the whole soil (by weight) is volcanic ash, cinders, and pumice; <35 percent (by volume) is 2 mm in diameter or larger; the fine-earth fraction is not thixotropic; the exchange complex is dominated by amorphous materials.
Medial-skeletal	Thirty-five percent or more (by volume) is rock fragments other than cinders 2 mm in diameter or larger; the fine-earth fraction is otherwise medial.
Thixotropic	Less than 35 percent (by volume) has diameter of 2 mm or larger; the fine-earth fraction is thixotropic; the exchange complex is dominated by amorphous materials.
Thixotropic-skeletal	Thirty-five percent or more (by volume) is rock fragments other than cinders 2 mm in diameter or larger; the fine earth fraction is otherwise thixotropic.

[1]Percentages by weight in these definitions are estimated from grain counts; generally a count of one or two dominant size fractions of the conventional mechanical analysis is enough for placement of soil.

section) that is used for application of particle-size classes.

Contrasting mineralogy modifiers are not recognized except where substitute modifiers have been used in place of particle-size class modifiers (Table 3.9). In those soils there is an overlay of ash or cinders or an upper medial or thixotropic layer, and the ashy, cindery, medial, or thixotropic layer extends at least 10 cm into the upper part of the control section. In identifying and naming the contrasting mineralogy modifiers in families of those soils, the seven particle-size classes are used to describe the lower part of the section. For example, a pair of contrasting layers is named "medial over loamy, mixed," not "medial over coarse-loamy, mixed".

If there are layers of contrasting particle-size in the control section, the mineralogy class of the upper part of the control section is definitive of the family mineralogy. For example, if there is fine-loamy material of mixed mineralogy over sandy material that is siliceous, the proper modifiers describing the family are "fine-loamy over sandy, mixed," not "fine-loamy, mixed, over sandy, siliceous".

Table 3.9 is a key to mineralogy classes, not a set of complete definitions. Mineral soils are placed in the first mineralogy class of the key that accommodates them although they also may seem to meet the requirements for other mineralogy classes. Substitute terms that connote both particle-size and mineralogy are based on combined texture, consistence, and mineralogy classes and are used to indicate important variations in Andaquepts; Andepts; andic, andaqueptic, and andeptic subgroups; cryic great groups of Spodosols; and cindery and ashy families of Aridisols and Entisols. Mineralogy classes are not named for Calciaquolls because the effect of the carbonates overshadows other differences in mineralogy, and they are not named for Quartzipsamments, which, by definition, are siliceous.

It is recognized that normally it is impossible to be certain of the percentages of the various kinds of clay minerals. Quantitative methods of identification are still subject to change. Although much progress has been made in the past few decades, an element of judgment enters into any estimation of the percentages. All the evidence does not need to come from X-ray, surface, and DTA determinations. Other physical and chemical properties suggest the mineralogy of many clayey soils. Changes in volume, cation-exchange capacity, and consistence are useful in estimating the nature of clay.

The description of clay mineralogy in naming families of clayey soils is based on the weighted average of the control section.

Calcareous and reaction classes

The presence or absence of carbonates and the reaction are discussed together because they are so intimately related. A calcareous horizon cannot be strongly acid. Calcareous classes are applied to the section between

Table 3.9. Key to mineralogy classes in the United States system of soil taxonomy (Soil Survey Staff, 1975)

Class	Definition	Determinant size fraction
	CLASSES APPLIED TO SOILS OF ANY PARTICLE-SIZE CLASS	
Carbonatic	More than 40 percent by weight carbonates (expressed as $CaCO_3$) plus gypsum, and the carbonates are >65 percent of the sum of carbonates and gypsum.	Whole soil, particles <2 mm in diameter, or whole soil <20 mm, whichever has higher percentage of carbonates plus gypsum.
Ferritic	More than 40 percent by weight iron oxide extractable by citrate-dithionite, reported as Fe_2O_3 (or 28 percent reported as Fe).	Whole soil, particles <2 mm in diameter.
Gibbsitic	More than 40 percent by weight hydrated aluminum oxides, reported as gibbsite and boehmite.	Whole soil, particles <2 mm in diameter.
Oxidic	Less than 90 percent quartz; <40 per cent any other single mineral listed subsequently; and the ratio, percent extractable iron oxide plus percent gibbsite to percent clay[1], is 0.20 or more. That is, $\frac{\text{extractable } Fe_2O_3 \text{ (pct.)} + \text{gibbsite (pct.)}}{\text{clay (pct.)}^1} \geqslant 0.20$	For quartz and other minerals, fraction 0.02 to 2 mm in diameter; for ratio of iron oxide and gibbsite to clay, whole soil <2 mm.
Serpentinitic	More than 40 percent by weight serpentine minerals (antigorite, chrysotile, fibrolite, and talc).	Whole soil, particles <2 mm in diameter.
Gypsic	More than 40 percent by weight of carbonates (expressed as $CaCO_3$) plus gypsum, and the gypsum is >35 percent of the sum of carbonates and gypsum.	Whole soil, particles <2 mm in diameter, or whole soil <20 mm, whichever has higher percentage of carbonates plus gypsum.
Glauconitic	More than 40 percent glauconite by weight.	Whole soil, particles <2 mm in diameter.
	CLASSES APPLIED TO SOILS THAT HAVE A SANDY, SANDY-SKELETAL, LOAMY, OR LOAMY-SKELETAL PARTICLE-SIZE CLASS	
Micaceous	More than 40 percent mica by weight.[2]	0.02 to 20 mm.

Siliceous	More than 90 percent by weight[2] of silica minerals (quartz, chalcedony, or opal) and other extremely durable minerals that are resistant to weathering.	0.02 to 2 mm.
Mixed	All others that have <40 percent of any one mineral other than quartz or feldspars.	0.02 to 2 mm.
	CLASSES APPLIED TO SOILS THAT HAVE A CLAYEY PARTICLE-SIZE CLASS	
Halloysitic	More than half halloysite[3] by weight and smaller amounts of allophane or kaolinite or both.	<0.002 mm.
Kaolinitic	More than half kaolinite, tabular halloysite, dickite, and nacrite by weight and smaller amounts of other 1:1 or nonexpanding 2:1 layer minerals or gibbsite.	<0.002 mm.
Montmorillonitic	More than half montmorillonite and nontronite by weight or a mixture that has more montmorillonite than any other one clay mineral.	<0.002 mm.
Illitic	More than half illite (hydrous mica) by weight and commonly >4 percent K_2O.	<0.002 mm.
Vermiculitic	More than half vermiculite by weight or more vermiculite than any other one clay mineral.	<0.002 mm.
Chloritic	More than half chlorite by weight or more chlorite than any other clay mineral.	<0.002 mm.
Mixed	Other soils.[4]	<0.002 mm.

[1]Percentage of clay or percentage of 15-bar water times 2.5, whichever is greater, provided the ratio of 15-bar water to clay is 0.6 or more in half or more of the control section.

[2]Percentages by weight are estimated from grain counts. Usually, a count of one or two of the dominant size fractions of a conventional mechanical analysis is sufficient for placement of the soil.

[3]Halloysite as used here includes only the tubular forms. What has been called tabular halloysite is grouped here with kaolinite.

[4]Sepiolitic, defined as containing more than half by weight of sepiolite, attapulgite, and palygorskite, should be named if found.

depths of 25 and 50 cm or between a depth of 25 cm and a lithic or paralithic contact that is below a depth of 25 cm but not as deep as 50 cm, or to some part of the soil above a lithic or paralithic contact that is shallower than 25 cm. Two classes, calcareous and noncalcareous, are used in selected taxa. The definitions follow.

Calcareous—The fine-earth fraction effervesces in all parts with cold dilute HCl.

Noncalcareous—The fine-earth fraction does not effervesce in all parts with cold dilute HCl. The term "noncalcareous" is not used as a part of a family name.

It should be noted that a soil containing dolomite is calcareous and that effervescence of dolomite, when treated with cold dilute HCl, is slow.

Reaction classes are applied to the control section that is defined for particle-size classes. Two classes, acid and nonacid, are used in selected taxa. The definitions follow.

Acid—The pH is < 5.0 in 0.01 M $CaCl_2$ (2:1) throughout the control section (about 5.5 in H_2O, 1:1).

Nonacid—The pH is 5.0 or more in 0.01 M $CaCl_2$ (2:1) in at least some part of the control section. The term "nonacid" is not used in family names of calcareous soils.

Reaction-class modifiers are used only in names of families of Entisols and Aquepts; they are not used in names of sandy, sandy-skeletal, and fragmental families of these taxa, nor are they used in names of Sulfaquepts and Fragiaquepts and families that have carbonatic or gypsic mineralogy.

Calcareous-class modifiers are used, if appropriate, in the names of the same taxa as reaction-classes and, in addition, are used in families of Aquolls except for Calciaquolls and for Aquolls that have an argillic horizon. Calcareous reaction-class modifiers are not used in family names of soils that have carbonatic or gypsic mineralogy. A calcareous soil is never acid. Calcareous therefore implies nonacid, and both modifiers are not used in the family name because nonacid would be redundant. Similarly, noncalcareous would be redundant in family names of acid soils.

Soil temperature classes

Soil temperature classes, as named and defined here, are used as family differentiae in all orders. The class names are used as family name modifiers unless the name of a higher taxon carries the same limitation. Thus, frigid is implied in all boric suborders and cryic great groups and is redundant in the name of a family.

The Celsius (centigrade) scale is the standard. Approximate Fahrenheit equivalents are indicated parenthetically. It is assumed that the temperature is that of a soil that is not being irrigated.

For soils in which the difference is 5°C (9°F) or more between mean summer (June, July, and August in the northern hemisphere) and mean winter (December, January, and February in the northern hemisphere) soil temperatures at a depth of 50 cm or at a lithic or paralithic contact, whichever is shallower, the following classes, defined in terms of the mean annual soil temperature are used.

Frigid—Less than 8°C (47°F).

Mesic—From 8° to 15°C (47° to 59°F).

Thermic—From 15° to 22°C (59° to 72°F).

Hyperthermic—More than 22°C (72°F).

For soils in which the difference is less than 5°C (9°F) between mean summer and mean winter soil temperature at a depth of 50 cm or at a lithic or paralithic contact, whichever is shallower, the following classes, defined in terms of the mean annual soil temperature are used.

Isofrigid—Less than 8°C (47°F).

Isomesic—From 8° to 15°C (47° to 59°F).

Isohyperthermic—More than 22°C (72°F).

The appropriate limit between isofrigid and isomesic cannot be tested in the United States and probably will need to be revised.

Other characteristics

Several soil characteristics other than those already discussed must be considered in particular taxa to provide reasonable groupings of series into families. Some of these seem to be logical family criteria. Others probably should have been used in higher categories, but the lack of information about them makes it much safer to use them as family differentiae at this time. These characteristics include soil depth, soil slope, soil consistence, moisture equivalent, and permanent cracks.

Soil depth classes—Classes of shallow and deep soils may be needed at the family level in all orders of mineral soils. Some distinctions in depth are made in great groups and in arenic and lithic subgroups, but some other soils should also be grouped in families according to depth. Some soils have a paralithic contact over soft rock such as clay shale that is too compact for penetration by roots. The classes of soil depth follow.

Micro. Less than 18 cm through diagnostic horizons. Used in cryic great groups but not in pergelic subgroups or in Entisols.

Shallow. Two depths are considered shallow:

1) Less than 50 cm to the upper boundary of a petrocalcic horizon or to a paralithic or a petroferric contact. Used in all great groups of Entisols, Inceptisols, Aridisols, Mollisols, Spodosols, Alfisols, and Ultisols, except pergelic subgroups of the cryic great groups (Cryaquepts, Cryumbrepts, Cryorthods, and so on). Note that lithic subgroups are also shallow, but the adjective "shallow" in a family name for them is redundant.

2) Less than 1 m to a lithic or paralithic or a petroferric contact. Used in families of Oxisols.

Soil slope or shape—Soils of aquic great groups normally have level or concave surfaces. They are mainly in places where ground water saturates the soil during some period of the year. A few, however, are on the sides of slopes where water cannot stand and are kept wet by more or less continuous precipitation and by seepage of water from higher areas. A very few aquic soils are kept wet by hydrostatic pressure. No consistent internal morphologic clues have yet been found that distinguish those sloping aquic soils if the dissolved oxygen content is low, but they generally are easily recognized in the field from their position in the landscape. It is proposed, therefore, in aquic great groups, particularly in Aquolls and Aquults, to use the shape of the soil as a family differentia. Classes of level and sloping soils, as these classes are defined in the Soil Survey Manual (1951), seem adequate. It may be necessary to use slope classes as family differentiae in other orders, but they should not be used as differentiae for families of Aquods or Albaqualfs. If no slope modifier is used in the family name, "level" is assumed in families of aquic soils.

Soil consistence—Some cemented horizons, for example, a duripan, are differentiae in the classification in categories above the family. Others, such as a cemented spodic horizon (ortstein) are not, but no single family should include both soils that have a continuous, shallow cemented horizon and soils that do not. In Spodosols, in particular, a cemented spodic horizon needs to be used as a family differentia. The following classes of consistence are defined for Spodosols:

Ortstein. All or part of the spodic horizon is at least weakly cemented, when moist, into a massive horizon that is present in more than half of each pedon.

Noncemented. The spodic horizon, when moist, is not cemented into a massive horizon in as much as half of each pedon.

Cementation of a small volume into shot or concretions does not constitute cementation that forms a massive horizon. The name of a family of noncemented Spodosols normally does not have a modifier that implies lack of cementation. The name of a family of cemented Spodosols contains the modifier "ortstein".

A cemented calcic or gypsic horizon is not identified in a family name. Many calcic and some gypsic horizons are weakly cemented and some are indurated. The recognition of a petrocalcic or petrogypsic horizon is expected to meet most, if not all, the needs for recognition of cementation in those horizons. Taxa of these cemented soils are not named at the family level.

Coatings—Despite the emphasis given to particle-size classes in the taxonomy, variability remains in the sandy particle-size class, which takes in sands and loamy sands. Some sands are very clean, almost completely free of silt and clay. Others are mixed with appreciable amounts of finer grains. A moisture equivalent of 2 percent makes a reasonable division of the sands at the family level. Two classes of Quartzipsamments are defined in terms of their moisture equivalent.

Coated. The moisture equivalent is 2 percent or more.

Uncoated. The moisture equivalent is <2 percent. The moisture retained at tension of 0.5 bar may be substituted for the moisture equivalent. Or, if moisture tension data are not available, the silt plus clay is $\leqslant 5$ percent.

The moisture equivalent for this distinction is the weighted average for the control section, weighted for the thickness of each horizon or layer.

Permanent cracks—Hydraquents consolidate after drainage and become Fluvaquents. In the process, they form polyhedrons, roughly 12 to 50 cm in diameter, depending on the *n*-value and particle-size. The polyhedrons are separated by cracks that range in width from 2 mm to 1 cm or more. The polyhedrons may shrink and swell with changes in moisture content of the soil, but the cracks are permanent and can persist for some hundreds of years even though the soils are cultivated. The cracks permit rapid movement of water through the soil either vertically or laterally. Yet the soils may have the same particle-size, mineralogy, and other family properties as soils that are not cracked or that have cracks that open and close with the seasons. The soils that have permanent cracks are so rare in the United States that only a provisional definition of their characteristics can be presented.

The modifier "cracked" is used only to designate families of Fluvaquents. It means that there are continuous, permanent, lateral and vertical cracks, at least 2 mm wide, spaced at average lateral intervals of 50 cm or less. If this modifier is not in the family name, permanent cracks are assumed to be absent.

3: 2.7 Soil Families of Histosols (Soil Survey Staff, 1975)

The order in which family modifiers are placed in the technical family names of Histosols follows. The differentiae chosen are those appropriate to the particular family.

Particle-size class
Mineralogy class, including nature of limnic deposits
Reaction class
Soil temperature class
Soil depth class

The control section

The control section in Histosols depends on the nature of the upper part of the soil. The control section extends to any layer of water present below

130 cm or 160 cm. If a lithic or paralithic contact is present at a depth of less than 130 cm, the control section extends to the contact. The control section extends to a depth of 160 cm if (1) the upper 60 cm of the soil is three-fourths or more fibers derived from *Sphagnum* or from *Hypnum* or other mosses or if (2) the upper 60 cm has a bulk density < 0.1. If none of the aforementioned conditions is present, the control section extends to a depth of 130 cm.

Particle-size classes

Particle-size modifiers are used in family names of Histosols only in Terric subgroups. The terms used are as follows:

Fragmental
Loamy-skeletal or clayey-skeletal
Sandy or sandy-skeletal
Loamy
Clayey

The meaning of each of these terms is the same as that defined for particle-size classes of mineral soils. The proper term is selected to describe the weighted average particle-size of the upper 30 cm of the mineral layer or that part of the mineral layer that is within the control section, whichever is thicker.

Mineralogy classes

Mineralogy classes of Histosols are of four kinds, based on the nature of the subgroup or great group.

Ferrihumic—Containing ferrihumic materials within the control section (applied to Fibrists, Hemists, and Saprists, except Sphagnofibrists and sphagnic subgroups of other great groups). Bog iron is present in some Histosols or in organic soil materials. It is called ferrihumic material. It consists of authigenic deposits (formed in place) of hydrated iron oxides mixed with varying kinds or amounts of organic materials. The iron in some places is present in large cemented aggregates. In other places it may be mostly dispersed and soft. Colors normally are shades of dark reddish brown, commonly mixed with black, and the colors change little on drying. The content of iron oxide ranges from 10 percent to >20 percent.

Ferrihumic material is either saturated with water for long periods (>6 months) or is in an artificially drained soil. The content of free iron oxide should exceed 10 percent (7 percent Fe), but the horizon may be either organic or mineral provided there is at least 1 percent organic matter. The material should have >2 percent (by weight) concretions of iron, which may range in size from fine (< 5 mm) to 1 m or more in the largest lateral dimension. Colors should be dark reddish brown or reddish brown or should be close to these colors. The presence of ferrihumic material within the control section is one of the family differentiae.

If ferrihumic is used as a modifier in the technical family name, no other mineralogy modifier is used because the presence of the iron is considered to be, by far, the most important characteristic.

Modifiers applied only to terric subgroups—The mineralogy modifiers used for mineral soils are applied to the mineral parts of the soil for which a particle-size modifier has been used if the mineralogy is not ferrihumic.

Clastic—More than 55 percent mineral matter (total ash after ignition) as a weighted average of the organic materials within the control section (applied to all subgroups, except hydric and terric, that do not have ferrihumic mineralogy).

Modifiers applied to limnic subgroups—If limnic materials are present in the control section, if they are 5 cm or more thick, and if the materials do not have ferrihumic mineralogy, the following modifiers are used:

Coprogenous. Limnic materials that consist of coprogenous earth are present.

Diatomaceous. Limnic materials that consist of diatomaceous earth are present.

Marly. Limnic materials that consist of marl are present.

Reaction classes

Modifiers to indicate reaction are used in all subgroups. The meanings follow:

Euic—The pH of undried samples is 4.5 or more (0.01 M $CaCl_2$) in at least some part of the organic materials in the control section.

Dysic—The pH is <4.5 (in 0.01 M $CaCl_2$) in all parts of the organic materials in the control section.

Soil temperature classes

Names and definitions of classes follow the rules given for soil temperature classes of mineral soils. Frigid, however, is redundant in boric and cryic great groups and is not used. No temperature modifier is used in pergelic subgroups.

Soil depth classes

Soil depth modifiers are used in all lithic subgroups of Histosols except in the suborder of Folists. It is assumed that lithic Folists have a shallow lithic contact. Other lithic Histosols have a lithic contact within the control section but it may be as much as 160 cm deep.

Shallow—Used in lithic subgroups to indicate a lithic contact between a depth of 18 cm and 50 cm.

Micro—Used to indicate a lithic contact shallower than 18 cm without regard to soil temperature. (In mineral soils, micro families are restricted to cryic great groups.)

3: 2.8 Soil Series

Names of series as a rule are geographic names. The name usually is taken from a place near the one where the series was first recognized. It may be the name of a town, a county, or some local feature. Some series in sparsely settled regions have coined names. Most of the series names have been carried over from earlier classifications.

In 1909 Whitney described the term *soil series,* although it had been used in soil mapping since 1900. At that time, in 1909, a soil series was determined on the basis of soil color and soil structure. The use of the soil series name plus the name of the texture of the surface determined the *soil type*. Examples of soil type names and the State of origin are: Gloucester sandy loam (Massachusetts), Cecil clay loam (North Carolina), Marshall silt loam (Iowa), and Kitchen Creek loam (California).

Whitney's publication in 1909 listed a total of 230 soil series and 700 soil types for the entire United States. Now there are more than 10,500 series but no estimate as to the number of soil types.

Soil series are hierarchical but not connotative. This means that each soil series belongs to only one soil family but this information cannot be inferred from the name of the series. By contrast, all other soil taxa names are both hierarchical and connotative. An example of a complete taxonomy is given in the facing Chart (Figure 3: 1, p. 61).

3: 3 OTHER MAJOR SOIL TAXONOMIES

3: 3.1 Soil Taxonomy in the U.S.S.R.

Twelve pages in Soil Survey Staff, 1975 (pages 444-455) are devoted to "A Systematic List of U.S.S.R. Soils" with these examples of abbreviated categories:

1) Ecological—genetic (bioclimatic group of classes).

2) Genetic orders.

3) Humate bound with Fe_2O_3 and Al_2O_3. Readily soluble salts and carbonates leached.

4) Humate bound with Fe_2O_3, Al_2O_3, and calcium. Readily soluble salts leached.

5) Humate bound with calcium and partly with Fe_2O_3 and Al_2O_3. Readily soluble salts leached out of profile or deposited in a lower horizon.

6) Humate bound with calcium. Readily soluble salts leached to lower and middle horizons.

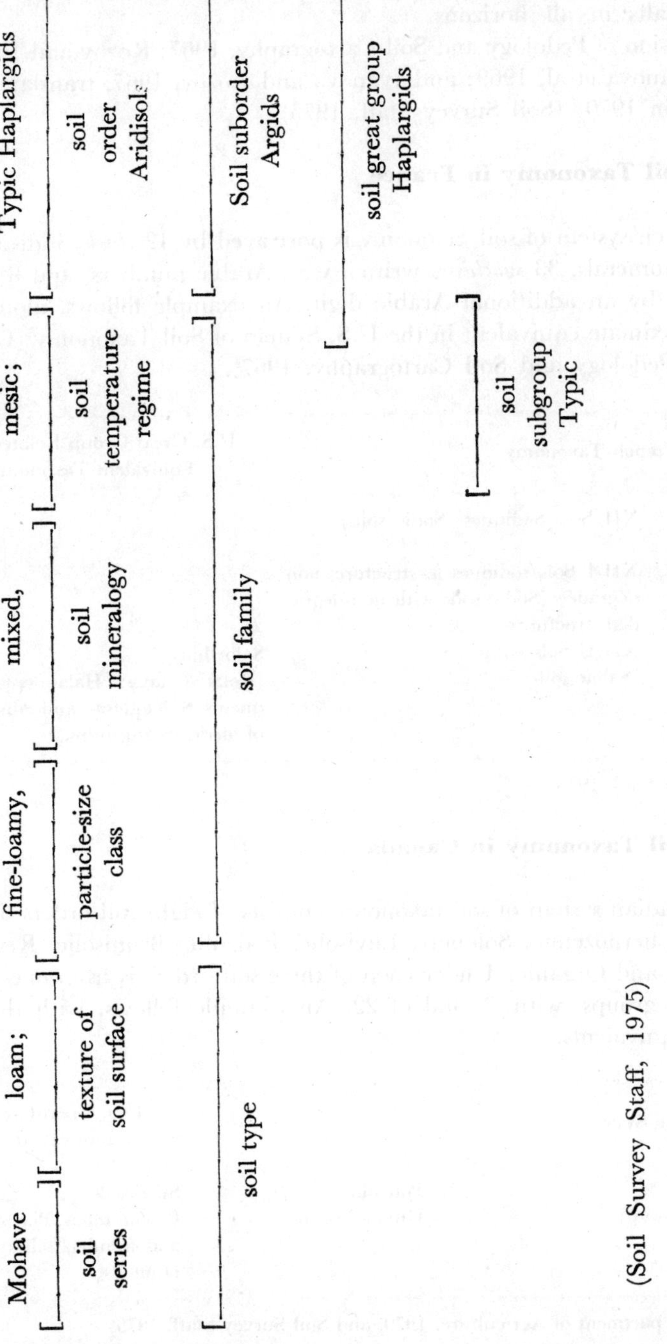

Fig. 3.1. Chart of hierarchical taxonomy of Mohave Soil Series.

7) Humate bound with sodium, magnesium, and calcium. Readily soluble salts in all horizons.
(Commission of Pedology and Soil Cartography, 1967; Rozov and Ivanova, 1967; Ivanova et al, 1969; and Ivanova and Rozov, 1967, translated from Russian in 1970) (Soil Survey Staff, 1975).

3: 3.2 Soil Taxonomy in France

The French system of soil taxonomy is portrayed by 12 *classes* indicated by Roman numerals, 33 *subclasses* written with Arabic numbers, and 81 *groups* indicated by an additional Arabic digit. An example follows, along with the approximate equivalent in the U.S. System of Soil Taxonomy (Commission of Pedology and Soil Cartography, 1967).

	French Taxonomy	U.S. Great Group Related and Equivalent Taxonomy
Soil Class:	XII Sols Sodiques (Sodic soils)	
Soil Subclass:	XII-I Sols sodiques à structure non dégradée (Sodic soils with non-degraded structure)	
Soil Group:	XII/II Sols salins (Saline soils)	Salorthids (Related taxa: Halaquepts, Sulfaquents, Sulfaquepts, and saline phases of torric great groups.)

(Soil Survey Staff, 1975)

3: 3.3 Soil Taxonomy in Canada

The Canadian system of soil taxonomy consists of eight soil orders listed as follows: Chernozemic, Solonetz, Luvisolic, Podzolic, Brunisolic, Regosolic, Gleysolic, and Organic. Under each of these soil orders is from one to four soil great groups, with a total of 22. An example follows, with the U.S. system equivalents.

Canadian System		U.S. Great Group Equivalent
Soil order:	4. Podzolic	Spodosols
Soil great group:	4.1 Humic Podzol	Cryohumods, Placohumods, and frigid families of other Humods

(Canada Department of Agriculture, 1970, and Soil Survey Staff, 1975)

3: 3.4 Soil Taxonomy in Australia

The Australian system of soil taxonomy has two solum classes:

I. Solum Undifferentiated
II. Solum Differentiated

Under II, Solum Differentiated, are two soil orders:
(A) Pedalfers and (B) Pedocals. Under Pedalfers are four suborders and 22 great groups. Whereas, under Pedocals are five suborders and 25 great groups.
(Stephens, 1962 and Buol, Hole, and McCracken, 1973)

3: 4 SOIL SURVEYS

3: 4.1 Soil Surveys in the United States

Soil surveys consist of soil maps and reports that describe the natural resources of an area, usually a county. Included in the soil survey report is a description of the climate, the principal agricultural enterprises, a generalized soil map and from 20 to 50 detailed folded soil maps on a photographic base. Also explained in the soil survey report are limitations for major land uses, interpretations for each soil map unit of productive potential for the major agricultural crops, and engineering uses for enhancing the human environment. Throughout all reports issued after 1965, each map unit is related to the U.S. soil taxonomy.

The first soil surveys in the United States were made in 1899. These included four areas: two in the irrigated regions of the Pecos River Valley of New Mexico and in the Salt Lake area of Utah; and two in the humid Connecticut River Valley of Massachusetts and Connecticut. Soil surveys in the irrigated areas were made to try to find answers to the questions of excessive salt accumulation on some soils in relation to permanence of irrigation agriculture. In the Connecticut River Valley, Sumatra tobacco was being introduced and was grown successfully on specific soils but was a failure on others.

In 1899 the soil surveys were made by the Bureau of Soils with 18 ha (40 acres) as the smallest map unit; now the smallest map unit is about half ha (one acre). The Bureau of Soils merged into the Bureau of Chemistry and Soils during the early 1920's. Detailed soil mapping was then done on a scale of one inch to one mile and reconnaissance mapping on a much smaller scale. Aerial photographs were used as base maps as soon as they became available in the 1930's (Soil Survey Staff, 1951).

In 1935 the newly-established Soil Conservation Service began mapping soils with a farm or ranch as the unit area. These maps were used primarily for farm and ranch planning as a means to reduce soil erosion.

The Soil Survey Division of the Bureau of Chemistry and Soils and the soil mapping unit of the Soil Conservation Service were integrated into a National Cooperative Soil Survey in 1952. This is the current organization responsible for all soil surveying in the United States.

The National Cooperative Soil Survey is a division within the Soil Conservation Service, United States Department of Agriculture. In each state, soil surveys are conducted on private land in cooperation usually with the State Land-Grant University. On public lands, the soil surveys are conducted in cooperation with the respective Federal agency responsible for managing the land. For example, soil surveys on land managed by the Bureau of Land Management, are conducted by the National Cooperative Soil Survey in cooperation with that Bureau.

Usually with a county as a unit, a detailed soil survey is most often made on a photographic base with a scale of 1:20,000 (about 3.16 inches per mile or 5 cm per km). Soil boundaries are marked on the nonglossy map with a pencil and later inked over.

The soil surveyor is usually a college graduate or a graduate student working toward an advanced degree. Typically he works alone and drives a pickup truck. He will first map soils along all roads and then walk over and maps the landscape between roads. On land posted against trespassing, the soil surveyor seeks out the owner and obtains his/her permission. He carries a soil legend prepared previously by the supervisor(s) from nearby completed county soil maps, supplemented with a study of soils in the county to be mapped.

In addition to the base map, the soil surveyor carries a six-foot soil auger, a hand (Abney) level for measuring slope, a pH kit, a Munsell color chip book, and a bottle of 10 percent hydrochloric acid for determining the presence of calcium and/or magnesium carbonate. By frequent borings he determines the correct mapping unit to draw on the photographic base map. This is done by observing and noting soil color, texture, structure, pH, and presence of lime by horizons. Slope percentage, degree of stoniness, and degree of erosion are also determined. All of these soil and land characteristics are integrated into a composite map symbol for each discrete soil map unit. For example, in the map unit symbol Me E_2, the Me stands for the soil type Memphis silt loam, the E for 14 to 30 percent slopes, and the two for eroded phase.

3: 4.2 Soil Surveys in India

The need and importance of soil survey in agricultural development in India have been recognized for many years. The scientific study of soils of the country was taken up as early as 1898 when four major soil groups occurring extensively were differentiated (National Commission on Agriculture, 1972).

With the initiation of agricultural research in the country the emphasis was on soil fertility. Soil profile studies started receiving attention only during the 1930s when soil genesis and development came to be recognized as significant factors for the purpose of soil classification. The standard comprehensive soil survey was started in 1956 when the All India Soil Survey and Land Use Organization was established. The modern system developed by the United States Department of Agriculture has been in use since 1969. A task of carrying out and coordinating the soil survey work in the country is done by the National Bureau of Soil Survey and Land Use Planning, Nagpur. The survey in progress is designed to furnish data about all important soil characteristics and associated features for the largest variety of users.

Soil survey is an arduous task involving field and laboratory work. The entire operation is carried out in three stages (Soil Survey Manual):

1) The pre-field operation consists of studying existing data with regard to the geological, agronomic and climatic aspects of the area to be surveyed; carrying out general field reconnaissance, interpretation of aerial photographs, if any, and designing and planning a field survey.

2) The second stage comprising field survey includes a preliminary study of the soils, preparation of the legend, identification of soils, plotting of boundaries and collection of soil samples for laboratory analysis.

3) The third stage includes revision of aerial photographs, interpretations, laboratory analysis of soil samples, analysis and evaluation of soil data and presentation in a report.

The entire operation is required to be carried out by well-trained staff. A work plan is prepared well in advance every year.

There are two main types of soil surveys: reconnaissance and detailed. In case of the former, the scale used for mapping is about 1 to 50,000. Soil profiles are located at intervals of 3 to 6 km depending on soil heterogeneity and they are examined as per standard procedure. Photographs of profiles as well as of landscapes are taken.

Detailed surveys aim at bringing out differences in respect of soil and terrain features to enable interpretation and classification of soils into land use classes, sub-classes and capability units. Base maps used are in the scale of 1 to 8,000 or aerial photographs in the scale of 1 to 20,000 or larger. Auger samples of soils are examined at every quarter to half km intervals depending on soil heterogeneity.

Annual turnout of work of detailed survey for each field party consists of a Soil Survey Assistant, Field Assistant, Tracer and a Helper can be about 16,000 hectares in favorable terrain and 8,000 hectares in difficult and hilly terrain. Recently aerial photographs are used wherever available to expedite the soil survey work.

Soil survey is in progress all over the country with the final objective of preparing a soil map of India on the scale of 1:1 million for use in the formulation of development plans at district and lower levels.

The final Soil Survey Report and maps are prepared in six sections:

1) Introduction.

2A) General description of the area with regard to location and extent, physiography, rivers, major streams and drainage, geology, climate, vegetation.

2B) Socio-economic conditions such as transport, marketing, educational and medical facilities.

3) Present land use and agriculture including the details of the farming and cropping systems adopted in the area.

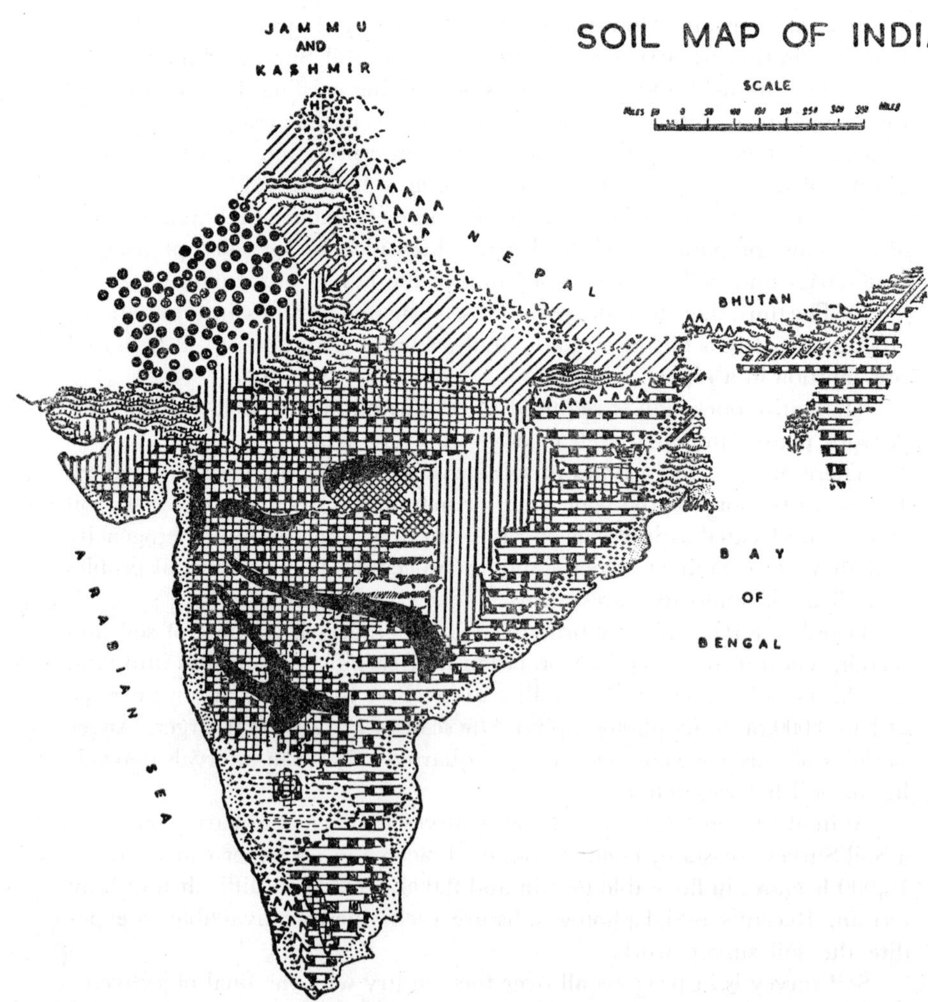

4) Soils giving the details of method of soil survey, soil mapping units, physical and chemical properties and land capability classification.

5) General problems of the area with broad suggestions and recommendations.

6) Summary and conclusion.

Details of the methods and procedures suggested for adoption for soil survey in India are to be found in the Manuals prepared by the National Bureau of Soil Survey and Land Use Planning, Nagpur, India.

Using a legend based primarily on geologic origin of parent material, soil scientists at the Indian Agricultural Research Institute made a Soil Map of India in the mid 1950's at a scale of one inch equals 250 miles (Fig. 3.2). This early map has been useful in broad land-use planning. In the 1970's a soil map of India at the Great Group level was made based on the United States System of Soil Taxonomy. The scale is one centimeter to 100 kilometers (Fig. 3.3).

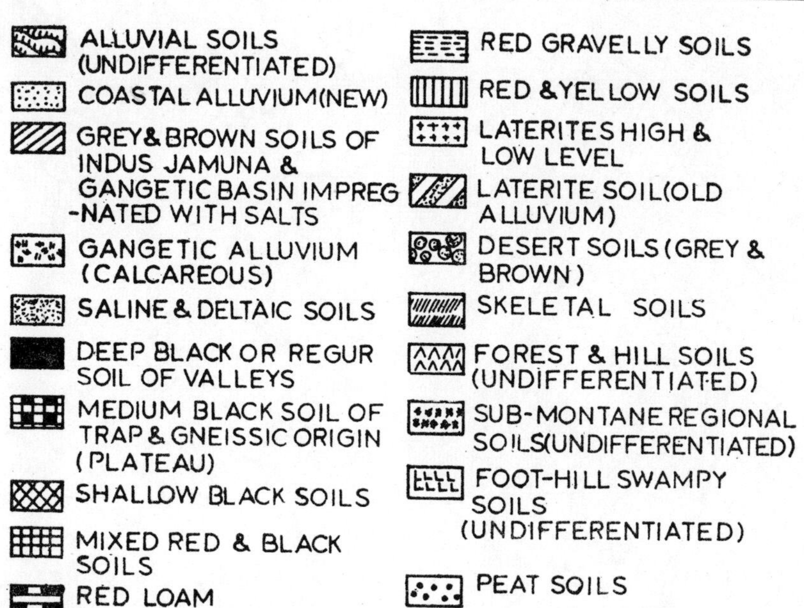

Fig. 3.2. One of the earliest of the Soil Maps of India. Note that the map unit names are based on geologic origin of parent material; its geographic location; and the depth, color, and texture of surface soil. Compare this map and legend with Figure 3.2, based on the U.S. System of Soil Taxonomy. (*Source:* Indian Council of Agricultural Research and appearing in: Arakeri, H. R., G. V. Chalam, and P. Satyanarayana, in collaboration with R. L. Donahue. *Soil Management in India.* Asia Publishing House, New Delhi and London, first edition 1959, opposite page 2.)

3: 4.3 United States Soil Map of the World (Soil Survey Staff, 1971)

Based on the United States System of Soil Taxonomy, the Soil Survey Staff, 1971, prepared a Soil Map of the World on a scale of 1:5,000,000 (Fig. 3.4). The map legend follows in Table 3.10. The shaded patterns and capital

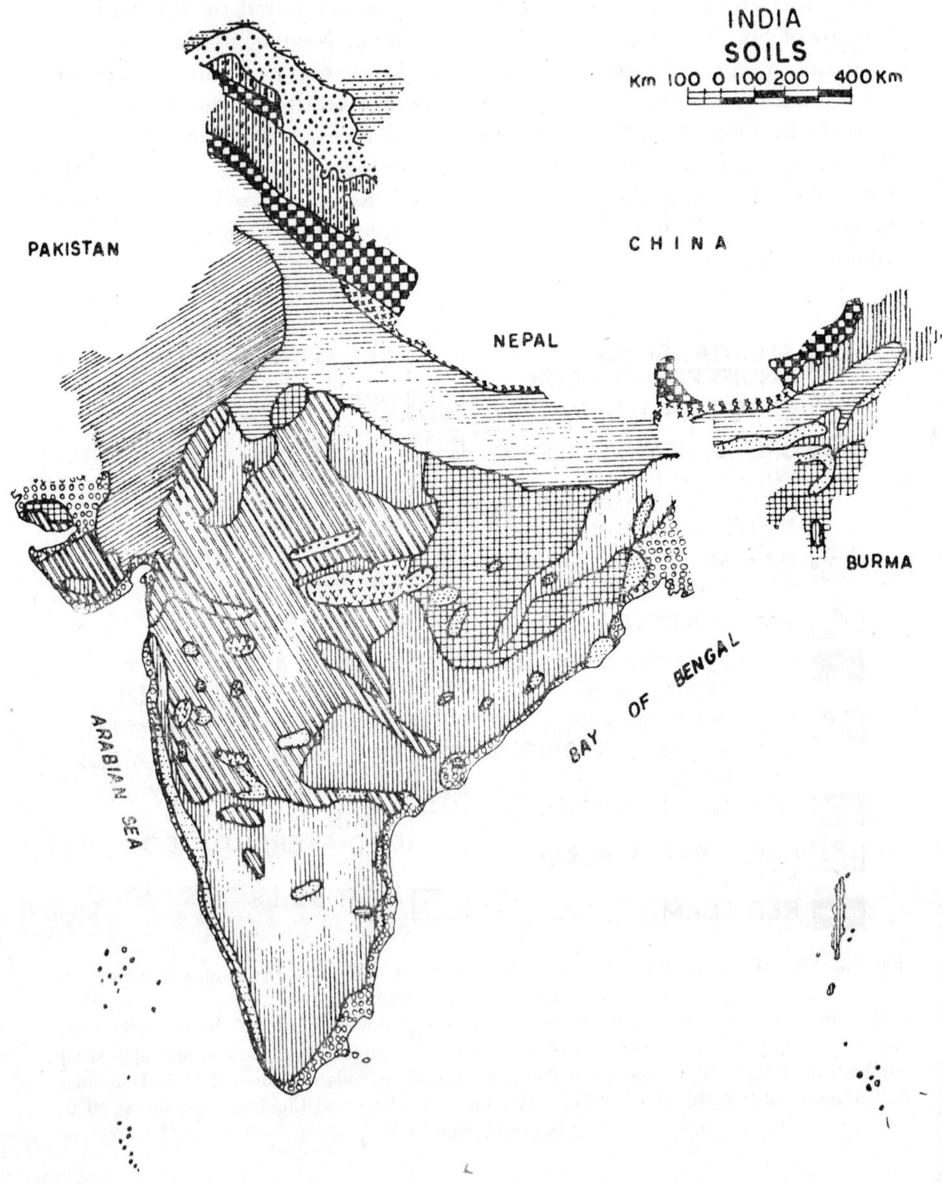

letters are soil orders; whereas, the numbers are suborders and the lower case letters in most instances stand for soil great groups. When no one soil great group predominates in the map unit, the lower case letter signifies an associated suborder. For example, in central India there is a large body of soil with the symbol V2c. The V means soil order of *Vertisols,* the 2 stands for suborder *Usterts,* and the c designates an associated suborder of *Ustalfs.*

Table 3.11 lists the square kilometers, square miles, and percentage of land area of the world for each map unit.

3: 4.4 FAO/UNESCO World Soil Map

From 1961 to 1969, soil scientists at the Food and Agriculture Organization worked with other soil scientists from around the world to prepare and publish a soil map by continents. The map units consist of a world "consensus" (meaning a compromised committee decision), its upper category is roughly equivalent to the great group of the U.S. system and to the soil

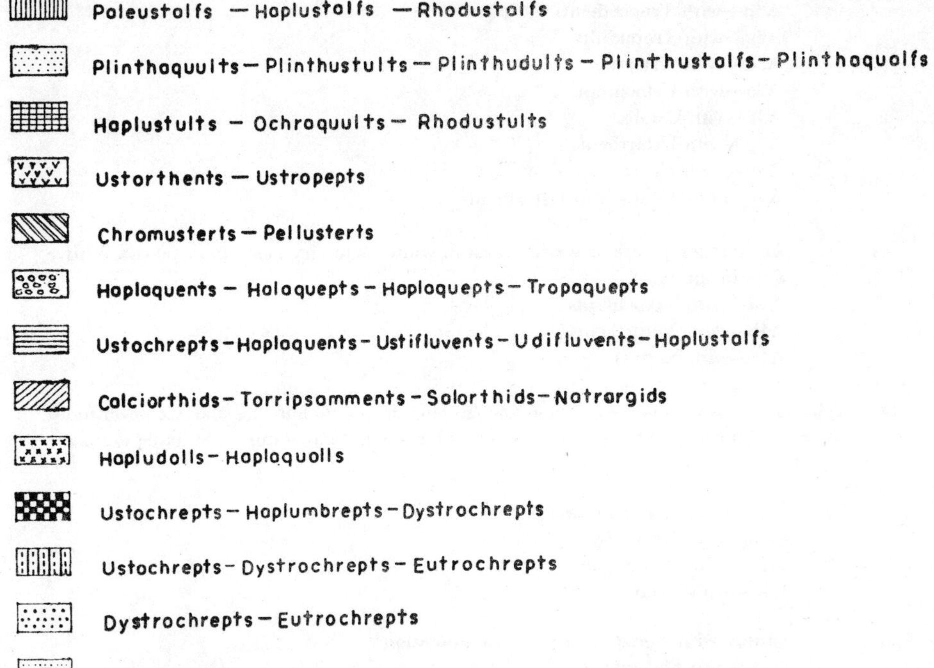

Fig. 3.3. The most recent Soil Map of India, based on the U.S. System of Soil Taxonomy. Note that the map units are names of Great Groups in the system. (*Source:* Indian Council of Agricultural Research, New Delhi.)

Table 3.10. Legend for Soil Map of the World (Soil Survey Staff, 1971)

A **Alfisols** Soils with subsurface horizons of clay accumulation and medium to high base supply; either usually moist or moist for 90 consecutive days during a period when temperature is suitable for plant growth

A1 BORALFS cool
Ala—with Histosols, cryic temperature regimes common
Alb—with Spodosols, cryic temperature regimes

A2 UDALFS temperate to hot, usually moist
A2a—with Aqualfs
A2b—with Aquolls
A2c—with Hapludults
A2d—with Ochrepts
A2e—with Troporthents
A2f—with Udorthents

A3 USTALFS temperate to hot, dry more than 90 cumulative days during periods when temperature is suitable for plant growth
A3a—with Tropepts
A3b—with Troporthents
A3c—with Tropudults
A3d—with Usterts
A3e—with Ustochrepts
A3f—with Ustolls
A3g—with Ustorthents
A3h—with Ustox
A3j—Plinthustalfs with Ustorthents

A4 XERALFS temperate or warm, moist in winter and dry more than 60 consecutive days in summer
A4a—with Xerochrepts
A4b—with Xerorthents
A4c—with Xerults

D **Aridisols** Soils with pedogenic horizons, usually dry in all horizons and are never moist as long as 90 consecutive days during a period when temperature is suitable for plant growth

D1 ARIDISOLS undifferentiated
D1a—with Orthents
D1b—with Psamments
D1c—with Ustalfs

D2 ARGIDS with horizons of clay accumulation
D2a—with Fluvents
D2b—with Torriorthents

E **Entisols** Soils without pedogenic horizons; either usually wet, usually moist, or usually dry

E1 AQUENTS seasonally or perennially wet
E1a—Haplaquents with Udifluvents
E1b—Psammaquents with Haplaquents
E1c—Tropaquents with Hydraquents

E2 ORTHENTS loamy or clayey textures, many shallow to rock
E2a—Cryorthents
E2b—Cryorthents with Orthods
E2c—Torriorthents with Aridisols
E2d—Torriorthents with Ustalfs
E2e—Xerorthents with Xeralfs

E3 PSAMMENTS sand or loamy sand textures
E3a—with Aridisols
E3b—with Orthox
E3c—with Torriorthents
E3d—with Ustalfs
E3e—with Ustox
E3f—with shifting sands
E3g—Ustipsamments with Ustolls

H Histosols Organic soils

H1 HISTOSOLS undifferentiated
H1a—with Aquods
H1b—with Boralfs
H1c—with Cryaquepts

I Inceptisols Soils with pedogenic horizons of alteration or concentration but without accumulations of translocated materials other than carbonates or silica; usually moist or moist for 90 consecutive days during a period when temperature is suitable for plant growth

I1 ANDEPTS amorphous clay or vitric volcanic ash or pumice
I1a—Dystrandepts with Ochrepts

I2 AQUEPTS seasonally wet
I2a—Cryaquepts with Orthents
I2b—Halaquepts with Salorthids
I2c—Haplaquepts with Humaquepts
I2d—Haplaquepts with Ochraqualfs
I2e—Humaquepts with Psamments
I2f—Tropaquepts with Hydraquents
I2g—Tropaquepts with Plinthaquults
I2h—Tropaquepts with Tropaquents
I2j—Tropaquepts with Tropudults

I3 OCHREPTS thin, light-colored surface horizons and little organic matter
I3a—Dystrochrepts with Fragiochrepts
I3b—Dystrochrepts with Orthox
I3c—Xerochrepts with Xerolls

I4 TROPEPTS continuously warm or hot
I4a—with Ustalfs
I4b—with Tropudults
I4c—with Ustox

I5 UMBREPTS dark-colored surface horizons with medium to low base supply
I5a—with Aqualfs

M Mollisols Soils with nearly black, organic-rich surface horizons and high base supply; either usually moist or usually dry

M1 ALBOLLS light gray subsurface horizon over slowly permeable horizon, seasonally wet
M1a—with Aquepts

M2 BOROLLS cool or cold
M2a—with Aquolls
M2b—with Orthids
M2c—with Torriorthents

M3 RENDOLLS subsurface horizons have much calcium carbonate but no accumulation of clay
M3a—with Usterts

M4 UDOLLS temperate or warm, usually moist
M4a—with Aquolls
M4b—with Eutrochrepts
M4c—with Humaquepts

M5 USTOLLS temperate to hot, dry more than 90 cumulative days in the year
M5a—with Argialbolls
M5b—with Ustalfs
M5c—with Usterts
M5d—with Ustochrepts

M6 XEROLLS cool to warm, moist in winter and dry more than 60 consecutive days in summer
M6a—with Xerorthents

O Oxisols Soils with pedogenic horizons that are mixtures principally of kaolin, hydrated oxides, and quartz, and are low in weatherable minerals

O1 ORTHOX hot, nearly always moist
O1a—with Plinthaquults
O1b—with Tropudults

O2 USTOX warm or hot, dry for long periods but moist more than 90 consecutive days in the year
O2a—with Plinthaquults
O2b—with Tropudults
O2c—with Ustalfs

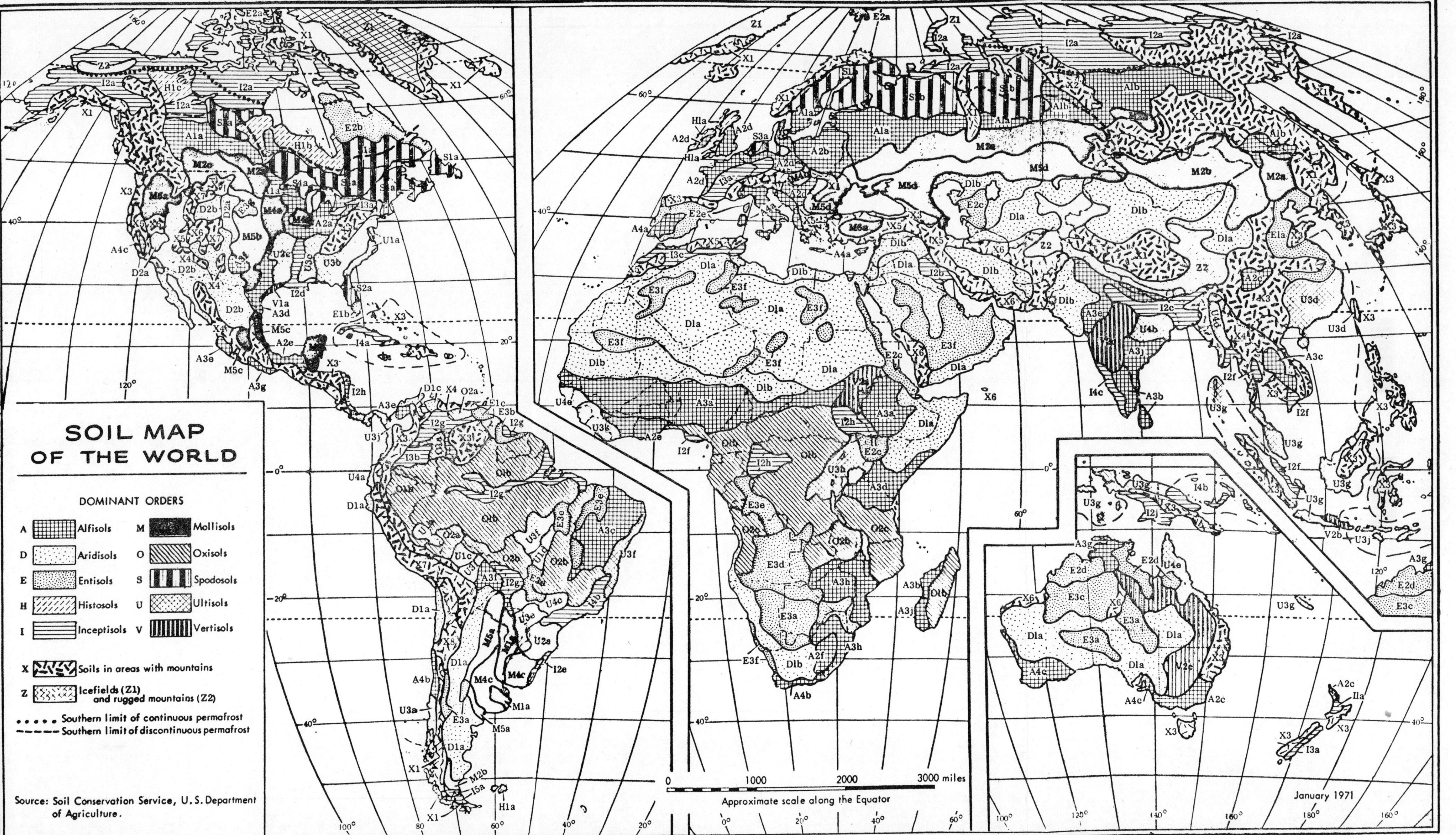

Fig. 3.4. Soil Map of the World (1971). Scale 1 : 50,000,000 (*Courtesy:* USDA—Soil Conservation Service).

S **Spodosols** Soils with accumulation of amorphous materials in subsurface horizons; usually moist or wet

S1 SPODOSOLS undifferentiated
S1a—cryic temperature regimes; with Boralfs
S1b—cryic temperature regimes; with Histosols

S2 AQUODS seasonally wet
S2a—Haplaquods with Quartzipsamments

S3 HUMODS with accumulations of organic matter in subsurface horizons
S3a—with Hapludalfs

S4 ORTHODS with accumulations of organic matter, iron, and aluminum in subsurface horizons
S4a—Haplorthods with Boralfs

U **Ultisols** Soils with subsurface horizons of clay accumulation and low base supply, usually moist for 90 consecutive days during a period when temperature is suitable for plant growth

U1 AQUULTS seasonally wet
U1a—Ochraquults with Udults
U1b—Plinthaquults with Orthox
U1c—Plinthaquults with Plinthaquox
U1d—Plinthaquults with Tropaquepts

U2 HUMULTS temperate or warm and moist all of year, high content of organic matter
U2a—with Umbrepts

U3 UDULTS temperate to hot, never dry more than 90 cumulative days in the year
U3a—with Andepts
U3b—with Dystrochrepts
U3c—with Udalfs
U3d—Hapludults with Dystrochrepts
U3e—Rhodudults with Udalfs
U3f—Tropudults with Aquults
U3g—Tropudults with Hydraquents
U3h—Tropudults with Orthox
U3j—Tropudults with Tropepts
U3k—Tropudults with Tropudalfs

U4 USTULTS warm or hot, dry more than 90 cumulative days in the year
U4a—with Ustochrepts
U4b—Plinthustults with Ustorthents
U4c—Rhodustults with Ustalfs
U4d—Tropustults with Tropaquepts
U4e—Tropustults with Ustalfs

V **Vertisols** Soils with high content of swelling clays; deep, wide cracks develop during dry periods

V1 UDERTS usually moist in some part in most years, cracks open less than 90 cumulative days in the year
V1a—with Usterts

V2 USTERTS cracks open more than 90 cumulative days in the year
V2a—with Tropaquepts
V2b—with Tropofluvents
V2c—with Ustalfs

X Soils in areas with mountains Soils with various moisture and temperature regimes; many steep slopes, relief and total elevation vary greatly from place to place. Soils vary greatly within short distances and with changes in altitude; vertical zonation common

X1 Cryic great groups of Entisols, Inceptisols, and Spodosols
X2 Boralfs and cryic great groups of Entisols and Inceptisols
X3 Udic great groups of Alfisols, Entisols, Inceptisols, and Ultisols
X4 Ustic great groups of Alfisols, Inceptisols, Mollisols, and Ultisols
X5 Xeric great groups of Alfisols, Entisols, Inceptisols, Mollisols, and Ultisols
X6 Aridisols, torric great groups of Entisols
X7 Ustic and cryic great groups of Alfisols, Entisols, Inceptisols, and Mollisols; ustic great groups of Ultisols; cryic great groups of Spodosols
X8 Aridisols, torric and cryic great groups of Entisols, and cryic great groups of Spodosols and Inceptisols

Z Miscellaneous

Z1 Icefields

Z2 Rugged Mountains—mostly devoid of soil (includes glaciers, permanent snow fields, and, in some places, small areas of soil)

Table 3.11. Areas of soils (measured from Soil Map of the World, 1 : 50,000,000)

Ice-free areas of world	132,037,400 sq km	51,043,000 sq mi
Perennial snow and ice	16,075,000 sq km	6,219,000 sq mi
Inland water	2,077,200 sq km	765,000 sq mi

Soils	% of land area	sq km	sq mi
A — Alfisols	13.1873	17,138,200	6,630,200
A1—Boralfs	3.5451	4,607,200	1,782,400
A1a	1.9410	2,522,400	975,900
A1b	1.6041	2,084,800	806,500
A2—Udalfs	2.3200	3,015,000	1,166,400
A2a	0.3784	491,800	190,200
A2b	0.4894	636,000	246,100

Table 3.11 (*Contd.*)

Soils	% of land area	sq km	sq mi
A2c	0.3515	456,800	176,700
A2d	0.6193	804,800	311,400
A2e	0.3392	440,800	170,500
A2f	0.1422	184,800	71,500
A3—Ustalfs	6.3842	8,296,800	3,209,800
A3a	2.4496	3,183,200	1,231,500
A3b	0.2721	353,600	136,800
A3c	0.8470	1,100,800	425,900
A3d	0.6808	884,800	342,300
A3e	0.5460	709,600	274,500
A3f	0.1828	237,600	91,900
A3g	0.1957	254,400	98,400
A3h	0.8815	1,145,600	443,200
A3j	0.3287	427,200	165,300
A4—Xeralfs	0.9380	1,219,200	471,600
A4a	0.4278	556,000	215,100
A4b	0.1403	182,400	70,500
A4c	0.3699	480,800	186,000
D—Aridisols	18.7626	24,384,000	9,433,600
D1—Aridisols	17.1726	22,317,600	8,634,200
D1a	11.5635	15,028,000	5,814,000
D1b	5.5204	7,174,400	2,775,600
D1c	0.0886	115,200	44,600
D2—Argids	1.5900	2,066,400	799,400
D2a	0.1822	236,800	91,600
D2b	1.4078	1,829,600	707,800
E—Entisols	8.2788	10,759,200	4,162,400
E1—Aquents	0.6186	804,000	311,000
E1a	0.5515	716,800	277,300
E1b	0.0191	24,800	9,600
E1c	0.0480	62,400	24,100
E2—Orthents	2.0406	2,652,000	1,026,000
E2a	0.1440	187,200	72,400

Table 3.11 (*Contd.*)

Soils	% of land area	sq km	sq mi
E2b	0.5935	771,200	298,400
E2c	0.5361	696,800	269,600
E2d	0.5128	666,400	257,800
E2e	0.2542	330,400	127,800
E3—Psamments	5.6196	7,303,200	2,825,400
E3a	1.2121	1,575,200	609,400
E3b	0.0652	84,800	32,800
E3c	0.6180	803,200	310,700
E3d	0.9055	1,176,800	455,300
E3e	0.6901	896,800	347,000
E3f	2.0721	2,692,800	1,041,800
E3g	0.0566	73,600	28,400
H—Histosols	0.9000	1,169,600	452,500
H1—Histosols	0.9000	1,169,600	452,500
H1a	0.0745	96,800	37,400
H1b	0.5885	764,800	295,900
H1c	0.2370	308,000	119,200
I—Inceptisols	8.8784	11,538,400	4,464,000
I1—Andepts	0.0271	35,200	13,600
I1a	0.0271	35,200	13,600
I2—Aquepts	7.4725	9,711,200	3,757,000
I2a	5.1001	6,628,000	2,564,200
I2b	0.1329	172,800	66,800
I2c	0.4204	546,400	211,400
I2d	0.1502	195,200	75,500
I2e	0.0302	39,200	15,200
I2f	0.2185	284,000	109,900
I2g	0.8206	1,066,400	412,500
I2h	0.4414	573,600	221,900
I2j	0.1582	205,600	79,600
I3—Ochrepts	0.7380	959,200	371,100
I3a	0.3527	458,400	177,400
I3b	0.1317	171,200	66,200
I3c	0.2536	329,600	127,500

Table 3.11 (*Contd.*)

Soils	% of land area	sq km	sq mi
I4—Tropepts	0.6057	787,200	304,600
I4a	0.1539	200,000	77,400
I4b	0.3349	435,200	168,400
I4c	0.1169	152,000	58,800
I5—Umbrepts	0.0351	45,600	17,700
I5a	0.0351	45,600	17,700
M—Mollisols	8.5743	11,143,200	4,310,900
M1—Albolls	0.3065	398,400	154,100
M1a	0.3065	398,400	154,100
M2—Borolls	4.0377	5,247,200	2,030,000
M2a	2.1367	2,776,800	1,074,200
M2b	1.5015	1,951,200	754,900
M2c	0.3995	519,200	200,900
M3—Rendolls	0.1520	197,600	76,400
M3a	0.1520	197,600	76,400
M4—Udolls	0.8642	1,123,200	434,500
M4a	0.2967	385,600	149,200
M4b	0.0683	88,800	34,300
M4c	0.4992	648,800	251,000
M5—Ustolls	2.8144	3,657,600	1,415,000
M5a	0.3681	478,400	185,100
M5b	0.5337	693,600	268,300
M5c	0.1243	161,600	62,500
M5d	1.7883	2,324,000	899,100
M6—Xerolls	0.3995	519,200	200,900
M6a	0.3995	519,200	200,900
O—Oxisols	8.5085	11,057,600	4,277,900
O1—Orthox	5.9011	7,668,800	2,966,900

Table 3.11 (*Contd.*)

Soils	% of land area	sq km	sq mi
O1a	0.1003	130,400	50,400
O1b	5.8008	7,538,400	2,916,500
O2—Ustox	2.6074	3,388,800	1,311,000
O2a	0.2129	276,800	107,000
O2b	1.4176	1,842,400	712,800
O2c	0.9769	1,269,600	491,200
S—Spodosols	4.2764	5,557,600	2,150,000
S1—Spodosols	3.1678	4,116,800	1,592,600
S1a	0.8045	1,045,600	404,500
S1b	2.3633	3,071,200	1,188,100
S2—Aquods	0.0665	86,400	33,400
S2a	0.0665	86,400	33,400
S3—Humods	0.1089	141,600	54,800
S3a	0.1089	141,600	54,800
S4—Orthods	0.9332	1,212,800	469,200
S4a	0.9332	1,212,800	469,200
U—Ultisols	5.5574	7,222,400	2,794,100
U1—Aquults	0.3643	473,600	183,200
U1a	0.0794	103,200	39,900
U1b	0.0855	111,200	43,000
U1c	0.0899	116,800	45,200
U1d	0.1095	142,400	55,100
U2—Humults	0.2253	292,800	113,300
U2a	0.2253	292,800	113,300
U3—Udults	4.0336	5,241,600	2,027,900
U3a	0.0683	88,800	34,300
U3b	0.4027	523,200	202,400
U3c	0.4107	533,600	206,500
U3d	0.5873	763,200	295,300

Table 3.11 (*Contd.*)

Soils	% of land area	sq km	sq mi
U3e	0.1994	259,200	100,300
U3f	0.4796	623,200	241,100
U3g	1.0214	1,327,200	513,500
U3h	0.4310	560,000	216,700
U3j	0.2246	292,000	112,900
U3k	0.2086	271,200	104,900
U4—Ustults	0.9342	1,214,400	469,700
U4a	0.0307	40,000	15,400
U4b	0.2185	284,000	109,900
U4c	0.1859	241,600	93,500
U4d	0.1298	168,800	65,200
U4e	0.3693	480,000	185,700
V—Vertisols	1.8006	2,340,000	905,300
V1—Uderts	0.0283	36,800	14,200
V1a	0.0283	36,800	14,200
V2—Usterts	1.7723	2,303,200	891,100
V2a	0.2622	340,800	131,800
V2b	0.0394	51,200	19,800
V2c	1.4707	1,911,200	739,500
X—Soils in areas of mountains	19.6814	25,578,000	9,895,500
X1	8.8175	11,459,200	4,433,300
X2	0.2308	300,000	116,000
X3	5.1287	6,665,200	2,578,600
X4	1.3727	1,784,000	690,200
X5	1.4515	1,886,400	729,800
X6	1.5131	1,966,400	760,800
X7	0.8353	1,085,600	420,000
X8	0.3318	431,200	166,800
Z—Miscellaneous			
Z2	1.5943	2,072,000	801,600

Summaries

Order	% of land area	sq km	sq mi
A—Alfisols	13.1873	17,138,200	6,630,200
D—Aridisols	18.7626	24,384,000	9,433,600
E—Entisols	8.2788	10,759,200	4,162,400
H—Histosols	0.9000	1,169,600	452,500
I—Inceptisols	8.8784	11,538,400	4,464,000
M—Mollisols	8.5743	11,143,200	4,310,900
O—Oxisols	8.5085	11,057,600	4,277,900
S—Spodosols	4.2764	5,557,600	2,150,000
U—Ultisols	5.5574	7,222,400	2,794,100
V—Vertisols	1.8006	2,340,000	905,300
X—Soils of mountains	19.6814	25,578,000	9,895,500
Z(Z2) Rugged mountains	1.5943	2,072,000	801,600
	100%	129,960,200	50,278,000

type of the U.S.S.R. system, and the lower category consists of contrasting intergrades. Diagnostic horizons have been used, similar to the diagnostic horizons of the U. S. system.

There are 25 major map units and 84 minor map units on the FAO/UNESCO World Soil Maps. One example will be given of one major map unit with five minor map unit subdivisions:

Major Map Unit: *Ferrasols* (rich in iron and aluminum sesquioxides)
Minor Map Units: Haplic
Ochric
Rhodic
Humic
Plinthic

(Dudal, 1969; and Buol, Hole, and McCracken, 1973)

3: 5 SUMMARY

Soil taxonomy is a systematic way of grouping soils of similar characteristics for the purpose of making them more useful. Some of the first soil taxonomies were developed in the U.S.S.R. where large land masses are conducive to such field studies. In the United States, extensive efforts were being made since 1900 to develop a system of soil taxonomy applicable to the world. In 1965, such a system was adopted and in 1971 the first Soil Map of the World, based on this system, was prepared.

The categories (taxa) in the United States System of Soil Taxonomy include, for the United States only, 10 soil orders, 47 suborders, 185 great groups, 970 subgroups, 4,500 soil families and 10,500 soil series. The origin and connotation of the name of each taxa are explained. Also a list is given of the names of all orders, suborders, and great groups in the United States system. A soil map of the world is presented, based on the U.S. taxonomy.

Other major soil taxonomies discussed are those developed in the U.S.S.R. France, Canada, and Australia.

Present position of soil survey is given.

Two soil maps of India are reproduced; one an early version and the other at the great group level of the United States system of soil taxonomy. Mention is also made of the world soil map published by continents with map units and legend developed by a committee of world renowned soil taxonomists.

CITED REFERENCES

Baldwin, M., C.E. Kellogg, and J. Thorp. "Soil Classification", *In* "Soils and Men, the 1938 Yearbook of Agriculture". U.S. Department of Agriculture, 1938, pages 979-1001.

Bidwell, O.W. and F.D. Hole. "Numerical Taxonomy and Soil Classification." Soil Science 1963, 97:58-62.

Buol, S.W., F.D. Hole, and R.J. McCracken. "Soil Genesis and Classification." The Iowa State University Press, Ames, Iowa, 1973, 360 pages.

Canada Department of Agriculture. "A System of Soil Classification for Canada." Queen's Printer for Canada, Ottawa, Canada, 1970.

Cline, M.G. "Basic Principles of Soil Classification." Soil Science, 1949, 67:81-91.

Commission of Pedology and Soil Cartography. "Classification of Soils." Laboratory of Geology and Pedology, National Superior School of Agronomy, Grignon, France, 1967.

Dudal, R. "About the Legend of the FAO/UNESCO Soil Map of the World." Technical Work-Planning Conference, National Cooperative Soil Survey, Charleston, South Carolina, 1969.

Glinka, K.D. "Die Typen der Boldenbilding. Ihre Klassifikation Und Geographische". Verbreitung. Berlin, 1914.

Glinka, K.D. "Dochuchaev's Ideas in the Development of Pedology and Cognate Science." *In* Russian Pedological Investigations No. 1, Academy of Science, USSR, Leningrad, 1927.

Hilgard, E.W. "Soils: Their Formation, Properties, Composition, and Relation to Climate and Plant Growth in the Humid and Arid Regions." Macmillan, New York, 1906.

Ivanova, E.N., et al., "Present Status of the Doctrine of Soil Genesis in the USSR", Soviet Soil Science,1969, 3:265-277.

Invanova, E.N. and N.N. Rozov, eds. "Classification and Determination of Soil Types."(Translated from Russian, 1970) Israel Program of Science Translations, Jerusalem, Israel, 1967, Numbers 1-5.

Jenny, H. "Factors of Soil Formation." McGraw-Hill, New York, 1941.

Johnson, W.M. "Soil Classification and the Design of Soil Surveys." *In* "Soil-Resource Data for Agricultural Development." Leslie D. Swindale, ed., Hawaii Agr. Exp. Sta., Univ. of Hawaii, Honolulu, Hawaii, 1978, pages 3-11.

Kellogg, E. "Soil Interpretations in the Soil Survey." Soil Conservation Service, U.S. Dept. of Agriculture, 1961.

Marbut, C.F. "The Great Soil Groups of the World and Their Development." Translated by C.F. Marbut from Glinka, K.D. Lithoprinter, Ann Arbor, Michigan, 1927, 235 pages.

Marbut, C.F. "Atlas of American Agriculture. Part III, Soils of the United States." U.S. Dept. of Agriculture, 1935, 98 pages.

National Commission on Agriculture. Interim Report on "Soil Survey and Soil Map of India." Government of India, Ministry of Agriculture 1972, pages 1-56.

Rozov, N.N. and E.N. Ivanova. "Classification of the Soils of the USSR", Soviet Soil Science, 1967, 2:147-156.

Simonson, R.W. "The Soil Series as Used in the USA." Transactions, 8th Intern. Congress of Soil Science, Bucharest, Romania, 1964, 5:17-24.

Smith, G.D., F. Newhall, and L.H. Robinson. "Soil Temperature Regimes, Their Characteristics and Predictability." SCS-TP-144, Soil Conservation Service, U.S. Dept. of Agr., 1964.

Soil Survey Staff. "Soil Survey Manual." U.S. Dept. of Agriculture Handbook 18, 1951.

Soil Survey Staff. "Soil Classification: A Comprehensive System, 7th Approximation." Supplement, U.S. Dept. of Agriculture, 1960 and 1964.

Soil Survey Staff. "Soil Map of the World," scale 1:50,000,000. USDA-Soil Conservation Service, 1971.

Soil Survey Staff. "Soil Series of the United States, Puerto Rico and the Virgin Islands: Their Taxonomic Classification." U.S. Dept. of Agriculture, 1972, 361 pages.

Soil Survey Staff. "Soil Taxonomy: A Basic System of Soil Classification for Making and Interpreting Soil Surveys." Agriculture Handbook 436, 1975, 754 pages.

Stephens, C.G., "A Manual of Australian Soils," 3rd Edition, CSIRO, Melbourne, Australia, 1962.

Thorp, J. "Geography of the Soils of China." National Geological Survey of China, Nanking, China, 1936.

Thorp, J. and G.D. Smith. "Higher Categories of Soil Classification." Soil Science, 1949, 67:117-126.

Whitney, M. "Soils of the United States." U.S. Department of Agriculture, Bulletin 55, 1909.

ADDITIONAL REFERENCES

Afanasiev, J.N. "The Classification Problem in Russian Soil Science." (Documenting Sibirtsevs Classification System, 1895). *In* Russian Pedological Invest., Acad. Sci., USSR, Leningrad, 1927.

Ahn, P.M. "West African Soils" Oxford University Press, London, England, 1970, 332 pages.

Arakeri, H.R., G.V. Chalam, P. Satyanarayana, and R.L. Donahue. "Soil Management in India." 2nd Edition, Asia Publishing House, Bombay, India, 1962, 609 pages.

Bridges, E.M. "World Soils." Cambridge University Press, 1970, 89 pages.

Donahue, R.L. "Ethiopia: Taxonomy, Cartography, and Ecology of Soils." Monograph No. 1, African Studies Center, Institute of International Agriculture, Michigan State Univ., East Lansing, Michigan, 1972, 44 pages.

Donahue, R.L. "Soils of Equatorial Africa and Their Relevance to Rational Agricultural Development." Research Report No. 7, Institute of International Agriculture, Michigan State Univ., East Lansing, Michigan, 1970, 52 pages.

Donahue, R.L., R.W. Miller, and J.C. Shickluna. "Soils: An Introduction to Soils and Plant Growth." 5th Edition, Prentice-Hall, Inc., Englewood Cliffs, New Jersey, 1983, 667 pages.

Lutgens, F.K. and J. Tarbuck. "The Atmosphere—An Introduction to Meteorology." Prentice-Hall, Inc., Englewood Cliffs, New Jersey, 1979, 413 pages.

Marbut, C.F. "Lectures on Soil Genesis and Classification." Graduate School. United States Dept. of Agriculture, Washington, D.C. 1928.

Mohr, E.G. Jul. "The Soils of Equatorial Regions With Special Reference to the Netherlands East Indies." (Indonesia), Translated by R.L. Pendleton. J.W. Edwards, Ann Arbor, Michigan, 1944, 766 pages.

Raychaudhuri, S.P. "Land and Soil." National Book Trust, India, New Delhi, 1966, 55 pages.

Raychaudhuri, S.P., et al. "Soils of India." Indian Council of Agricultural Research, New Delhi, 1963, 496 pages.

"Soil: The Yearbook of Agriculture, 1957." United States Dept. of Agriculture, Washington, D.C., 784 pages.

Swindale, L.D. "Soil-Resource Data for Agricultural Development." Hawaii Agr. Exp. Station, University of Hawaii, 1978, 306 pages.

Tamhane, R.V., D.P. Motiramani, Y.P. Bali, and R.L. Donahue.

"Soils: Their Chemistry and Fertility in Tropical Asia." 2nd Edition, Prentice-Hall of India, Private Limited, New Delhi, India, 1966, 475 pages.

Young, A. "Tropical Soils and Soil Survey". Cambridge University Press, Cambridge, 1980, 468 pages.

CHAPTER 4

Soil Physical Properties

4:1 INTRODUCTION

The physical properties of soils are influenced by the soil particles: *sands, silts, clays, gravels,* and *coarser fragments.* The relative proportion of these soil separates in a soil sample determines the soil's textural class, such as a *loam.* The cohesion of these individual particles to form aggregates is called soil *structure.* The spaces between and among individual soil particles and structural aggregates are termed *pore spaces.* (Engineers call them *voids.*) Soil consistence has reference to the relative stability of soil aggregates. Other physical properties which are self-explanatory are soil *temperature* and soil *color.*

For maximum production of *upland plants* (not rice), the soil must be porous enough to simultaneously hold the right amount of air and water. On a volume basis, the right amount for upland plants on most agricultural soils would be 25 percent each of air and water. The other 50 percent is mineral (sand, silt, clay) and organic matter (Fig. 4.1). Coarse-textured soils such as sands have enough *large* pore spaces to facilitate adequate air exchange from the atmosphere to plant roots. However, pore spaces in sands may be too large to hold adequate water. In contrast many clay soils may have more *total* pore space but the pores may be so *small* and so often filled with water that plant roots do not get enough oxygen for optimum growth.

Roots of lowland plants such as rice need less soil air because oxygen from the atmosphere is transmitted through the stems to the roots.

4:2 SOIL PARTICLES (SOIL SEPARATES)

Most natural field soils are composed of mineral particles, including coarse fragments, gravel, sands of varying sizes, silt, and clay. In addition, most field soils contain organic matter in all stages of decomposition. There may be recognizable twigs, leaves, and grass blades on the soil surface as

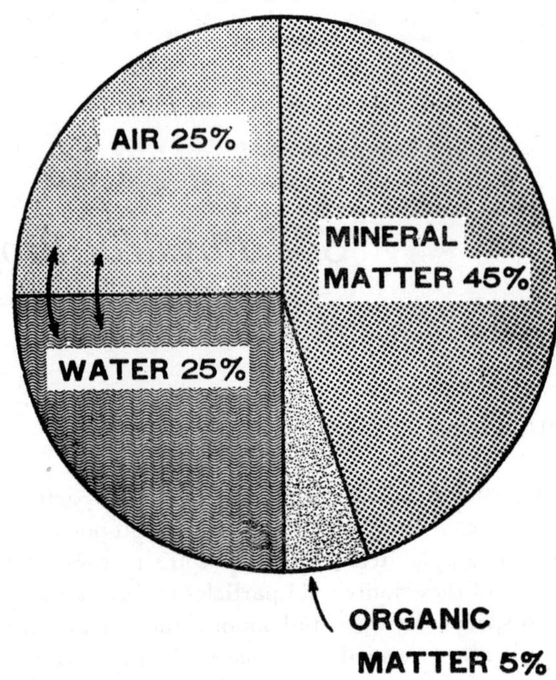

Fig. 4.1. Volume composition of average mineral soil in good tilth is half solids and half pore spaces. When the soil moisture is adequate for normal plant growth, approximately half of the pore spaces will be filled with water and the other half with air. (*Courtesy:* Texas Agricultural Education Teaching Materials Center.)

well as partially decomposed litter whose origin is not identifiable. Beneath these accumulations may be dark brown to black highly decomposed organic residues known as *humus*. Humus is composed mostly of carbon, hydrogen, and oxygen. Unlike most clays, humus is amorphous and not crystalline. Contrastingly, most clays of temperate regions are crystalline and composed of aluminum, silicon, and oxygen. Many Opisols clays are amorphous iron and aluminum.

The two dominant systems for classifying soil particles were developed by the International Society of Soil Science and the United States Department of Agriculture. Each will be explained, followed by the Soil Survey Staff's classification of coarse fragments; i.e., particles larger than 2 mm in diameter, the upper limit for clay in both systems.

The International Society of Soil Science recognizes five classes of soil separates (soil particles) based on size. These are, in millimeters (mm) in diameter: clay, <0.002; silt, 0.002–0.02; fine sand, 0.02–0.2; coarse sand, 0.2–2.0; and gravel, >2.0 (Fig. 4.2). In contrast, the United States Department of Agriculture has adopted eight classes, as follows (in mm in diameter):

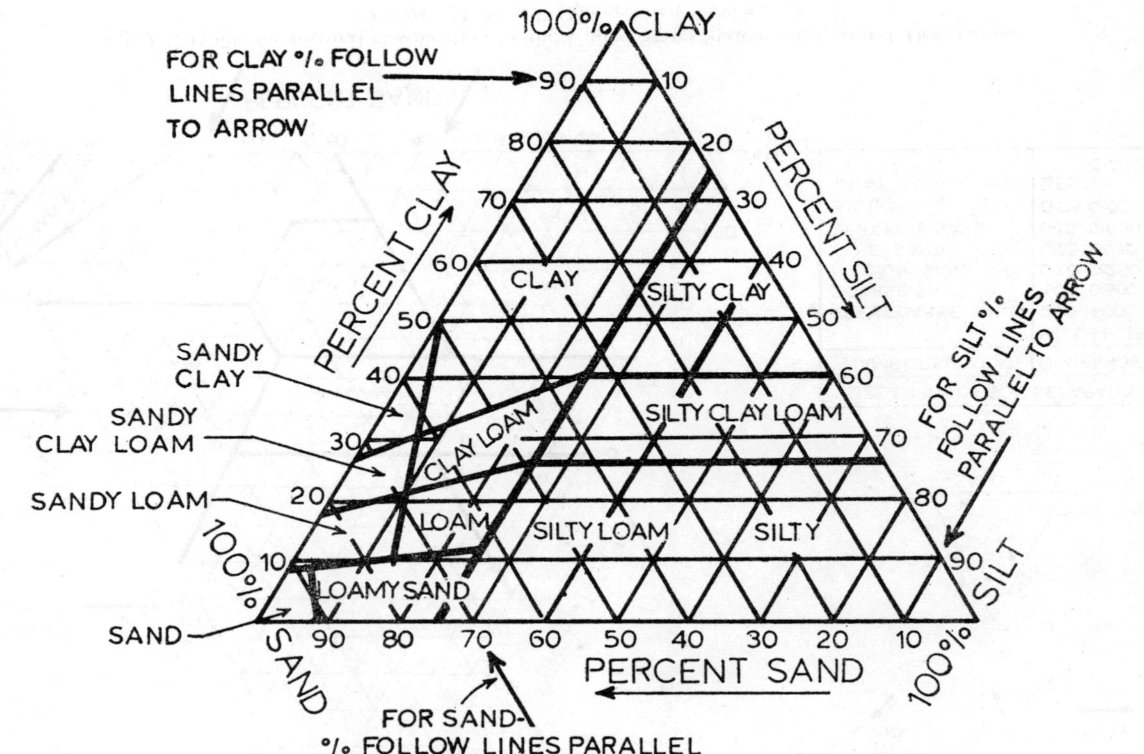

Fig. 4.2. Guide for textural classification by the International System for Textural Designations.

Source: Marshall, T.J., *Mechanical Composition of Soils in Relation to Field Description of Texture.* Commonwealth of Australia, Council for Scientific and Industrial Research, Melbourne, Australia, Bulletin 224, p. 20, 1947.

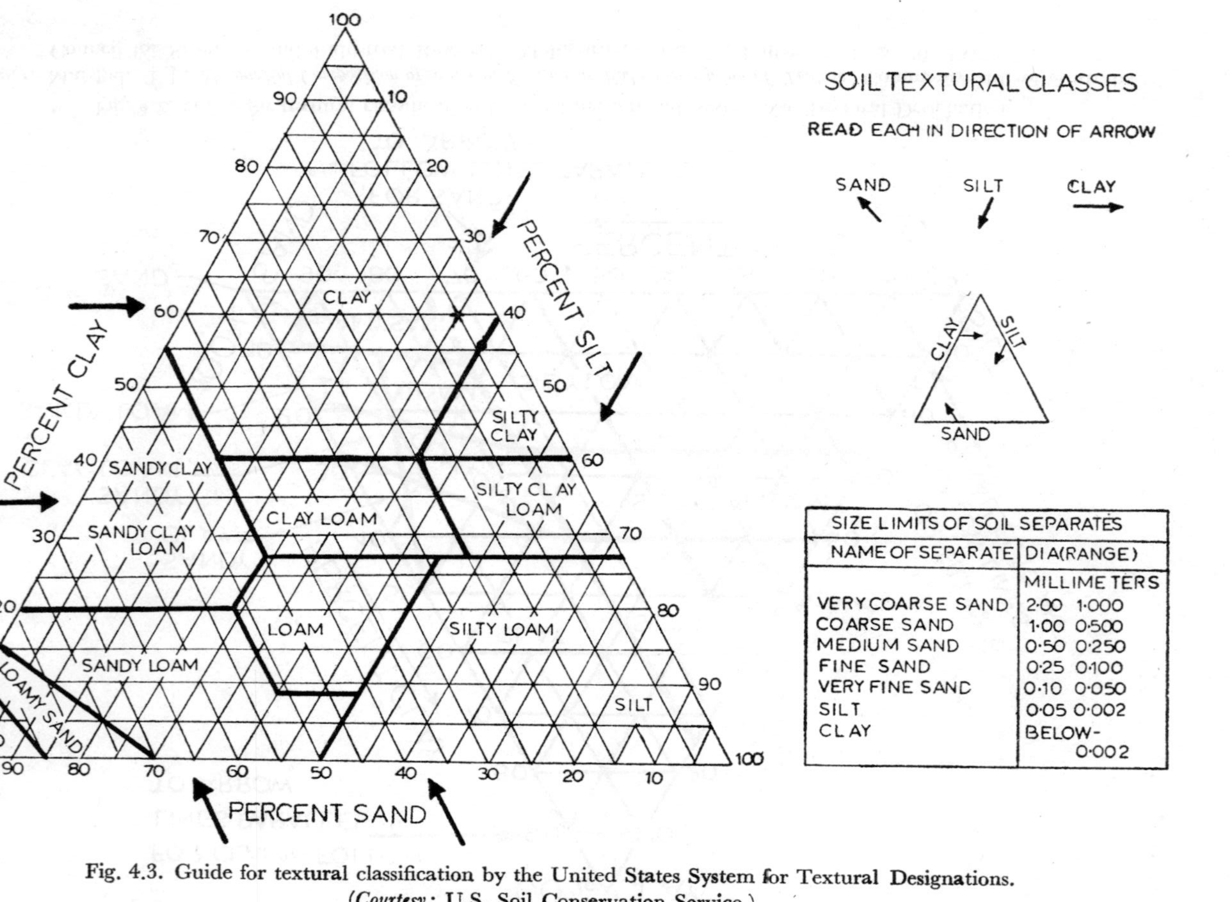

SIZE LIMITS OF SOIL SEPARATES	
NAME OF SEPARATE	DIA(RANGE)
	MILLIMETERS
VERY COARSE SAND	2·00 1·000
COARSE SAND	1·00 0·500
MEDIUM SAND	0·50 0·250
FINE SAND	0·25 0·100
VERY FINE SAND	0·10 0·050
SILT	0·05 0·002
CLAY	BELOW-0·002

Fig. 4.3. Guide for textural classification by the United States System for Textural Designations. (*Courtesy:* U.S. Soil Conservation Service.)

clay, < 0.002; silt, 0.002–0.5; very fine sand, 0.05–0.10; fine sand, 0.10–0.25; medium sand, 0.25–0.5; coarse sand 0.5–1.0; very coarse sand 1.0–2.0; and gravel, > 2.0 (Fig. 4.3).

It can thus be observed that both systems of soil particle classification define gravel as particles larger than 2 mm in diameter. It is obvious that these classification systems are laboratory techniques because field soils often contain coarse fragments too large to be called gravel. Superimposing a system of classifying coarse fragments made for soil surveys, the upper limit for gravel would be 10 mm (1 cm). The complete designations for coarse fragments, as used by the USDA—Soil Conservation Service, are presented in Table 4.1 (The International Society of Soil Science does not have a system for differentiating gravel from other coarse fragments.)

Table 4.1. Classification of coarse fragments (> 2 mm in diameter) in soils (Soil Survey Staff, 1975, page 472)

Shape of fragment	Kind of fragment	Size and name of fragment		
		2–10 mm (1 cm) in diameter	1–4 cm in diameter	> 4 cm in diameter
Rounded	Any kind	Gravelly	Cobbly	Stony
Angular	Chert	Cherty	Coarse cherty	Stony
Angular	Other than chert	Angular gravelly	Angular cobbly	Stony
Thin, flat	Sandstone, limestone, or schist	Channery 2 mm–2 cm long	Flaggy 2–6 cm long	Stony > 6 cm long
Thin, flat	Slate	Slaty	Flaggy	Stony
Thin, flat	Shale	Shaly	Flaggy	Stony

4:3 SOIL TEXTURAL CLASSES

Soils throughout the world contain an infinite combination of sands, silt, and clays. For this reason, various names are assigned to soils with specific percentages of each of these soil particles.

There are several techniques for determining the percentages of sands, silt, and clay in a sample of soil. Such a determination is called *particle-size analysis* (formerly known as mechanical analysis). Particle-size analysis may be conducted by sedimentation, sieving, and/or micrometry. The sedimentation or micrometric method gives the percentages of total sand, silt, and clay. The five grades of sand in the USDA system or the two in the international system must then be determined by sieving.

After the percentages of sands, silt, and clay are known, one of two textural triangles are used for determining the textural class name. When the particle-size distribution has been determined for the soil separates as defined by the International Society of Soil Science, the textural classes can be determined with the aid of the triangle in Fig. 4.2. Correspondingly, Fig. 4.3 is used for designating soil textural classes by the system used by the United States Department of Agriculture (USDA).

The principal soil textural classes recognized, ranked according to increasing amounts of fine particles are: sand, loamy sand, sandy loam, loam, silt, silt loam, sandy clay loam, clay loam, silty clay loam, sandy clay, silty clay, and clay. The classes of sand, loamy sand, and sandy loam may be further modified by the terms *coarse, fine,* or *very fine* inserted before the word "sand". When the fineness of the sand is not specified, it is assumed to be "medium".

The textural triangle can be used to designate the principal textural classes from a mechanical analysis. However, in the United States system, the sand, loamy sand, and sandy loam classes are further subdivided, based on the fineness of the sand. Since this detail is beyond the limits of the triangle in Figure 4.3, it will be set forth here.

Sand

Soil material that contains 85 percent or more of sand; percentage of silt, plus 1.5 times the percentage of clay, shall not exceed 15.

Coarse sand—25 percent or more very coarse and coarse sand, and < 50 percent any other one grade of sand.

Sand—25 percent or more very coarse, coarse, and medium sand, and < 50 percent fine or very fine sand.

Fine sand—50 percent or more fine sand (or) < 25 percent very coarse, coarse, and medium sand and < 50 percent very fine sand.

Very fine sand—50 percent or more very fine sand.

Loamy sand

Soil material that contains at the upper limit 85 to 90 percent sand, and the percentage of silt plus 1.5 times the percentage of clay is not less than 15; at the lower limit it contains not less than 70 to 85 percent sand, and the percentage of silt plus twice the percentage of clay does not exceed 30.

Loamy coarse sand—25 percent or more very coarse and coarse sand, and < 50 percent any other one grade of sand.

Loamy sand—25 percent or more very coarse, coarse, and medium sand, and < 50 percent fine or very fine sand.

Loamy fine sand—50 percent or more fine sand (or) < 25 percent very coarse, coarse, and medium sand and < 50 percent very fine sand.

Loamy very fine sand—50 percent or more very fine sand.

Sandy loam

Soil material that contains either 20 percent clay or less, and the percentage of silt plus twice the percentage of clay exceeds 30, and 52 percent or more sand; or < 7 percent clay, < 50 percent silt, and between 43 percent and 52 percent sand.

Coarse sandy loam—25 percent or more very coarse and coarse sand and < 50 percent any other one grade of sand.

Sandy loam—30 percent or more very coarse, coarse, and medium sand, but < 25 percent very coarse sand, and < 30 percent very fine or fine sand.

Fine sandy loam—30 percent or more fine sand and < 30 percent very fine sand (or) between 15 and 30 percent very coarse, coarse, and medium sand.

Very fine sandy loam—30 percent or more very fine (or) >40 percent fine and very fine sand, at least half of which is very fine sand and < 15 percent very coarse, coarse, and medium sand.

Field soil textural class names may be further modified based on the relative proportion and kinds of coarse fragments present. These terms ususally precede the textural class name; for example, *gravelly* fine sandy loam, *cobbly* loam, or *stony* clay (see Table 4.1).

4: 4 SOIL STRUCTURE

Soil structure refers to the arrangement of individual soil particles or clusters of soil particles into aggregates. Structural aggregates may be held together by chemical or biological agencies or both. Chemical bonding includes, in temperate region soils, the attraction of adsorbed cations at the edges of clay minerals to their negatively-charged surfaces. In well-drained soils of the tropics, on old land surfaces, structural aggregates are held together by the bonding of positively-charged iron and aluminum hydrous oxides with negatively-charged silicate clay minerals. In any environment, biological bonding may be caused by gelatinous (sticky) exudates of such soil fauna and flora as earthworms, bacteria, actinomycetes, fungi, and plant roots; the physical entwining of fibrous roots of higher plants and fungal hyphae; and chemical bonding of organic molecules from plant and animal residues.

An aggregate formed in nature is called a *ped*; one formed anthropogenically (by people manipulating the soil) is a *clod*. A *fragment* is a ped broken across natural planes of weakness, and a *concretion* consists of groups of soil particles irreversibly cemented in nature by compounds such as iron, aluminum, silica, calcium carbonate, and/or calcium sulfate.

Soil structure is more readily understood when it is categorized as *grade* (distinctness), *class* (size) and *type* (shape).

Grade of soil structure is a term expressing the degree or distinctness of aggregation. Common terms for describing grade are:

Structureless—That condition in which there is no observable aggregation or no definite orderly arrangement of natural lines of weakness. *Massive* if coherent; *single grain* if noncoherent.

Weak—That degree of aggregation characterized by poorly formed indistinct peds that are barely observable in place. When disturbed, soil material that has this grade of structure breaks into a mixture of few entire peds, many broken peds, and much unaggregated material. If necessary for comparison, this grade may be subdivided into *very weak* and *moderately weak.*

Moderate—That grade of structure characterized by well-formed distinct peds that are moderately durable and evident but not distinct in undisturbed soil. Soil material of this grade, when disturbed, breaks down into a mixture of many distinct entire peds, some broken peds, and little unaggregated material.

Strong—That grade of structure characterized by durable peds that are quite evident in undisplaced soil, that adhere weakly to one another, and that withstand displacement and become separated when the soil is disturbed. When removed from the profile, soil material of this grade of structure consists very largely of entire peds and includes few broken peds and little or no unaggregated material. If necessary for comparison, this grade may be subdivided into *moderately strong* and *very strong.*

Class of soil structure refers to the size range of the aggregates. The smaller sizes designate platy and granular types of structure and the larger sizes prismatic and columnar. The relative class size names, along with their absolute size ranges follow:

Very fine or *very thin,* <1 mm to <10 mm
Fine or *thin,* 1–2 mm to 10–12 mm
Medium, 2–5 mm to 20–50 mm
Coarse or *thick,* 5–10 mm to 50–100 mm
Very coarse or *very thick,* >10 mm to >100 mm

Type of soil structure means the shape. The principal types are as follows: (Fig. 4.4)

Platy (laminated)
Prismatic (vertical axes of aggregates longer than the horizontal axes)
Columnar (prisms with dome-shaped tops)
Blocky (angular or subangular)
Granular (like chocolate cake crumbs; the ideal soil structure for plant growth)

Field descriptions of soil structure use these three kinds of soil structural names in this sequence: grade, class, and type. Thus a soil horizon may be:

Grade—weakly aggregated
Class—fine (1–2 mm in diameter)
Type—granular (like chocolate cake crumbs)

With these characterizations, the soil structure would be described as: *weak*, *fine*, and *granular*.

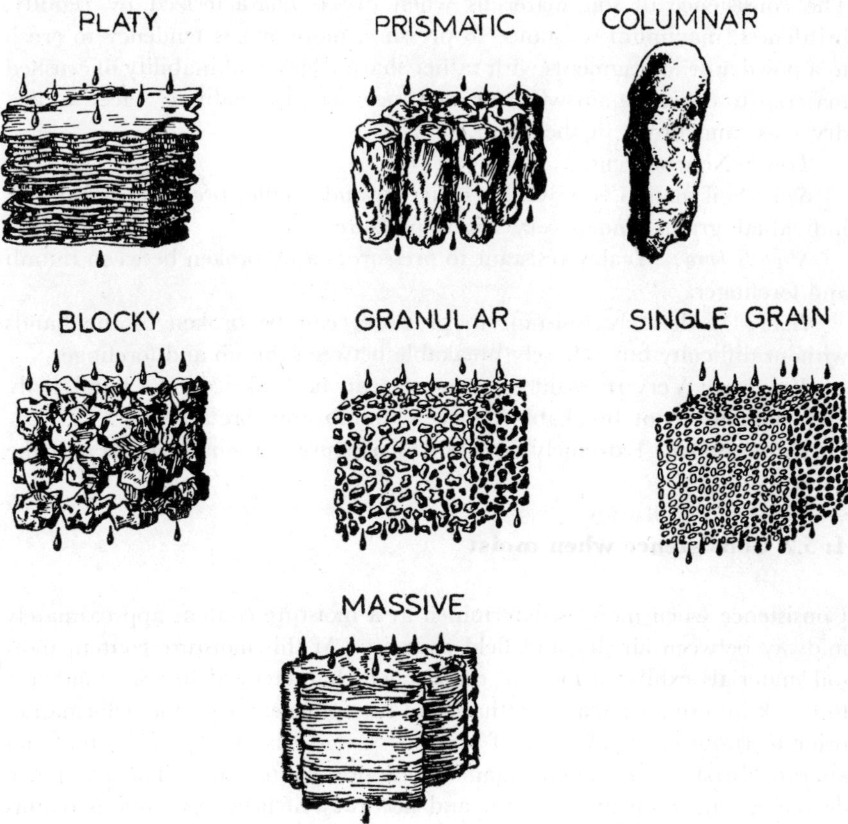

Fig. 4.4. Principal types of soil structure. Water and plant growth relationships are most favorable with granular structure. (*Courtesy:* United States Department of Agriculture.)

4: 5 SOIL CONSISTENCE

Whereas soil structure refers to the degree of distinctness (grade), size (class), and shape (type) of soil aggregates, soil consistence means relative cohesive *strength* of the aggregates to resist rupture or deformation when an external force is applied, such as with the thumb and forefinger. Unless otherwise stated, consistence terms apply to undisturbed soil horizons as observed from a freshly-dug soil pit.

The ability of soil aggregates to withstand external pressure is influenced by its relative water content. For this reason, different terms are used at three different moisture contents: dry, moist, and wet. Three degrees of consistence for *cemented* aggregates are also given (Soil Survey Staff, 1975).

4: 5.1 Consistence when dry

The consistence of soil materials when dry is characterized by rigidity, brittleness, maximum resistance to pressure, more or less tendency to crush to a powder or to fragments with rather sharp edges, and inability of crushed material to cohere again when pressed together. To evaluate, select an air-dry mass and break in the hand.

Loose: Noncoherent.

Soft: Soil mass is very weakly coherent and fragile; breaks to powder or individual grains under very slight pressure.

Slightly hard: Weakly resistant to pressure; easily broken between thumb and forefinger.

Hard: Moderately resistant to pressure; can be broken in the hands without difficulty but is barely breakable between thumb and forefinger.

Very hard: Very resistant to pressure; can be broken in the hands only with difficulty; not breakable between thumb and forefinger.

Extremely hard: Extremely resistant to pressure: cannot be broken in the hands.

4: 5.2 Consistence when moist

Consistence when moist is determined at a moisture content approximately midway between air dry and field capacity. At this moisture content most soil materials exhibit a form of consistence characterized by: (a) tendency to break into smaller masses rather than into powder, (b) some deformation prior to rupture, (c) absence of brittleness, and (d) ability of the material after disturbance to cohere again when pressed together. The resistance decreases with moisture content, and accuracy of field descriptions of this consistence is limited by the accuracy of estimating moisture content. To evaluate this consistence, select and attempt to crush in the hand a mass that appears slightly moist. Moist soil consistence terms are:

Loose: Noncoherent.

Very friable: Soil material crushes under very gentle pressure but coheres when pressed together.

Friable: Soil material crushes easily under gentle to moderate pressure between thumb and forefinger, and coheres when pressed together.

Firm: Soil material crushes under moderate pressure between thumb and forefinger but resistance is distinctly noticeable.

Very firm: Soil material crushes under strong pressure; barely crushable between thumb and forefinger.

Extremely firm: Soil material crushes only under very strong pressure; cannot be crushed between thumb and forefinger and must be broken apart bit by bit.

The term *compact* denotes a combination of firm consistence and close packing or arrangement of particles and should be used only in this sense. It can be given degrees by use of "very" and "extremely".

4: 5.3 Consistence when wet

Consistence when wet is determined at or slightly above field capacity.

Stickiness

Stickiness is the quality of adhesion to other objects. For field evaluation of stickiness, soil material is pressed between thumb and finger and its adherence noted. Degrees of stickiness are described as follows:

Nonsticky: After release of pressure, practically no soil material adheres to thumb or finger.

Slightly sticky: After pressure, soil material adheres to both thumb and finger but comes off one or the other rather cleanly. It is not appreciably stretched when the digits are separated.

Sticky: After pressure, soil material adheres to both thumb and finger and tends to stretch somewhat and pull apart rather than pulling free from either digit.

Very sticky: After pressure, soil material adheres strongly to both thumb and forefinger and is decidedly stretched when they are separated.

Plasticity

Plasticity is the ability to change shape continuously under the influence of an applied stress and to retain the impressed shape on removal of the stress. For field determination of plasticity, roll the soil material between thumb and finger and observe whether or not a wire or thin rod of soil can be formed. If helpful to the reader of particular descriptions, state the range of moisture content within which plasticity continues, as plastic when slightly moist or wetter, plastic when moderately moist or wetter, and plastic only when wet, or as plastic within a wide, medium, or narrow range of moisture content. Express degree of resistance to deformation at or slightly above field capacity as follows:

Nonplastic: No wire is formable.

Slightly plastic: Wire formable but soil mass easily deformable.

Plastic: Wire formable and moderate pressure required for deformation of the soil mass.

Very plastic: Wire formable and much pressure required for deformation of the soil mass.

4: 5.4 Cementation

Cementation of soil material refers to a brittle hard consistence caused by some cementing substance other than clay minerals, such as calcium carbonate, silica, or oxides or salts of iron and aluminum. Typically the cementation is altered little if any by moistening; the hardness and brittleness persist in the wet condition. Semireversible cements, which generally resist moistening but soften under prolonged wetting, occur in some soils and give rise to soil layers having a cementation that is pronounced when dry but very weak when wet. Some layers cemented with calcium carbonate soften somewhat with wetting. Unless stated to the contrary, descriptions of cementation imply that the condition is altered little if any by wetting. If the cementation is greatly altered by moistening, it should be so stated. Cementation may be either continuous or discontinuous within a given horizon.

Weakly cemented: Cemented mass is brittle and hard but can be broken in the hands.

Strongly cemented: Cemented mass is brittle and too hard to be broken in the hand but is easily broken with a hammer.

Indurated: Very strongly cemented; brittle, does not soften under prolonged wetting, and is so extremely hard that for breakage a sharp blow with a hammer is required; hammer generally rings as a result of the blow.

4: 6 PARTICLE DENSITY AND BULK DENSITY

Density of individual soil particles and of soil bulk are reported in relation to the density of water, which is 1 gram per cubic centimeter (1 g/cc). Solid soil particles, such as grains of sand, are composed mostly of the mineral quartz. Its particle density is 2.65 g/cc, meaning that its weight (mass) is 2.65 times that of water. Clay minerals have a particle density slightly less than 2.65 and soil humus about 0.5.

A given bulk of soil such as a cubic centimeter, a cubic foot, or a "sample" of soil is not all solid; on a volume basis it may contain about 50 percent pore space occupied by air and water (see Fig. 4.1). For this reason, bulk density is always less than particle density. If soil particles with a density of exactly 2.65 comprised a "sample" of soil in which the pore space was exactly 50 percent, the bulk density of the sample would be one-half of 2.65 = 1.375 (note: all soil calculations are on an oven-dry basis).

The bulk density of soils in the field vary from about 0.5 for peat to 1.9 for a sandy clay artificially compacted to "waterproof" it for use as a foundation for a road bed. Ideal bulk densities for the best growth of plants, however, vary from about 1.2 for a clay soil to about 1.4 for a sandy soil. Vehicular traffic in a cotton field in southern United States has been reported to increase the bulk density of the surface of a clay loam soil from 1.3 to 1.67; and at a depth of 25 cm, from 1.5 to 1.7 (Trouse, 1971; Donahue, Miller, Shickluna, 1983).

The principle of, and approximate determination of, the bulk density of a field soil can be performed in this way. Push a cylinder (such as a tin can with one end cut out) into the soil flush with the soil surface. Dig out the can with a shovel in such a way that the can is full of soil in its natural state of compaction. Put the can of soil in the oven at 105°C until it loses no more water; i.e., until it has attained a constant weight with two 24-hour successive weighings. The calculation of bulk density follows:

Volume of a can $= \pi r^2 \times h$, where pi is 3.1416, r is radius of the can in cm and h is height of the can in cm. If the particular can used has a radius of 4 cm and a height of 10 cm, its volume is $3.1416 \times 16 \times 10 = 502.656$ cubic cm.

Oven-dry weight of soil in can = 676.8 gm

$$\text{Soil bulk density} = \frac{\text{dry weight of soil}}{\text{volume of soil}} = \frac{676.8 \text{ gm}}{502.656} = 1.35$$

4:7 PORE SPACES

Soil pores are those parts of soil bulk (soil "sample" or horizon) not occupied by solid soil particles. They are also called pore volume, interstices, and voids. In a field soil the pores are always filled with water, air, carbon dioxide, or other gases. The volume percentage of the total bulk of a soil not occupied by solid soil particles is known as porosity (Soil Science Society of America, 1979).

Porosity (percent pore space) may be better understood by a sample calculation, using the bulk density in the previous problem and average particle density of 2.65.

$$\text{Porosity} = 100 - \frac{\text{bulk density}}{\text{particle density}} \times \frac{100}{1} = \frac{1.35}{2.65} = 50.9$$

$$100 - 50.9 = 49.1 \text{ percent}$$

This porosity of nearly 50 percent is considered ideal for most agricultural soils. However, *total* pore space is not always a good criterion for judging the plant-producing capacity of a soil.

Pore spaces are the channels through which water and gases move through the soil to nourish plant roots. This implies that the pores must be connected and of sufficient size for ready movement of air and water.

Because pore spaces are fragile and are disrupted when taking a sample of soil to a laboratory, such scientific studies must be conducted in the field. However, direct field studies are extremely variable because the number, size, continuity, orientation, and shape of pore spaces vary greatly. For example, an earthworm burrow, an old root channel, or a vertical soil crack in the area studied would skew the results of all aeration studies.

One scientific but indirect method of study of soil aeration is to measure the depth and abundance of rooting of key plants. Such field studies were conducted in the Adirondack Mountains of New York State and in Ethiopia and Kenya. In these studies soil morphology was related to the abundance and maximum depth of rooting of wild and crop plants. It was concluded that both abundance of roots and maximum depth of rooting were positively correlated with soil aeration, desirable soil structure, and potential productivity for plants (Donahue, 1940, 1970, 1972 and Kline, Green, Donahue, and Stout, 1969).

However, a special problem was encountered with these relationships in western Africa. Soils that harden into ironstone are porous but not productive because plant roots, water, and air cannot penetrate them. Similar soils are also common in South India, as first reported by Buchanan, 1807.

Guidelines for field studies of roots and soil pores are given on pages 479–481 in Soil Survey Staff, 1975.

4: 8 SOIL TEMPERATURES

Soil temperature regulates all physiological functions such as seed germination, microbial activity, root and shoot growth, and nutrient availability. Especially where growing seasons are short, it is important to plant a crop as early in the spring as possible. For this reason, some enlightened farmers use a soil thermometer to measure temperature at seeding depth to determine when the soil has warmed sufficiently to germinate the seed. In temperate countries for fall-seeded winter wheat, the soil should *cool* to the critical temperature indicated.

For proper germination and growth, favorable soil temperatures at seeding depth for the following crops are:

4–10°C—wheat and peas
10–29°C—corn
16–21°C—potatoes
27°C —sorghums, melons, and most other warm-season crops.

Winter wheat is usually planted in the U.S.A. at about the time of the first freeze in *fall* and peas at about the last freeze in spring. The *earliest* planting date for corn is about ten days *after* the average last freeze in spring. In India wheat sowing in the beginning of winter season has to be delayed until the soil temperatures come down.

Because potato seed pieces have more food reserves than corn, a sprouting potato can recover more readily from a freeze. For this reason, potatoes are usually planted about 10 days *before* the average last freeze in spring. Sorghums, melons, and most other warm-season crops should not be planted earlier than two weeks *after* the average last freeze in spring. In India too soil temperatures affect crop production in some parts. In the northern part soil temperature in summer is excessively high and restricts the growth of summer crops. Studies have been carried out to reduce the soil temperature through mulching, irrigation and tillage. Mulching reduces soil temperature by a few degrees and expedites the emergence of soybean and cotton. Irrigation is also observed to reduce rapidly and substantially maximum soil temperature in summer with beneficial effects. It is attributed to the lower temperature of irrigation water than that of soil, high specific heat of water and greater evaporative cooling (Choudhary and Sandhu, 1982).

Soil temperatures are so important that they are used as one criterion for differentiating soil family classes, as discussed in Section 3:2.6.

Each group of soil microorganisms has its critical temperature. For example, the actinomyces involved in decomposing manure compost are most abundant at 55 to 65°C. However, most species proliferate abundantly at 25 to 30°C. This is also the optimum temperature for most species of bacteria. Fungi are more abundant when the soil is about 37°C. Nitrogen-fixing organisms grow and reproduce fastest at a soil temperature of about 36°C (Alexander, 1977).

4: 9 SOIL COLOR

Soil color may be *lithochromic* (inherited from the color of parent material) or *pedochromic* (resulting from soil-forming processes).

Color of geologic formations (lithochromic) are most contrasting in sedimentary rocks in arid and semiarid regions, especially in western United States. The rocks on the walls of the Grand Canyon of the Colorado River in Arizona vary from gray through purple, brown, red, buff, and green. The Painted Desert in Arizona exhibits such contrasting colors as gray, purple, and pink. Sedimentary rocks in Bryce Canyon in Utah are predominantly pink. The Permian Red Beds in Northern Texas are among the oldest sedimentary rocks known.

Soil color may therefore be inherited from lithochromic color (parent material) or a result of soil-forming (pedochromic) processes. The principal pedochromic processes are dominated by organic matter and its stage of decomposition and iron and its state of oxidation and hydration.

In humid regions, very poorly drained soils usually have a dark, humified surface and a uniformly gray subsurface. The dark color is due to humified organic matter and the gray subsurface to iron in the ferrous (Fe^{2+}) form. In contrast, well-drained soils on old land surfaces in temperate humid regions probably have a brown surface and a uniformly colored yellowish brown to red subsurface. Again in humid temperate regions, soils of intermediate drainage (poorly drained, somewhat poorly drained, and moderately well-drained) have a surface soil color of dark brown and somewhere in the profile a mottled horizon of gray, yellow, brown, and/or red. This mottling indicates a zone of fluctuating water table. Whitish colors are caused by quartz, kaolin, calcium carbonate, magnesium carbonate, calcium sulfate (gypsum), and sodium chloride. Most difficult to explain is the dark color of Vertisols whose organic matter seldom exceed 3 percent. Here the colors are imparted by reduced iron (Fe^{2+}), elemental carbon, and compounds of manganese and magnetite. Also difficult to explain are the very dark colors of sodic soils. In these soils the humus is highly dispersed; thus it has the property of masking other soil colors.

Until the Munsell system was adopted by most soil scientists of the world, it was impossible to describe soil colors with any valid degree of communication. The Munsell system of color notation was developed by A.H. Munsell of the United States in 1905. It has been adopted around the world to standardize the identification of soil colors. The Munsell charts for soil description consist of 175 different colored chips (papers) arranged according to their notation in this sequence: *hue, value,* and *chroma.*

When using the Munsell chips, a sample of soil is held a few centimeters above the chip that most nearly approximates it in color. Then the hue, value, and chroma are noted, such as 5YR 5/6 (bright reddish brown). This means:

hue = 5YR, on a scale of 0 to 10 from yellow to red
value = 5, on a scale of 0 to 10
chroma = 6, on a scale of 0 to 20

Because soil moisture darkens a soil sample, the relative moisture content should be indicated at the time of recording the Munsell color notation.

4: 10 SUMMARY

Soil physical properties are just as critical in plant growth as soil chemical properties. Physical properties, however, appear to be more difficult to study and to correlate with the growth of plants.

Soil particles include sands, silt, and clay. Coarse fragments recognized are gravel, chert, sandstone, limestone, schist, slate, and shale.

Soil textural classes refer to the relative proportion of sands, silt, and clay in a given "sample" of soil. Textural triangles of both the International and the United States systems are given for comparison. It is explained how these textural triangle names are further modified by the fineness of the sand and/or the presence and abundance of coarse fragments.

Soil structural terms are explained by three categories: grade (distinctness of aggregates), class (size of aggregates), and type (shape of aggregates). Soil consistence means the relative strength of the aggregates; usually applied to soils in the field.

Particle density is the weight of individual soil particles in relation to the weight of water. Bulk density is a term applied to the weight of a volume of soil in relation to the weight of an equal volume of water.

Pore spaces are the spaces in a volume of soil not occupied by solid mineral and humus particles. These spaces are always full of water and/or air. The most productive soils are about half pore spaces. The presence or absence of plant roots of wild plants or weeds is a good criterion for judging whether pores are satisfactory for growth of commercial plants.

Soil temperatures determine seed germination, microbial decomposition of organic residues, nutrient availability and plant growth. Soil temperatures are also used in describing soil families in the United States system of soil taxonomy.

Soil color may be inherited from the color of the parent material. This is called lithochromic color. Color developed from soil-forming processes is known as pedochromic. Humus and the state of oxidation/hydration of iron are the dominant substances determining soil color. The Munsell color notation system is now used worldwide to designate soil color in the sequence of hue, value, and chroma.

CITED REFERENCES

Alexander, M. "Introduction to Soil Microbiology." John Wiley & Sons, New York, 2nd Edition, 1977, 467 pages.

Buchanan, H.F. "Journey from Madras, Canara, and Malabar", London, 1807. (Quoted from Fox, C.S. Records, Geological Survey of India 69389, 1936).

Choudhary, T.N. and B.S. Sandhu. "Soil Temperature and Plant Growth" Review of Soil Research in India. Proceedings of 12th GCSS., New Delhi, India, 1982, pages 48-59.

Donahue, R. L. "Ethiopia: Taxonomy, Cartography, and Ecology of Soils." African Studies Center, Institute of International Agriculture, Michigan State University, East Lansing, Michigan, 1972, 43 pages.

Donahue, R.L. "Forest-Site Quality Studies in the Adirondacks. I. Tree Growth as Related to Soil Morphology." Cornell University Memoir 229, 1940, Ithaca, New York, 44 pages.

Donahue, R.L. "Soils of Equatorial Africa and Their Relevance to Rational Agricultural Development." Institute of International Agriculture, Michigan State University, East Lansing, Michigan. Research Report No. 7, 1970, 52 pages.

Donahue, R.L., R.W. Miller and J.C. Shickluna. "Soils: An Introduction to Soils and Plant Growth." Prentice-Hall, Inc., Englewood Cliffs, New Jersey, 5th Edition, 1983, 667 pages.

Gupta, R.P. and Y.N. Rao. "Soil Structure and its Management". Review of Soil Research in India. Proceedings of 12th GCSS., New Delhi, India, 1982, pages 60-76.

Kline, C.K., D.A.G. Green, R.L. Donahue, and B.A. Stout. "Agricultural Mechanization in Equatorial Africa." Institute of International Agriculture, Michigan State University, East Lansing, Michigan. Research Report No. 6, 1969, 648 pages.

Soil Science Society of America. "Glossary of Soil Science Terms." Madison, Wisconsin, 1979, 34 pages.

Soil Survey Staff. "Soil Taxonomy: A Basic System of Soil Classification for Making and Interpreting Soil Surveys." United States Department of Agriculture Handbook 436, 1975, page 472.

Trouse, A.C., Jr. "Soil Conditions as They Affect Plant Establishment, Root Development, and Yield." *In* "Compaction of Agricultural Soils." American Society of Agr. Eng. Monograph, 1971, page 234.

ADDITIONAL REFERENCES

Arakeri, H.R., G.V. Chalam, P. Satyanarayana, and R.L. Donahue. "Soil Management in India." Asia Pub. House, Bombay and London, 2nd Edition, 1962.

Brady, Nyle C. "The Nature and Properties of Soils." Macmillan Pub. Co., Inc. New York, 8th Edition, 1974, 639 pages.

Fujihira Industry Co., Ltd. "Standard Soil Color Charts." Tokyo, Japan, undated.

Tamhane, R.V., D.P. Motiramani, Y.P. Bali, and R.L. Donahue. "Soils: Their Chemistry and Fertility in Tropical Asia." Prentice-Hall of India, Private Limited, New Delhi, 2nd Edition, 1966, 475 pages.

Thompson, L.M. and F.R. Troeh. "Soils and Soil Fertility." McGraw-Hill Book Co., New York, 4th Edition, 1978, 516 pages.

CHAPTER 5

Soil Chemical and Colloidal Properties

5: 1 INTRODUCTION

Efficient soil and water management is essential for luxuriant plant growth, and efficient crop production requires a practical and scientific knowledge of the chemical and colloidal properties of soil. This chapter explains colloidal clay minerals and their characteristics in relation to adsorbed nutrient ions, buffering, soil pH and its amelioration, plant nutrition, soil testing, and special problem soils.

5: 2 CLAY MINERALS

Clay is defined as particles less than 0.002 mm in diameter in both the United States' system and that of the International Society of Soil Science. Furthermore, *most* clays in temperate regions are more than just small mineral particles; they are crystallized aluminosilicates, with a permanent negative charge. In the tropics and subtropics, iron and aluminum sesquioxide clays are common in Oxisols and Ultisols; these have a variable charge, either positive or negative depending on their pH. Some sesquioxides are crystallized, but most are amorphous. Amorphous clays may, however, occur in any climatic zone.

The principal crystallized clay minerals of the world are chlorite, halloysite, illite, kaolinite, montmorillonite, and vermiculite (Table 5.1). Each clay mineral will be described briefly.

Amorphous clays have originated from recent volcanic ash; this means they have not had time to develop fully into crystals. Their net charge may be positive below the pH of zero charge or negative when the pH is above the point of zero charge. These clays are very fertile because their leaching has been minimal.

Chlorite consists of clays with a 2:2 ratio of two silica tetrahedra, an alumina octahedra, and a magnesium octahedra. The clays developed from marine sediments are not fertile.

Table 5.1. Principal clay mineral groups (< 0.002 mm in diameter) and their composition, shrink/swell potential, and environment where usually formed (Adapted from Donahue, Miller, Shickluna, 1983)

Clay mineral group	Usual chemical formula/general composition	Relative shrink/swell potential	Environment where usually formed
Amorphous	Mixed alumino silicate	low	Any temperature, humid; young volcanic ash
Chlorite	Platy hydrous silicates of aluminum, ferrous iron, and magnesium	low	Temperate zone, humid/subhumid, young marine sediments
Halloysite	$Al_2Si_2O_5(OH)_4 \cdot 2H_2O$	low	Subtropical zone, humid/subhumid
Illite	Complex silicates of potassium, aluminum, iron, and magnesium	low to moderate	Temperate zone, subhumid, from slightly weathered mica
Kaolinite	$Al_2(Si_2O_5)(OH)_4$	low	Subtropical zone, humid/subhumid
Montmorillonite	$Al_2Si_4O_{10}(OH)_2$	very high	Any temperature zone, humid/arid, limited leaching
Sesquioxides	Oxides of iron and aluminum	low	Tropical zone, humid, highly leached
Vermiculite	$(Mg, Fe, Al)_8 (Al, Si_4) O_{10}(OH)_2 \cdot 4H_2O$	high	Temperate zone, humid/subhumid, from mica

Halloysite is the name for a common clay mineral. It has a 1:1 ratio of silica tetrahedral sheets to alumina octahedral sheets. Both tubular (slender hollow tubes) and tabular (like the pages of a tablet) forms of halloysite are recognized by mineralogists. These clays are not fertile.

Illite is a 2:1 type clay mineral with an alumina octahedra between two silica tetrahedra. Potassium ions hold the adjacent sheets so tightly that water cannot penetrate between them. For this reason, when wetted, illite expands very little. Such clays are moderately fertile.

Kaolinite is a 1:1 type clay mineral, consisting of one sheet of silica tetrahedra and one of alumina octahedra. No water penetrates between the sheets, therefore, the clay does not expand when wet. Acid conditions favor its formation. Fertility is low.

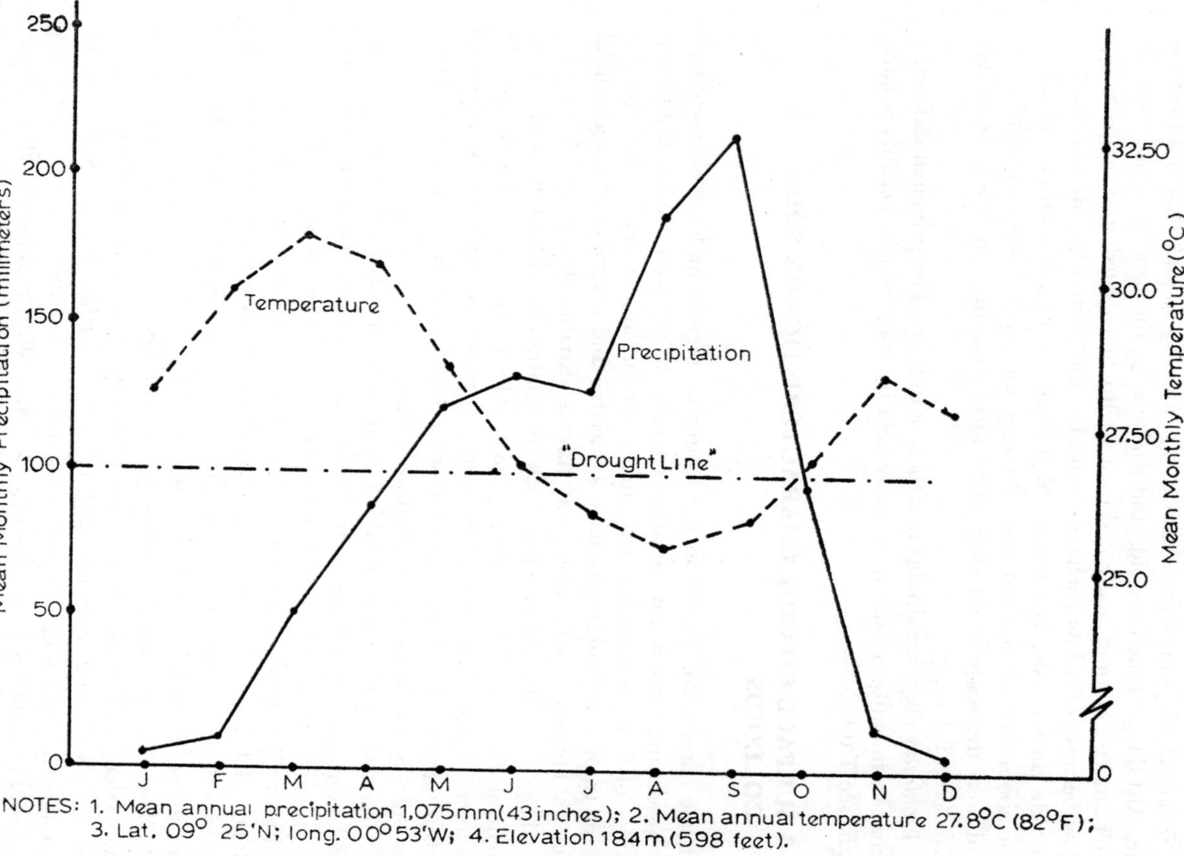

Fig. 5.1. Mean monthly precipitation and mean monthly temperature in Tamale, Ghana (Western Africa) (10-year average). Under these conditions sesquioxide clays form readily (Donahue, 1970).

Montmorillonite is a 2:1 swelling and sticky clay because water can penetrate the layers of the clay lattice. Alkaline conditions favor its formation. Fertility is high.

Sesquioxide clays are mixtures of iron oxide, Fe_2O_3, and aluminum hydroxide, $Al(OH)_3$, formed on old land surfaces in the tropics. They may be either amorphous or crystalline, do not swell when wetted, and their fertility is low because of a low exchange capacity and high toxic aluminum. Sesquioxide clays usually form under high temperature and high precipitation, with about half of the months "drought months". Under these climatic conditions the sesquioxide clays often form ironstone (laterite) (Donahue, 1975) (Fig. 5.1).

Vermiculite clays are similar in structure to illite. The principal difference is that vermiculite crystals are weakly held by magnesium. Fertility is fairly high (see Table 3.8).

5:3 SURFACE CHARGE CHARACTERISTICS ON SOIL COLLOIDS

Silicate clays occur mostly in the temperate regions and are characterized by possessing permanent negative charges. In contrast, colloidal hydrous oxides of iron, aluminum, manganese, silicon, and titanium that develop in the tropics and subtropics have a variable and reversible electrochemical charge. Humus in all regions may have a variable charge.

The 2:1 layer silicate clays such as montmorillonite, illite, and vermiculite and the 2:2 layer silicate clay, chlorite, have permanent negative charges. These electrochemical charges result because of isomorphous substitution of Al^{3+} for Si^{4+} in the silica tetrahedral layers and/or of Mg^{2+} for Al^{3+} in the alumina octahedral layers.

Clay minerals with a variable charge occur mostly in the humid tropics and subtropics on old and well-drained land surfaces. Such soils are placed in the soil orders of Oxisols (comprising 8.51 percent of all world soils) and Ultisols (5.56 percent of world soils). They are characterized by the abundance of 1:1 layer kaolinite and halloysite in mixture with hydrous oxides of mostly iron, aluminum, and silicon. These oxides may occur in amorphous or crystalline form (Uehara, 1978).

The electrochemical charge on variable charge clay minerals may be dependent on the pH. Examples of minerals with a pH-dependent charge are the oxides and hydrous oxides of iron (hematite, goethite, lepidocrosite) aluminum (gibbsite, boehmite), titanium (anatase, rutile), manganese (pyrolusite), and silicon (quartz). Common silicate minerals whose charge is dependent on pH are kaolinite, halloysite, and aluminum interlayered chlorite (Uehara, 1978).

Variable charge of clay minerals was first demonstrated by Mattson in

1931 and later confirmed by many soil scientists. The variable charge is characteristic of most clays in Oxisols and Ultisols. It means that a given clay may have a negative or a positive charge, depending on pH. The presence of aluminum and iron oxides and hydrous oxides comprising the clay minerals has been credited with this variation in charge.

Clays with a pH-dependent charge implies that at some pH the clay is neither positive nor negative but neutral in charge. This pH is called the point of zero charge, and it varies with the mineral. For example, the pH at which minerals have no (zero) charge is given here for selected minerals (Isbell, 1978).

Mineral	*pH of Zero Charge*
Quartz	1–3
Montmorillonite	< 2.5
Kaolinite	3
Rutile	3.5–6.7
Magnetite	6.5
Goethite	5.9–7.2
Hematite	8.3–9.0
Iron oxide (amorphous)	8.5
Gibbsite	7.8–9.5
Boehmite	6.5–9.4
Aluminum hydroxide (amorphous)	7.5–8.0

At pH values *below* the point of zero charge, the mineral has a net positive charge and at a pH *above* the zero charge, the mineral has a net negative charge.

The pH of zero charge of several highly weathered soils from tropical and subtropical regions is shown in Table 5.2.

5: 4 CATION/ANION EXCHANGE

Clay minerals in temperate regions have a permanent net negative charge. Most sesquioxide clay minerals and some amorphous clays have a variable charge. Because of the unsatisfied negative charges on clay minerals, positive ions (cations) are attracted. This attraction is strong enough to hold the adsorbed cations against leaching by low-cation water such as rainwater and distilled water. However, when a concentrated solution of *any* cation is added to these clay minerals, by *mass action*, the added cation replaces some of the adsorbed cations on the clay minerals. This is known as cation exchange. When variable charge clays have a net positive charge, they are capable of adsorbing anions such as sulfates, phosphates, and nitrates. This is anion exchange.

Examples of cation exchange follow: When fertilizer ammonium (NH_4^+) is added to a soil, by mass action, the ammonium will replace a

Table 5.2. Point of zero charge values for a range of weathered soils from subtropical and tropical regions (Isbell, 1978)

Soil great group*	Organic carbon (%)	Dominant† minerals	pH at point of zero charge pH	pzc‡ (a)	(b)
Acrorthox A	2.5	Gi, Go, K	5.3	3.9	3.5
Acrorthox B	0.7	Gi, Go, K	5.9	6.2	6.0
Acrohumox A	1.9	K, Gi, Go	4.9	3.6	2.1
Acrohumox B	0.3	K, Gi, Go	4.9	4.2	4.4
Tropudalf A	2.3	K, Go, Gi	6.3	3.4	1.9
Tropudalf B	1.0	K, Go, Gi	6.7	3.8	2.7
Gibbsihumox A	2.87	—	5.0	4.4	—
Gibbsihumox B	0.99	—	5.0	5.7	—
Gibbsihumox A	1.22	Gi, Go, He, K	5.0	6.3	6.0
Tropohumult A	4.70	K, Go	5.9	3.0	—
Tropohumult B	0.60	K, Go	5.8	3.4	—
Paleustalf B	0.6	K, Go, Gi, He	4.8	3.7	—
Acrorthox A	4.0	K, Gi, Go	3.8	—	2.6
Acrorthox B	0.6	K, Gi, Q, Go	4.8	—	5.4
Tropudult A	1.7	K, In, Gi, Q, Go	4.4	—	1.4
Tropudult B	0.4	K, In, Gi, Q, Go	4.5	—	4.2
Tropuldalf A	3.4	K, M, Gi, Q, Go	6.0	—	1.8
Tropuldalf B	0.7	K, M, In, Gi, Q, Go	5.0	—	4.2
Acrohumox A	6.3	Go, Gi, K, V, I	5.2	4.8	3.8
Acrohumox B	0.2	K, Go, Gi	4.8	6.4	7.0
Haplustox§ A	1.9	K, V, Q	5.2	4.2	3.0
Haplustox B	0.1	K, Q	5.3	4.4	3.8

*Soil Survey Staff (1975); A=surface horizon, B=subsoil horizon. †Gi=gibbsite; Go=goethite; He=hematite; I=illite; K=kaolinite; M=montmorillonite; Q=quartz; In=interstratified minerals; V=vermiculite. ‡(a) pzc value determined by potentiometric titration; (b) pzc value determined by adsorption of indifferent electrolyte. §Alternative classification if argillic horizon present is Paleustult.

large amount of the adsorbed cations such as calcium, magnesium, hydrogen, potassium, sodium, and aluminum. In like manner, when calcium (Ca^{2+}), magnesium (Mg^{2+}), or potassium (K^+) are applied to the soil, the large number of cations of the added element will replace large numbers of adsorbed cations. Anion exchange is almost always smaller in magnitude than cation exchange.

The adsorbed cations and anions on the surface of clay minerals are *available* to plants by plant roots releasing hydrogen ions in exchange for the adsorbed nutrient ions, calcium, magnesium, potassium, and ammonium; and hydroxide ions for nutrient anions. This root-soil mechanism is also called cation/anion exchange.

In addition to the property of cation adsorption, amorphous, sesquioxide, and kaolinite clays also adsorb smaller amounts of anions such as phosphates and sulfates. Other environmental factors being comparable, the greater the cation exchange capacity the more productive the soil.

Humus has a large cation exchange capacity and usually a small anion exchange capacity.

5: 5 BUFFERING

Buffering in soil science means a resistance to change in pH. Substances in the soil that buffer it are clay, humus, and compounds such as carbonates and phosphates. Even the type of clay greatly influences the buffer capacity of soils. Montmorillonite minerals have the greatest buffer capacity because of the very high exchange capacity, and sesquioxide clays the least buffer and exchange capacities.

The close relationship of buffer capacity and exchange capacity can be explained in this way: pH measures *active* acidity, and exchangeable acidity is the *reserve* acidity. When lime is added to a soil it first neutralizes the active acidity. However, the active and reserve acidity always tend to be in equilibrium. So when active acidity is neutralized, more hydrogen ions come from the reserve acidity. Thus, the more exchangeable (reserve) acidity present, the more lime is needed to cause an increase in soil pH. This explains the reason for the fact that the finer the soil texture and/or the more humus, the more lime that is needed to raise the pH.

5: 6 SOIL pH AND ITS AMELIORATION

The term "pH" (from French, *Pouvoir hydrogéne*, hydrogen power) was proposed by Sorensen to indicate acidity. It is defined as the logarithm of the reciprocal of the hydrogen ion concentration in gram atoms (moles) per litre. Thus:

$$pH = \log \frac{1}{[H^+]}$$

Table 5.3. The entire pH scale from 0 to 14, the pH of common products, and the hydrogen ion concentration at each pH

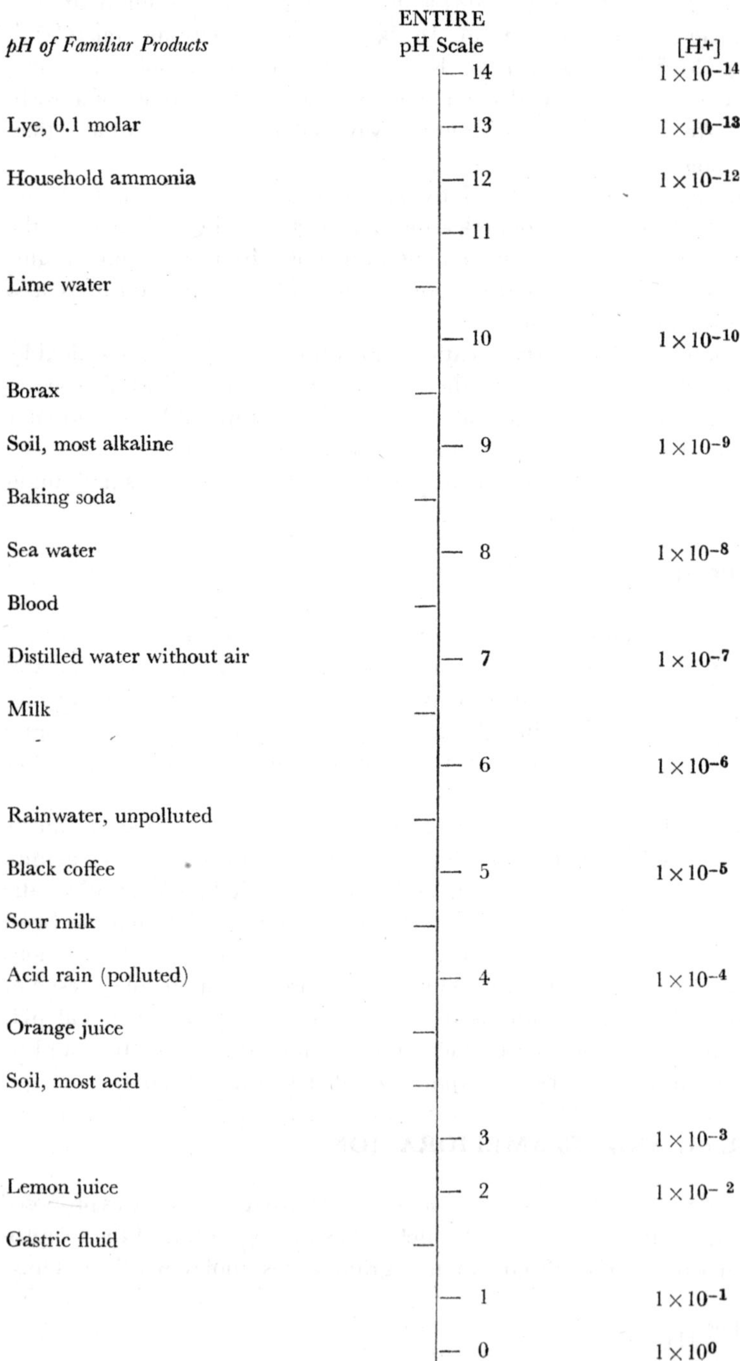

pH of Familiar Products	ENTIRE pH Scale	[H+]
	14	1×10^{-14}
Lye, 0.1 molar	13	1×10^{-13}
Household ammonia	12	1×10^{-12}
	11	
Lime water		
	10	1×10^{-10}
Borax		
Soil, most alkaline	9	1×10^{-9}
Baking soda		
Sea water	8	1×10^{-8}
Blood		
Distilled water without air	7	1×10^{-7}
Milk		
	6	1×10^{-6}
Rainwater, unpolluted		
Black coffee	5	1×10^{-5}
Sour milk		
Acid rain (polluted)	4	1×10^{-4}
Orange juice		
Soil, most acid		
	3	1×10^{-3}
Lemon juice	2	1×10^{-2}
Gastric fluid		
	1	1×10^{-1}
	0	1×10^{0}

Also expressed as the negative logarithm of the H^+ concentration in moles per litre.

$pH = -\log [H^+]$

The logarithm (log) of a number is the power to the base 10 to which the number 10 must be raised to give that number. Therefore, the log of 10 is 1; of 100 is 2; of 0.01 is −2. If the number is not an exact multiple of 10, a logarithm table is required. (For some persons it is easier to remember that pH stands for *p*ower (logarithmic) of the *h*ydrogen ion concentration).

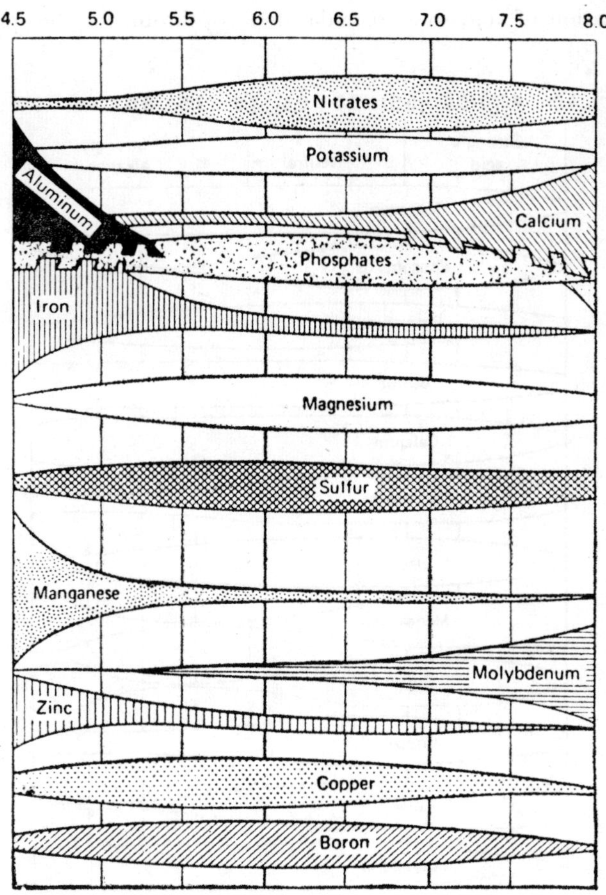

Fig. 5.2. The relative availability of 12 essential plant nutrients in well-drained *mineral* soils in temperate regions in relation to soil pH. A pH range between 6 and 7 (between heavy lines) is considered ideal for most plants. The thirteenth essential plant nutrient from the soil, chlorine, is not shown because its availability is not pH-dependent. Aluminum is not an essential nutrient for plants but it is shown because it may be toxic below a soil pH of 5.2. (*Source:* "Liming Acid Soils." Leaflet AGR-19, 1978, University of Kentucky.)

The entire pH scale extends from 0 to 14. From 0 to 7 the solution is acid, and from 7–14 it is alkaline. At exactly pH 7 the number of hydrogen and hydroxide ions are equal. Note that the scale is not arithmetic but logarithmic, i.e., each whole unit is 10 times the adjacent whole unit. For example, at a pH of 5 there are 10 times more hydrogen ions present than at a pH of 6 and 100 times more than at a pH of 7 (Table 5.3).

Availability of plant nutrients varies with soil pH (Figs. 5.2 and 5.3). Likewise, most plants have a wide pH tolerance and a narrower optimum pH (McCall, 1978) (Table 5.4).

Amelioration of acid soils to make them optimum for the species to be

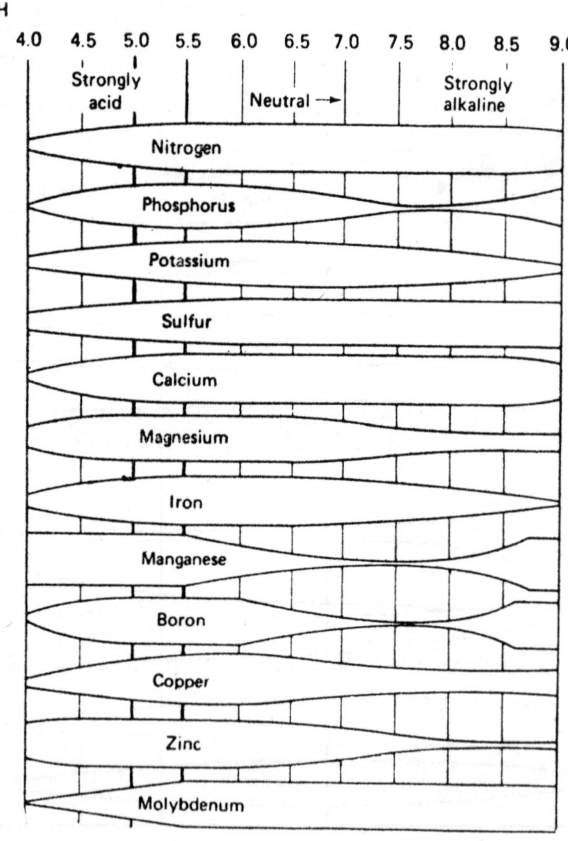

Fig. 5.3. The relative availability of essential plant nutrients from *organic* soils (Histosols). A pH range of 5.0 to 5.5 is considered ideal for the optimum growth of most plants (between heavy lines). Deduction: The more the organic matter in a *mineral* soil, the lower the "ideal" soil pH. *Note:* Until more data are available, the authors are suggesting that this figure can also be used for pH-plant growth relationships on Oxisols and Ultisols in the tropics and subtropics. (*Source:* R.E. Lucas and J.F. Davis, Michigan State University.)

Plate 1. Furrow Irrigation near Hyderabad, Andhra Pradesh, India. (*Courtesy:* USAID/India.)

Plate 2. A wide shovel is being used to make furrows for furrow irrigation of a row crop in Central India. (*Courtesy:* USAID/India.)

Plate 3. Tubewell irrigation water near Nalanda, India. (*Courtesy:* USAID/India.)

Plate 4. Clay soils crack heavily on drying. (*Courtesy:* Indian Council of Agricultural Research—ICAR, New Delhi, India.)

Plate 5. Transplanting rice seedlings.

Plate 6. The International Fertilizer Development Center assists in discovering, processing and testing fertilizers (India). (*Courtesy:* Frank Shuman, University of Illinois.)

Plate 7. Wooden plow is the only implement available with most of the farmers in India. It is being used for sowing seed. (*Courtesy:* Directorate of Extension, Department of Agriculture, Ministry of Agriculture, Government of India, New Delhi, India.)

Plate 8. Application of fertilizer in an early stage of rice crop (*Courtesy:* ICAR, New Delhi, India.)

Plate 9. Application of fertilizers in line for sugarcane crop. (*Courtesy:* Directorate of Extension, Deptt. of Agriculture, Ministry of Agriculture, New Delhi, India.)

Plate 10. Severe gully erosion in evidence in red soil region of Karnataka. (*Courtesy:* Karnataka State, Department of Agriculture, Bangalore, India.)

Plate 11. Terracing is a must for cultivation on steep slopes to control erosion.
(*Courtesy:* ICAR, New Delhi, India.)

Plate 12. Contour wattling, mulching and planting.
(*Courtesy:* **ICAR**, New Delhi, India.)

Plate 13. Asphalt pond to hold water from small water sheds. Water stored can be used for giving critical life-saving irrigation. (*Courtesy:* ICAR, New Delhi, India.)

Plate 14. Large pond for storing water for giving one or two irrigations at a critical time. (*Courtesy:* ICAR, New Delhi, India.)

Table 5.4. The optimum and tolerance pH range for common plants (McCall, 1978)

Plant	Suggested pH	pH tolerance	Plant	Suggested pH	pH tolerance
		Field Crops			
Alfalfa	6.5–7.5	6.0–8.0	Rice	5.0–6.5	4.5–8.0
Castor Bean	6.0–7.5		Sorghum	5.5–7.0	5.0–8.5
Field Corn	5.5–7.0	5.0–7.5	Sugar Cane	6.0–7.0	4.5–8.0
Kaimi Clover	5.5–6.5	4.5–7.0	Taro	5.5–7.5	
Kikuyu Grass	5.5–6.5		Trefoil	5.5–6.0	5.0–7.5
Pangola Grass	5.5–6.5		White Clover	6.0–7.0	5.5–8.0
		Flowering Plants			
Anthurium	5.5–6.5	5.0–7.5	Hibiscus	6.0–7.0	5.0–8.0
Azalea	4.5–5.0		Ixora	6.0–7.5	5.0–8.0
Begonia	5.5–7.0		Jacaranda	6.0–7.5	
Bougainvillea	5.5–7.0	5.0–8.0	Lantana	5.5–7.0	
Camellia	4.5–5.5		Magnolia	5.5–6.5	5.0–7.0
Carnation	6.0–7.5	5.0–8.0	Marigold	5.5–6.5	4.5–7.5
Chrysanthemum	6.0–7.5	5.0–8.0	Oleander	6.0–7.5	
Flame Grass	5.5–6.5	5.0–7.5	Orchid	4.0–5.0	
Gardenia	5.0–6.0	4.5–7.5	Poinciana	6.0–7.5	
Geranium	6.0–7.0	5.5–8.0	Poinsettia	6.0–7.5	
Ginger	6.0–7.0	5.0–8.0	Pomegranate	6.0–7.5	
Honeysuckle	6.5–7.5	5.5–8.0	Roses	5.5–7.0	
		Nuts			
Coconut	6.0–8.0		Macadamia	5.0–6.0	
Coffee	5.0–6.0				
		Fruits			
Avocado	5.5–7.0	5.0–8.0	Lime	6.0–7.5	5.5–7.5
Banana	6.0–7.5	5.5–8.0	Lychee	5.5–6.5	4.5–7.5
Breadfruit	5.0–6.0	4.5–8.0	Mango	5.5–6.5	5.0–7.5
Date	6.5–8.0		Orange	6.0–7.0	5.5–8.0
Fig	6.0–7.0		Papaya	6.0–7.5	
Grapefruit	6.0–7.5		Passion Fruit	5.0–6.0	4.5–8.0
Guava	5.5–7.0	5.0–7.5	Pineapple	5.5–6.5	5.0–7.0
Kumquat	6.0–7.5		Pummelo	5.5–6.5	5.5–7.0
Lemon	6.0–7.0	5.5–7.5	Tangerine	6.0–7.0	5.5–8.0
		Ornamentals			
Alamanda	5.5–6.5		Mock Orange	6.0–7.0	6.0–8.0
Banyan	5.0–7.5	4.5–8.0	Mondo Grass	6.0–7.0	5.0–8.0
Boxwood	6.0–7.0		Monkeypod	6.0–7.0	5.5–7.5
Calinga	5.5–6.5	5.0–7.5	Moss rose	6.0–7.0	5.0–8.0
Caladium	6.0–7.5		Palms	6.0–7.5	4.5–8.0
Coleus	6.0–7.5	5.0–8.0	Pandanus	6.0–7.5	4.5–8.0
Croton	5.5–6.5	5.0–7.5	Portulaca	5.5–6.5	5.0–7.5

Table 5.4 (*Contd.*)

Plant	Suggested pH	pH tolerance	Plant	Suggested pH	pH tolerance
Eucalyptus	6.0–7.0	5.0–8.0	Sunflower	6.0–7.0	5.5–8.0
Ironwood	6.0–7.0	5.0–8.0	Stephanotus	6.0–7.0	5.5–7.5
Jade Vine	6.0–7.5				
		Turf			
Bentgrass	6.0–7.0		St. Augustinegrass	5.5–6.5	5.0–7.5
Bermudagrass	6.0–7.0	5.0–8.0	Zoysiagrass	6.0–7.0	5.5–8.0
Centipedegrass	6.0–7.0	5.5–7.5			
		Vegetables			
Asparagus	5.5–7.0	5.0–8.0	Lima Beans	5.5–6.5	5.0–7.0
Beets	6.0–7.0	5.5–7.5	Mint	7.0–8.0	5.0–8.0
Bell Peppers	5.5–6.5	5.0–7.0	Muskmelon	5.5–6.5	5.0–7.0
Bitter Melon	5.5–6.5	5.0–7.0	Mustard	6.0–7.0	5.5–7.5
Broccoli	6.0–7.5	5.5–7.5	Okra	6.0–7.5	5.5–8.0
Cabbage	6.0–7.0	5.5–7.0	Onions	6.0–6.5	5.5–7.0
Cantalopes	5.5–6.5	5.0–7.0	Parsley	5.0–6.0	4.5–7.5
Carrots	5.5–6.5	5.0–7.0	Peanut	5.5–6.5	5.0–7.5
Cauliflower	6.0–7.0	5.5–7.5	Peas	5.5–6.5	5.0–7.0
Celery	5.8–7.0	5.0–7.5	Pole Beans	5.5–6.5	5.0–7.0
Chili Pepper	5.5–6.5	5.0–7.0	Potato	5.0–5.5	4.5–7.5
Cowpeas	5.5–7.0	5.0–8.0	Radish	5.5–6.5	5.0–7.0
Cucumbers	5.5–6.5	5.0–7.0	Snap Beans	5.5–6.5	5.0–7.5
Daikon	5.5–6.5	5.0–7.0	Squash	5.5–6.5	5.0–7.0
Dasheen	5.5–6.5	5.0–7.0	Strawberry	5.0–6.5	5.0–8.0
Eggplant	5.5–6.5	5.0–7.0	Sweet Corn	5.5–7.0	5.0–8.0
Ginger Root	6.0–7.5		Sweet Potato	5.0–6.0	5.0–7.0
Goard	6.0–7.0	5.0–7.5	Tomato	5.5–7.0	5.0–7.5
Gobo	5.5–7.0	4.5–8.0	Turnip	5.5–6.5	5.0–7.0
Kai Choy	5.0–6.0	4.5–6.5	Won Bok	6.0–7.0	5.0–7.5
Leek	6.0–7.0	5.5–8.0	Watercress	6.0–7.0	
Lettuce	6.0–7.0	5.5–7.5	Watermelon	5.0–6.5	5.0–7.0
		Weeds			
Crabgrass	6.0–7.0	5.0–7.5	Purslane	5.0–6.0	4.5–7.0
Dandelion	5.5–7.0	4.5–8.0	Spiny Amaranth	4.0–8.0	
Nutgrass	4.0–8.0		Spurge	5.0–7.5	4.5–8.0

grown is usually accomplished by adding ground limestone. Liming materials may also include calcium oxide and calcium hydroxide, although these materials are powdery, caustic, and difficult to apply on windy days. Also used as liming materials are ground oyster shells, basic slag from steel mills, marl (deposits in fresh water) and chalk (deposits in sea water). Most common of all liming materials are calcic limestone (impure calcium carbonate) and dolomitic limestone (impure calcium and magnesium carbonate).

The effectiveness of any lime to raise soil pH is due to two characteristics: purity and fineness. In evaluating purity, pure calcium carbonate is assumed to be 100. When a lime has 10 percent sand, chert, iron, clay or other impurities, the lime would have a purity rating of 90. Although it seldom exists in nature, pure magnesium carbonate would have a calcium carbonate equivalent of 119. This is because the molecular weight of magnesium carbonate is 84 compared with 100 for the molecular weight of calcium carbonate ($100 \div 84 = 1.19$). A compensating factor is the fact that magnesium carbonate is less soluble than calcium carbonate.

Fineness of ground limestone determines the rate of reaction in soil. To be effective in neutralizing acidity, calcitic limestone should pass a 40-mesh (425 micron) sieve or finer, dolomitic limestone a 60- to 80-mesh (180 to 250 micron) sieve or finer, and liming materials too coarse to pass through a 6- to 8-mesh (3.35 to 2.36 millimeter) sieve have little value (Voss, 1980).

5: 7 PLANT NUTRITION

All seed-bearing plants require 16 elements for growth and reproduction. (Lower forms of plants have similiar but not identical requirements.) Although most higher plants absorb many more than 16 elements, highly refined research has confirmed that most of them are not essential.

Sources of the essential elements are air, water, soil, lime, and fertilizer, as follows: (Table 5.5).

- Carbon, oxygen—from air through plant leaves
- Hydrogen—from water through roots to plants
- Nitrogen—from air through microbial fixation, organic decomposition and from fertilizer; to soil through roots to plants
- Calcium, magnesium—from soil minerals and lime through roots to plants
- Phosphorus, potassium, sulfur, boron, chlorine, copper, iron, manganese, molybdenum—from soil minerals and fertilizer to soil through roots to plants

Plant roots absorb nutrients through one or more of three mechanisms: *mass flow, diffusion,* and *root interception.* Mass flow absorption takes place when plant nutrients dissolved in the soil solution are absorbed along with the water. Diffusion absorption may be *active* or *passive.* In active absorption, ions and molecules move into the roots against a concentration gradient, using energy from respiration. This means a higher concentration of any particular element such as calcium in the root cells than in the soil solution. In passive absorption, each nutrient anion or cation moves independently from a higher concentration in the soil solution into root cells with a lower concentration of that element. Root interception refers to the extension and

Table 5.5. The 16 elements essential for plant growth, their source(s), the form(s) in which absorbed and mechanism of absorption (Donahue, Miller, Shickluna, 1983)

Essential element	Source(s)	Form(s) absorbed by plants and mechanism of absorption
Carbon	Air	CO_2; mostly through leaves by diffusion of gasses
Hydrogen	Water	H^+, HOH; mostly through roots by mass flow of soil solution
Oxygen	Air	O^{2-}, OH^-, CO_3^{2-}, SO_4^{2-}; mostly through leaves by diffusion of gasses
Nitrogen	Air/fertilizer to soil to plants	NH_4^+, NO_3^-; mostly through roots by mass flow of soil solution
Phosphorus	Soil/fertilizer	$H_2PO_4^-$, HPO_4^{2-}; mostly through roots by diffusion through soil solution
Potassium	Soil/fertilizer	K^+; mostly through roots by diffusion through soil solution
Calcium	Soil/lime	Ca^{2+}; mostly through roots by mass flow of soil solution
Magnesium	Soil/lime	Mg^{2+}; mostly through roots by unknown mechanism
Sulfur	Soil/fertilizer	SO_4^{2-}; mostly through roots by mass flow of soil solution
Boron	Soil/fertilizer	H_3BO_3, $H_2BO_3^-$, $B(OH)_4^-$; mostly through roots by unknown mechanism
Chlorine	Soil/fertilizer	Cl^-; mostly through roots by unknown mechanism
Copper	Soil/fertilizer	Cu^{2+}; mostly through roots by unknown mechanism
Iron	Soil/fertilizer	Fe^{2+}, Fe^{3+}; mostly through roots by unknown mechanism
Manganese	Soil/fertilizer	Mn^{2+}; mostly through roots by unknown mechanism
Molybdenum	Soil/fertilizer	MoO_4^{2+}; mostly through roots by mass flow of soil solution
Zinc	Soil/fertilizer	Zn^{2+}; mostly through roots by unknown mechanism

growth of roots into fresh supplies of plant nutrients in the soil and the absorption by either active or passive diffusion and/or mass flow.

Corn roots absorb most of their phosphorus and potassium by diffusion and most of their manganese by root interception. Mass flow is the principal mechanism of uptake of boron, calcium, copper, iron, magnesium, and zinc (Barber, 1966).

The ability of a plant to absorb adequate nutrients for optimum growth and reproduction can be reduced by the following negative factors: (Corey and Schulte, 1973).

- Low or unbalanced concentration of nutrients in the soil
- Low oxygen concentration in the soil
- Low or high soil or air temperature
- Antagonism of nutrients, such as high available potassium and ammonium suppressing the uptake of magnesium
- Toxic substances such as excess total soluble salts

Available nutrients in the soil in excess of plant needs may be absorbed by certain plants in excess of their requirements. The phenomenon is called *luxury consumption.* This is true especially with those cations loosely held on the clay and humus surfaces such as ammonium and potassium. It is also true with excess nitrates in the soil solution.

Besides being false economy, excessive ammonium and/or potassium may decrease absorption of magnesium in forage crops and cause grass tetany (hypomagnesemia) in animals because of low magnesium in the blood. Luxury nitrate absorption by crops may cause methemoglobinemia in livestock and human babies (Follett, Murphy, Donahue, 1981).

5: 8 CHEMICAL PROBLEM SOILS OF THE WORLD

The recent soil map of the world has been used to estimate the hectarage of soils having common plant toxicities and deficiencies (Dudal, 1977).

An estimated 22.47 percent of world soils have such a toxicity or deficiency for plant growth. Leading in total area are the Oxisols with 8.11 percent. Common toxicities on Oxisols are aluminum and manganese toxicity and a common deficiency of phosphorus, calcium, magnesium, potassium, and molybdenum (Table 5.6).

5: 9 SOIL TESTING

Soil testing is a chemical evaluation of the capabilities of soils in a particular field for the purpose of determining needs for lime or fertilizers. In a technical sense, soil testing attempts to determine the nutrient supplying capacity of the soil for a particular plant or plants. These technical data are then interpreted into the needs for lime and fertilizers to produce maximum

Table 5.6. Soils of the world: common mineral toxicities and deficiencies by soil taxa (Dudal, 1977)

United States taxon	FAO equivalent	Common mineral toxicity/ deficiency	Total area in world (000 ha)	Percentage of world soils
Andepts	Andosols	Toxicity of Al, Mn, Fe Deficiency of N	100,640	0.76
Oxisols	Ferrasols	Toxicity of Al, Mn Deficiency of P, Ca, Mg, K, Mo	1,068,450	8.11
Spodosols	Podzols, Podzoluvisols	Toxicity of Al Deficiency of N, P, K, Cu	741,820	5.63
Ultisols (Part)	Acrisols, Nitosols	Toxicity of Al, Fe, Mn Deficiency of N	1,049,890	7.97
		Total	2,960,800	22.47

economic returns from the crops grown. In recent years, soil testing has been used to determine suspected excess or toxic accumulations of fertilizers.

Most countries of the world now have a soil testing service for farmers. However, continuing research is needed to improve its accuracy for predicting lime and fertilizer needs. The principal problems involve the chemical methods of testing, methods of field sampling of soil, and correlation with actual field response (Melsted and Peck, 1973).

5: 10 SALINE AND SODIC SOILS

Saline soils are defined as having an exchangeable sodium percentage of less than 15, a conductivity more than 4 mmhos/cm, and a pH less than 8.5. A sodic soil has an exchangeable sodium percentage of more than 15, a conductivity less than 4 mmhos/cm, and a pH greater than 8.5. A saline-sodic soil is a sodic soil with an electrical conductivity of more than 4 mmhos/cm.

Plants sensitive to salt concentrations of 2 to 4 mmhos include beans, banana, all citrus, soybeans, and sugar cane. Plants that tolerate high salt concentrations of 10 to 16 mmhos include barley, bermudagrass, coconut, sugar beets, palms, rye, and zoysiagrass. Other plants are intermediate in salt tolerance (Table 5.7) (See Chapter 10).

Table 5.7. Relative salt tolerance of selected plants (McCall, 1976)*

Low Tolerance		Moderate Tolerance	High Tolerance	
millimhos per cm at 25°C in soil solution				
0	2	4	10	16
Little or no effect. Any plant can be grown	Very sensitive plants will be affected	Low tolerance plants cannot be grown	Only tolerant plants can be grown	Only a few very tolerant plants can be grown
green beans	avocado	broccoli	asparagus	sansevieria
	banana	cabbage	bermudagrass	
	celery	cantalope	bougainvillea	
	grapefruit	carrot	coconut	
	lemon	carnations	date palm	
	lime	castor beans	garden beets	
	orange	cauliflower	ornamental palms	
	papaya	corn, field	spinach	
	radish	corn, sweet	zoysiagrass	
	soybeans	chrysanthemum		
	sugar cane	cucumber		
	tangerine	fig		
	coleus	grape		
		guava		
		lettuce		
		lychee		
		macadamia nut		
		mango		
		onion		
		passion fruit		
		peas		
		pepper, hot		
		pepper, sweet		
		pineapple		
		pomegranate		
		potatoes, irish		
		potatoes, sweet		
		pummelo		
		rice		
		St. Augustine-grass		
		sorghum		
		squash		
		sunflower		
		tomato		
		most flowering plants		
		most ornamental plants		

**Note:* Plants in each salinity range can be grown under salinity conditions lower than those shown but not at higher salinity levels.

Crops sensitive to exchangeable sodium include beans, clovers, citrus, and avocado. Most tolerant to sodium are alfalfa, barley, beets, cotton, crested wheatgrass, and tomato. Most other crops are intermediate in tolerance.

Soil scientists and plant breeders are successfully screening and breeding rice varieties and other crops for greater tolerance to salinity and alkalinity (Ponnamperuma, 1977, Yadav 1976).

Reclamation of saline soils involves leaching the salts downward below plant root depth with irrigation water low in salt content. Reclamation of sodic and saline-sodic soils requires the replacement of exchangeable sodium by calcium, then leaching the sodium salts below root depth. Usually gypsum (impure calcium sulfate) is used to supply the calcium.

5: 11 SUMMARY

Most clays of temperate regions are aluminosilicates with a permanent net negative charge; whereas the highly weathered clays of the tropics and subtropics (Oxisols and Ultisols) are amorphous iron and aluminum sesquioxides with a variable and pH-dependent charge. The pH of zero charge for Oxisols and Ultisols varies from 3.8 to 6.7. For each specific soil, the net charge is positive at lower pH's and negative at higher pH's. Such soils would therefore adsorb cations at pH's higher than the pH of zero charge and anions at pH's lower than the pH of zero charge.

The greater the cation exchange capacity of a soil the more highly the soil is buffered and the more resistance to change in pH. For example, a clay loam soil at a pH of 5.5 may require 5 tons of limestone to change the pH to 6.5; whereas, it may require only 2 tons to make the same change in pH in a sandy loam. The clay loam would therefore be more highly buffered.

Plants absorb carbon and oxygen from the air through the leaves; hydrogen from water mostly through roots; nitrogen from microbial fixation from air, organic decomposition, and from fertilizer; and other nutrients mostly from soil minerals and fertilizers through roots.

Chemical evaluation of the available nutrient supplying capacity of soils is a world-wide practice. Sampling techniques, extractants, and correlation of soil test results with field response are a continuing research need.

Saline and sodic soils can be made more productive by breeding and selecting resistant plants, adding calcium to replace sodium, and by leaching salts downward below the root zone.

CITED REFERENCES

Barber, S.A. "The Role of Root Interception, Mass Flow, and Diffusion in Regulating the Uptake of Ions by Plants from Soil." Technical Reporting Service, International Atomic Energy Agency No. 65, 1966, pages 39–45.

Beeson, K.C. and G. Matrone. "The Soil Factor in Nutrition." Marcel Dekker, Inc., New York, 1976, 152 pages.

Bell, L.C. and G.P. Gillman. "Surface Charge Characteristics and Soil Solution Composition of Highly Weathered Soils." *In* "Workshop on the Mineral Nutrition of Legumes on Tropical and Subtropical Soils." Brisbane, Australia, Jan. 16–21, 1978, pages 37–57.

Corey, R.B. and E.E. Schulte. "Factors Affecting the Availability of Nutrients to Plants." *In* Leo M. Walsh and James D. Beaton, (eds.). "Soil Testing and Plant Analysis." Soil Science Society of America, 1973, pages 23–33.

Donahue, R.L. "Soils of Equatorial Africa and Their Relevance to Rational Agricultural Development." Institute of International Agriculture, Michigan State University, Research Report No. 7, 1970, 52 pages.

Donahue, R.L., Raymond W. Miller, and John C. Shickluna. "Soils: An Introduction to Soils and Plant Growth." Prentice-Hall, 4th Edition, 1983, page 86–112.

Dudal, R. "Inventory of the Major Soils of the World With Special Reference to Mineral Stress Hazards." *In* "Plant Adaptation to Mineral Stress in Problem Soils." Special Publication, Cornell University, Ithaca, New York, 1977, pages 3–13.

Ferris, A.P. and W.B. Jepson. "The Exchange Properties of Kaolinite and the Preparation of Homoionic Clays." Journal of Colloidal and Interface Science, Vol. 51, 1975, pages 245–259.

Follett, R.H., Larry S. Murphy, and R.L. Donahue. "Fertilizers and Soil Amendments." Prentice-Hall, 1981, pages 1–4.

Isbell, R.F. "Characteristics of Tropical and Subtropical Soils." *In* "Workshop on the Mineral Nutrition of Legumes on Tropical and Subtropical Soils." Brisbane, Australia, Jan. 16–21, 1978, pages 1–19.

Marbut, C.F. "Atlas of American Agriculture, Part III, Soils of the United States." United States Department of Agriculture, 1935, 98 pages.

Mattson, S. "The Laws of Soil Colloidal Behavior. IV. Amphoteric Behavior." Soil Science, Vol. 32, 1931, pages 343–365.

McCall, Wade W. "The pH Preference of Plants." University of Hawaii, Honolulu, General Home-Garden Series No. 18, 1978, 2 pages.

McCall, Wade W. "The Salt Tolerance of Plants." General Home-Garden Series No. 21. University of Hawaii, Honolulu, 1976, 2 pages.

Melsted, S.W. and T.R. Peck. "The Principles of Soil Testing." *In* "Soil Testing and Plant Analysis," Leo M. Walsh and James D. Beaton, (eds.). Soil Science Society of America, 1973, pages 13–33.

Ponnamperuma, F.N. "Screening Rice for Tolerance to Mineral

Stresses." IRRI Research Paper Series No. 6, March, 1977, International Rice Research Institute, Manila, Philippines.

Smith, B.H. and W.W. Emerson. "Exchangeable Aluminum in Kaolinite." Australian Journal of Soil Research, Vol. 14, 1976, pages 45–53.

Uehara, G. "Mineralogy of the Predominant Soils in Tropical and Subtropical Regions." *In* "Workshop on the Mineral Nutrition of Legumes on Tropical and Subtropical Soils." Brisbane, Australia, Jan. 16–21, 1978, pages 21–36.

Voss, Regis D. "What Constitutes An Effective Liming Material." Paper presented at the National Conference on Agricultural Limestone, Nashville, Tennessee, Oct. 16–18, 1980.

Yadav, J.S.P. "Saline, Alkaline and Acid Soils in India and their Management." Fertiliser News. Vol. 15, No. 9, Fertiliser Association of India, New Delhi, 1976, pages 15–23.

ADDITIONAL REFERENCES

Ahn, P.M. "West African Soils." Oxford University Press, London, England, 1970, 332 pages.

Arakeri, H.R., G.V. Chalam, P. Satyanarayana and R.L. Donahue. "Soil Management in India." Asia Publishing House, London, England, 2nd Edition, 1962.

Bhumbla, D.R. and R. Chhabra. "Chemistry of Sodic Soils." Review of Soil Research in India. Proc. 12th ICSS., New Delhi, India. 1982.

Bornemisza, E. and A. Alvarado, (eds.). "Soil Management in Tropical America." Soil Science Dept., North Carolina State Univ., Raleigh, North Carolina, 1975, 565 pages.

Dass, S.C. and R.K. Chatterjee. "Chemical Composition of Soils in India." Review of Soil Research in India. Proc. 12th ICSS., New Delhi, India, 1982, pages 83–109.

DeDatta, S.K. "Principles and Practices of Rice Production." John Wiley & Sons, New York, 1981, 618 pages.

Pooniyan, S.R. and Raj Pal. "Cation Exchange in Soils." Review of Soil Research in India. Proc. 12th ICSS., New Delhi, India, 1982, pages 101–122.

Tamhane, R.V., D.P. Motiramani, Y.P. Bali, and R.L. Donahue. "Soils: Their Chemistry and Fertility in Tropical Asia." Prentice-Hall of India Private Limited, New Delhi, India, 2nd Edition, 1966, 475 pages.

Wynne, D.W. and M.D. Thorne. "Soil, Water, and Crop Production." Avi Publishing Co., Westport, Conn., 1979, 353 pages.

CHAPTER 6

Tillage

6: 1 INTRODUCTION

Soil is the medium in which crops are grown. To ensure proper growth of plants, soil has to be maintained in proper physical, chemical and biological condition. Tilling of soil has been considered as one of the numerous soil management practices which are adopted for ensuring proper soil health. Tillage means manipulating or stirring of soil. The word is derived from the Anglo-Saxon words *tilian* and *teolian*, meaning to plow and prepare soil for seed, to sow, to cultivate and to raise crops. The objective is to obtain proper tilth. Tilth is the physical condition of the soil resulting from tillage. Soil is in good tilth when it is mellow, friable and adequately aerated. Soils with such good tilth are supposed to permit rapid infiltration of rain water without being too open to lose excessive water by evaporation and to offer very little resistance to root penetration.

Tillage is an oldest art associated with the development of agriculture. Despite considerable improvement in various aspects of art and science of raising crops, tillage has continued to be the most difficult and labor consuming item of work although the new minimum or no tillage concept is becoming a practical proposition in some parts of the world.

6: 1.1 Tillage Objectives

Tillage is one of the most expensive of the operations in raising crops. The purposes of tillage should, therefore, be studied to try to reduce this cost. The world over, there are eight reasons for tillage for upland crops (Donahue, Follett, Tulloch, 1983).

1) To prepare a mellow but firm seedbed that permits the incorporation of organic matter, lime, and fertilizers and a uniform planting depth for uniform seedling emergence.

2) To control weeds that rob crop plants of water, nutrients, and sunlight.

3) To improve the physical condition of the soil, to increase aeration and to warm up soil.

4) To conserve moisture by breaking the surface crust and thereby increase infiltration of rainwater and irrigation water.

5) To remove stubbles of previous crops with a view to preparing land for the next crop.

6) To cover crop residues so that seeding and cultivating equipment can operate more efficiently.

7) To control certain insects and diseases by plowing under of certain crop residues.

8) To control wind erosion by establishing cloddy ridges at right angles to erosive winds.

Tillage can, however, be a hazard to soil productivity, as explained here:

1) In preparing a mellow but firm weed-free seedbed, there is a danger that natural and desirable peds will be fractured, lose their water-stability, and develop into hard clods. This usually results from excessive tillage on fine-textured soils when they are tilled too wet. Furthermore, herbicides are becoming increasingly available around the world to control weeds.

2) Proper tillage at the right soil moisture content does immediately increase aeration and water infiltration. However, most long-term studies indicate that growing crops with extensive root systems (forage crops for instance) results in the best soil physical condition.

3) Although tilling does break the surface crust and increases infiltration, over the years there are fewer crusts and greater water infiltration when some crops with good root system are grown with *no tillage.*

4) Covering crop residues does help to bury crop residues so that they will not interfere with subsequent seeding and tillage. However, equipment is now made to permit satisfactory seeding *through* surface crop residues.

5) Hard pans are man-made compacted layers at plow depth that restrict water movement and root development. They develop when the soil is plowed too wet, with heavy machinery, and at the same depth each year.

6: 2 TRADITIONAL TILLAGE

Man took the first step towards civilization, when he learned and practiced the art of raising plants of his choice in place of the natural vegetation. The initial stage was the removal of the natural vegetation using available hand tools and implements. In spite of considerable developments that have taken place during the last two centuries with regard to design of tools and implements, control of unwanted vegetation has remained one of the main objectives of tillage. It is only in recent years that potent chemicals are being utilized to achieve this objective in some parts of the world. Tillage operations have been carried out in a routine that has been established as a result of experience through ages. The routine has included primary tillage like plowing, secondary tillage like clod crushing, leveling, harrowing, smoothening etc., and inter-tillage or after tillage operations in the standing crops.

Plowing is the basic tillage operation. Its essential purpose has been considered to be to loosen, turn and mix the soil so that any vegetation or manure on the surface is buried. A layer of soil from below is also brought to the surface and exposed to the action of weathering agents and other implements.

A wooden plow is one implement that is available with almost every farmer in India and plowing operation consumes as much as 70-75 percent of the total energy expended in carrying out field operations. Attempts made so far to either improve it or replace it with an iron plow has not yielded desired results. Only about 10 percent of the plows in the country are of iron type although it is shown that an iron plow is more efficient in many respects than the wooden plow. To get the same soil condition that is obtained with a single pass with an iron plow, the wooden plow has to be worked at least four times.

The results obtained so far indicate that plowing helps in the reduction of weed population, and in improving aeration and water absorption capacity. Plowing has proved more beneficial in humid areas where soils are fine-textured and are prone to crusting and packing.

A blade harrow is used as the primary tillage implement in place of the plow in some areas especially where the soils are deep Vertisols. It breaks clods and smoothens land when worked after plowing. It is an effective implement for destroying weeds and in creating mulch. Shovel tooth cultivators of various kinds are available for use under special circumstances, with different attachments like sweeps, furrowers, etc. The disc harrow is another implement that is proving useful and popular in some parts of India. It is used instead of the plow for preparing land quickly.

Various kinds of clod crushers are used to break clods. While in some situations simple wooden planks are sufficient to break clods, heavy spiked implements are necessary to deal with large and hard clods raised because of plowing when soil moisture condition is much below the optimum level.

Leveling and smoothening operations are carried out with various kinds of gadgets to ensure uniform spread of rain water. Under some situations compacting of soil becomes necessary to get better germination of seeds. It is possible to achieve this objective with the use of simple planks, blade harrow or various kinds of rollers.

In the traditional system, cultivation continues even after sowing until it is almost impossible to do anything because of the spread of the crop. Thereafter cultivation is carried out between rows of crops. This operation is done by means of either hand tools of various kinds or hoes or cultivators worked with bullocks or machines.

The main source of power used for farming in India is animal (Arakeri et al., 1959). In recent years mechanical power is being increasingly employed in some parts. Power availability is about 0.4 horse power per hectare as against 0.8 considered optimum the world over. In some parts of the world especially in some African countries human beings are the main source of power.

6:3 TILLAGE AND PLANT GROWTH (Donahue, Follett, and Tulloch, 1983)

There are five interrelated soil physical conditions important to plant growth that are influenced by tillage. These are soil temperature, soil moisture, bulk density, granulation, and porosity.

Soil temperature when cool is increased by tillage primarily by increasing the evaporation of soil water. Tillage can also help to bury crop residues and thus increase soil temperature by absorption of more heat from the sun. Each species of plant has an optimum soil temperature at which it germinates. For example, planted beans will emerge in 16 days at 15°C but in six days at 30°C. Corn (maize) emerges in 12 days at 15°C but in four days at 30°C.

Soil moisture and tillage are related in two important ways. Tillage at appropriate time helps the soil to dry out on the surface and planting can be done earlier; and it also increases the amount of infiltration and water storage. Contrastingly, excessive tillage can cause the surface of the soil to become too dry to germinate seeds.

Bulk density refers to the weight of a given volume of soil, usually in grams per cubic centimeter. Bulk densities of about 1.1 contain sufficient pore volume to supply adequate oxygen and water to plant roots. Bulk densities above 1.5 usually have too little total pore volume capacity for air and water. Tillage immediately decreases bulk density by increasing pore volume, however, after a few rains the bulk density may rise again.

Granulation is a general term used to characterize soil structure. The soil structural units are groups of soil particles held together by humus, iron, or gypsum. Natural structural units are called *peds* and anthropogenic structural units are *clods*. Peds are usually more water-stable than clods and can withstand heavy rains without disintegration (slaking). Minimum tillage preserves many peds, but excessive tillage turns peds into clods. Organic mulches, animal manures, and sewage sludges increase ped formation. Peds make a better seedbed than clods because peds more uniformly surround each seed and crop root to supply more adequate water, air, and nutrients.

Porosity is a term closely related to granulation and bulk density. Porosity means pores or openings between individual particles of sand, silt, clay, and organic matter (humus) as well as opening inside of and among peds and clods. Large pores permit rainwater and irrigation water to move into the soil, and if there is enough water, some of it percolates to replenish water tables. Medium-size pores hold water against the pull of gravity and is available for absorption by the plant roots for growth and reproduction. The smallest pores hold water so tightly that it is not available to plant roots. Too little porosity and a soil is said to be compacted.

6: 4 SOIL COMPACTION

Soil compaction refers to the fact that soil consists, on a volume basis, of too little pore space and too much solid matter such as sand, silt and clay. A soil in extremely good physical condition for plant growth may have a bulk density of 1.1. This density may increase by 50 percent to 1.5 if the soil is plowed too much and especially when plowed too wet.

Compacted soils may also occur in nature as claypan horizons, siltpan horizons, or indurated horizons cemented by iron, aluminum, silica, calcium carbonate, calcium sulfate (gypsum) or humus. However, most compacted soils are anthropogenic (man-induced). Fine-textured soils are often compacted when tilled too wet or by wheels when driven over with heavy loads. Two terms are used for anthropogenic compacted layers: *Induced pans,* which are formed at plow depth, 15 to 20 cm below the surface by tillage or heavy wheel traffic and *induced crusts* which are compacted soil at the soil surface about 1 cm thick caused by raindrop splash.

All tillage eventually results in soil compaction. It is true that tillage immediately increases soil aeration; long term results, however, show that after a lapse of some time they lose porosity and productivity.

For example, in a deep, mellow, well-aerated soil, cotton roots can grow nearly two meters deep and spread one meter laterally. In contrast, on a well-tilled soil in Alabama, cotton roots were restricted to a depth of 20 cm and a lateral spread of 33 cm. The root restriction was caused by a tillage pan at 20 cm and tractor wheel compaction between the rows. Furthermore, a soil in California was so compacted by tractor tires that water infiltration was only 1 cm/hour as compared with 4 cm/hour where the tractor did not run (Donahue, Follett, Tulloch, 1983).

Soil compaction problem (surface crusts and tillage pans) can be overcome by one or more changes in cultural practices, as follows:

- o Rotate intensively cultivated crops with soil building crops having profuse root system like forage crops wherever possible.
- o Practice minimum tillage.
- o Reduce the number of times any tractor, implement, or wheeled

vehicle passes over the field. This includes motorcycles and recreation vehicles.
- o Increase the amount of organic residues added to the soil and leave it *on the surface*.
- o Use a chisel instead of a turning plow. Use the chisel when the soil is *dry* to shatter induced pans and crusts.
- o Vary the depth of tillage from year to year.
- o Never use a field as an access road or as a footpath or cattle trail.

6: 5 TILLAGE CONFIGURATIONS

Tillage cannot be separated from the various practices of laying out land for soil and water conservation and also for planting. At the close of preparatory tillage operations, the land can either be left flat until it is sown or laid into ridges and furrows, flat beds, tie-ridges or raised beds. Plowing leaves the land clody if soil moisture content at the time of plowing is much less than optimum. If plowing is carried out at optimum condition it is likely that the land surface will be just wavy with small ridges and furrows. Both these conditions are favorable for increased penetration of rain water.

As a result of further working of soil with clod crushers, levelers and harrows the land is likely to be left in flat condition. With the receipt of rain, when the land surface is flat and without any plant residue on it, the soil is likely to crust soon and obstruct infiltration of water leading to increased runoff and soil erosion. To get over these problems land can be laid eventually into some sort of configuration that will aid in soil and water conservation.

Laying the land into ridges and furrows, preferably across the slope along the contour, with suitable implements will help in increasing infiltration in initial stages. Once the soil is saturated, water runoff and soil erosion may take place as usual. To improve the situation further, with regard to holding of water uniformly all over the field, checks are provided in each furrow at fixed interval. The system is known as the tie-ridge method.

Scooping, with implements specially designed for the purpose, is suggested with a view to creating pockets or depressions all over the field to hold water. The entire field can also be laid into beds by a running ridger or a bund former criss-cross at a regular interval.

All these methods help in increasing infiltration of water and reduce soil erosion up to a certain limit, beyond which the results have been observed to be the same as if not worst than what is obtained without any configuration. There are other disadvantages too like uneven wetting which hinders other cultural operations at later stages. It is for these reasons that none of the configurations have become popular with farmers so far.

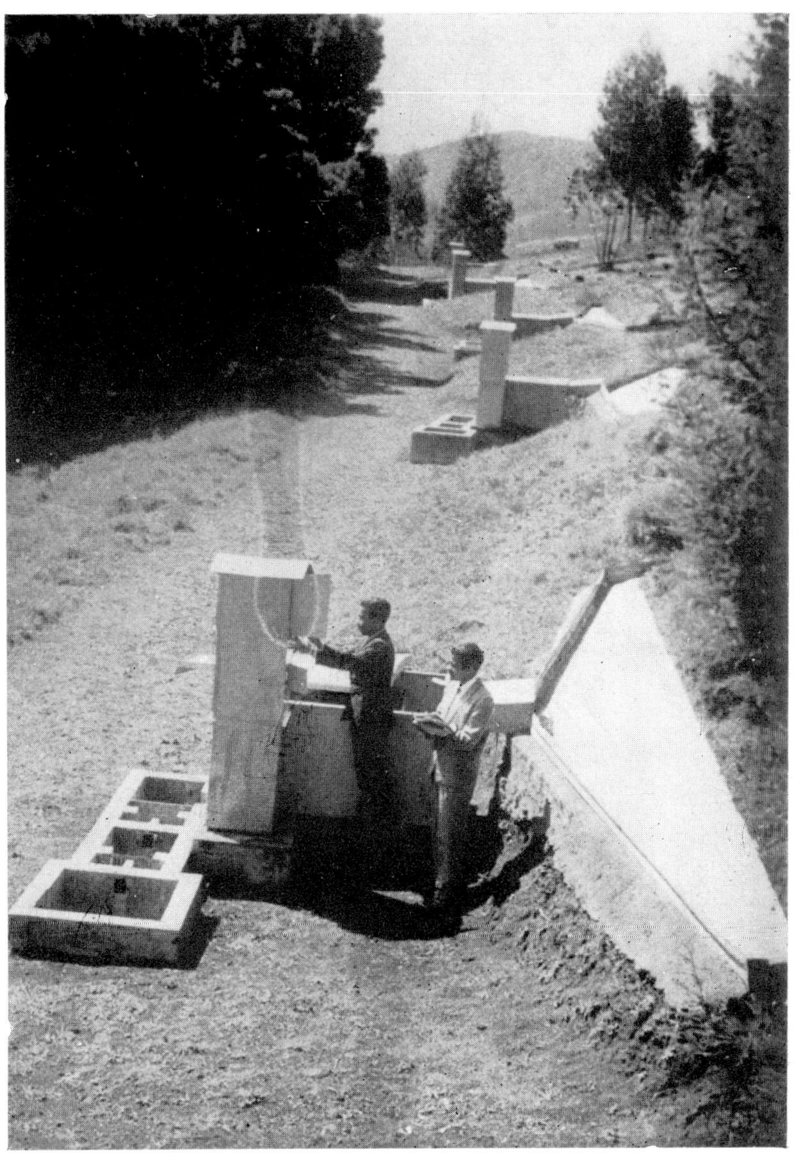

Plate 15. Set up for measurement of runoff and soil loss from experimental plots at the Soil Conservation Research Centre, Ootacamund, India. (*Courtesy:* ICAR, New Delhi, India.)

Plate 16. An irrigation channel well lined to prevent loss in transit. (*Courtesy:* ICAR, New Delhi, India.)

Plate 17. Uniform water spread is possible when land is laid out and leveled properly. (*Courtesy:* ICAR, New Delhi, India.)

Plate 18. Water management is easy when land is methodically laid out and fitted with necessary structures. (*Courtesy:* ICAR, New Delhi, India.)

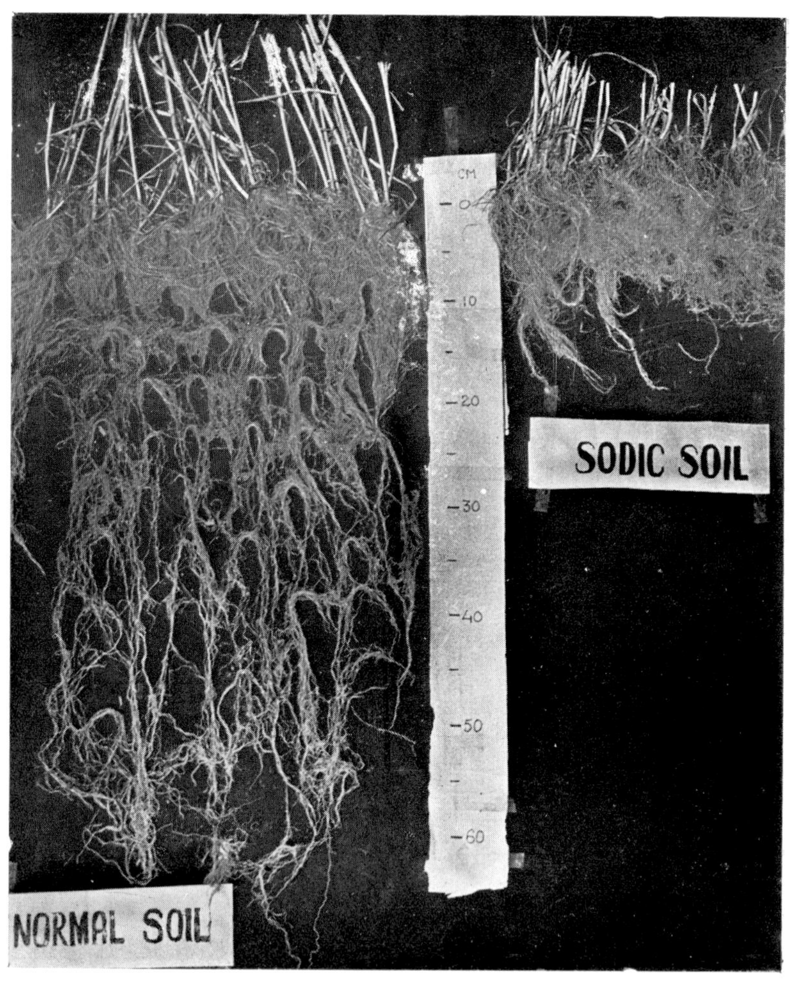

Plate 19. Root development of wheat crop in a normal and sodic soil. (*Courtesy:* Central Soil Salinity Research Institute, Karnal, India.)

Recently research in Hyderabad, Andhra Pradesh, India on medium-deep Vertisols resulted in higher yields and greater market value for maize (corn) and pigeonpea when planted on beds 150 cm wide as compared with planting on 75 cm beds or flat-planting. The increase in Rupee value of maize plus pigeonpea on 150 cm beds was 14 percent greater than on flat planting and 25 percent greater than on 75 cm beds. (Table 6.1 and Fig .6.1) (ICRISAT, 1976-1977).

Table 6.1. Effect of land management on runoff, erosion, and yield on medium deep Vertisols at ICRISAT Center, 1976-1977

Land treatment	Runoff	Erosion	Yields		Values*
			Maize	Pigeonpea	
	(mm)	(kg/ha)	(kg/ha)	(kg/ha)	(Rs/ha)
Flat planting	14	10	2700	530	3780
Narrow ridges (75 cm)	19	20	2470	480	3445
Broad ridges (150 cm)	17	20	3030	620	4310

*Total value of maize and pigeonpea.

6: 6 ALTERNATIVES TO CLEAN TILLAGE

Throughout the history of agriculture, tillage has been taken for granted. It has been accepted that some tillage operations are necessary to grow crops. The development of tillage equipment has been done more as an engineering feat rather than from crop needs. Traditional tillage practices have been assumed to be satisfactory and machines designed to do them better. It is only in the middle of 1940s that the wisdom of plowing the land and clean tillage was questioned. Clean tillage means plowing and cultivating to kill weeds and bury all crop residues. Such tillage is very expensive, causes soil compaction, induced pans, induced crusts, and results in erosion. By 1960 chemical seed bed preparation and no tillage technique was proposed but the difficulty of placing the seed in a trashy field was posed. To overcome this difficulty new types of seeding implements have been developed and put to use.

Alternatives to clean tillage have already become popular in many countries on upland crops as well as on rice in recent years. 'No Till' protagonists have projected that this technique would be put to practice on a wide scale in the world before the close of the century.

Alternatives to clean tillage on upland crops are as follows (Donahue, Follett, Tulloch, 1983):

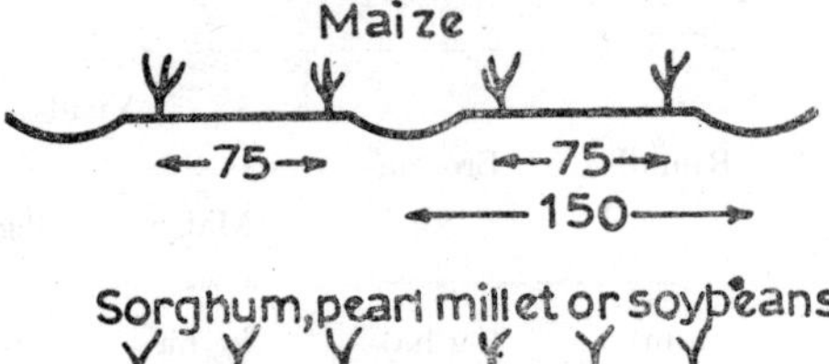

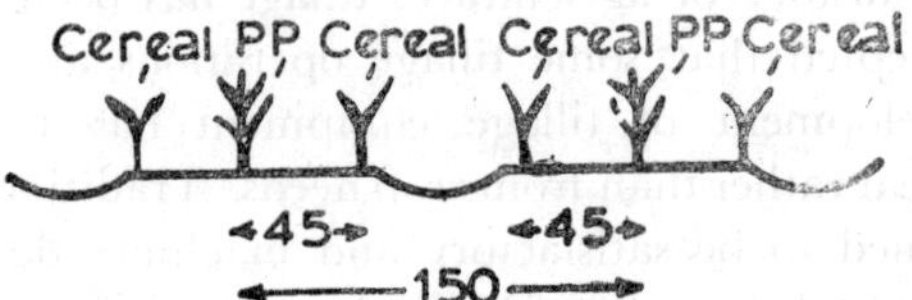

Fig. 6.1. Cropping patterns and row spacings on 75- and 150-cm beds

No-tillage (zero tillage)

Till-planting (strip tillage). A wide sweep and trash bars clear a strip over the previous crop row and a narrow planter shoe opens a narrow strip into which seeds are planted. There is no previous tillage and no tillage between rows.

Sweep tillage. A wide sweep moves through the soil such as after a small grain crop has been harvested, killing all weeds, mellowing the soil, and leaving all plant residues on the surface. The sweep may move through the soil several times to control weeds until the next grain crop is planted. There is no additional tillage.

Chisel tillage. A narrow chisel 5 to 10 cm wide is run through the soil at a depth of 15 to 30 cm leaving all plant residues on the surface. The chisel shatters tillage pans and surface crusts. Planting is done *through* the residues with special planters.

Plow-plant. After the soil is plowed, a special planter is used and in one pass over the field the seed is planted. There is no secondary tillage after plowing.

Herbicides-crop residues. Sometimes suitable herbicides can be used economically to control weeds. When herbicides are used in combination with plant residues left on the surface, soil productivity can be maintained with minimum or no tillage.

Approaches to the problems of tillage in countries like India are showing trends of new directions. Minimum or no tillage technique would probably be most welcome in these countries where power availability for farming is far below the optimum considered necessary for efficient production and where sowing and planting operations are delayed or carried out in a hurried manner on poor seed beds. The technology, if perfected and offered to farmers having no animal or machine power at their command, may prove very advantageous.

Studies carried out so far in India and other tropical countries during the last decade have indicated that minimum tillage may prove to be a dependable and attractive alternative to conventional tillage (Khan, Roy and Chatterjee, 1981; Sandhu, and Brar, 1979, Singh, Bhan and Singh, 1971; Gautaman and Sankaran 1976; De Datta, Botton and Lin, 1979).

6: 7 TILLAGE FOR RICE

Contrary to popular opinion, not all world rice is grown by wet land system. In India dry and semidry systems are also adopted on a large scale. Rice is generally grown either as a wetland or an upland crop, in deepwater, under rainfed conditions, or is direct-seeded and irrigated. Tillage for rice varies with the system of production used.

Tillage for rice grown under the following systems will be discussed separately: flooded, dry system, semidry system, deepwater, and alternatives to clean tillage (De Datta, 1981 and Arakeri, Cholam, Satyanarayana and Donahue, 1959).

6: 7.1 Flooded Paddy Tillage

When rice is grown under the wetland system a bund (levee) of soil is constructed around leveled fields. The height of the bund is normally about 25 cm. The area inside the bund varies with the slope of the land. On level land, several hectares may be enclosed by one bund. On steep land, however, bunds enclose only a fraction of a hectare to permit the field within the bund to be leveled. On sloping lands, bunds can be constructed along the contour to minimize leveling. The requirement for a level paddy field is to permit a uniform level of water to be maintained, usually at a depth of 5 to 10 cm.

When the season is declared satisfactory for starting tillage within paddy fields and irrigation water is available, a few centimeters of water is let into the field to soften the soil. After a few days, the field is plowed repeatedly and often cross-plowed to establish a soupy-mud puddle.

Puddling of soils in rice fields is done to accomplish these objectives:

1) Less power is required in tillage.

2) Ease of transplanting rice. Plants are pushed into the mud with thumb and forefinger.

3) Weed control. Buried weed seeds and plants do not sprout as readily.

4) Increase in availability of nutrients, especially phosphorus, iron, and manganese.

5) Reduced loss of water by deep percolation because of the formation of a tillage pan.

Disadvantages of puddling wetland rice soils include:

1) A high water requirement (up to 175 percent more, as compared with nonpuddling).

2) Soil structure is destroyed.

3) Root development is restricted.

4) Rotation of rice with upland crops is difficult because such crops grow best with no tillage pan and good soil structure.

5) Toxic soil accumulation of iron, hydrogen sulfide, and some toxic organic compounds especially on acid sulfate soils.

6: 7.2 Dry Systems

In some of the rice-growing areas rice soils are plowed when dry, the rice seed is sown and then the field is flooded with water. This system is also common in other parts of tropical Asia, the United States, Australia, most of Latin America and southern Europe. Weed control is attempted with chemicals or suitable intercultivating implements. The system is adopted on uplands in good rainfall areas or under irrigation.

Advantages of tillage when the soil is *moist* (but not with standing water as in puddling) include:

1) Desirable soil structure is maintained or improved.

2) Large power units can be used.

3) Crop rotations with other crops is easier.

4) Plant root development is favored.

5) Less water is used.

Disadvantages of dryland rice tillage are:

1) Higher fertilizer requirements.

2) Weed control is not as effective.
3) Higher draft requirements.

6: 7.3 Semi-Dry System

Rice is produced in medium high rainfall areas in India and in many other countries by adopting a semi-dry system. No irrigation is used. Land is tilled as soon as the first rains soften the soil. Often weeds are allowed to sprout and are killed by a second tillage. Rice seed is then drill sown or broadcast by hand. Weeds are always difficult to control. Intercultivation is possible in a drill sown crop with suitable implements. In broadcast sown crops hand weeding is attempted. When sufficient water accumulates in the field and when rice seedlings are 20 to 25 cm in height, soil is stirred with implements to create a semi puddled condition. Thus the crop is grown partly under dry system and partly under wet system in mid lying or low lying fields. Yields are low.

6: 7.4 Deepwater Rice Tillage

Along rivers during the dry season, land is prepared for deepwater rice varieties by tillage similar to that for upland rice. Seed is sown on dry soil. During the rainy period the rice elongates as the river rises and floods.

Many other tillage variations exist throughout the world, including minimum tillage systems.

6: 7.5 Alternatives to Clean Tillage for Rice (De Datta, 1981)

Rice is grown in tropical and subtropical regions where heavy, beating rains cause severe raindrop splash erosion. Furthermore, soil manipulation for rice is time-consuming and costly. In addition, if two or three rice crops are grown on the same field in a 12-month period, the time taken between crops for soil preparation must be shortened.

Dalapon was used in the 1950's in many rice-growing areas to control weeds and thus to reduce the need for some of the time-consuming tillage used to control weeds. Dalapon was replaced by Paraquat and Glyphosate in the late 1970's because they killed more kinds of weeds and left fewer toxic residues.

Minimum tillage for rice includes the use of Paraquat or Glyphosate as a nonresidual, broad-spectrum, preplant herbicide on soil to control volunteer rice and other weeds. Fields are then flooded and puddling and leveling are accomplished, followed by transplanting of rice. Substituting herbicides for tillage-to-control-weeds saves about two weeks of time and uses about 20 percent less irrigation water.

6:8 ALTERNATIVES TO CLEAN TILLAGE IN WESTERN AFRICA

Surface applied organic mulches of 4 to 6 tonnes / ha in Nigeria, western Africa, as compared with conventional tillage, increased yields of maize (corn) by 50 percent, sweet potatoes by 25 percent, cowpeas by 23 percent, soybeans by 21 percent, and pigeonpeas by 5 percent (Bornemisza and Alvarado, 1975). In these studies, besides increasing yields the organic mulch reduced soil temperatures by as much as 8°C, reduced soil water loss by evaporation, increased soil nitrate nitrogen and phosphorus availability, increased numbers of earthworms, increased rate of infiltration of rainwater, reduced erosion, and resulted in a more desirable soil tilth. The mulch was as effective in soil restoration as 10 to 15 years of bush-fallow in the traditional system of shifting cultivation.

6:9 TILLAGE IN EQUATORIAL AFRICA (Kline, Green, Donahue, and Stout, 1969)

Tillage sytems in relation to mechanization were studied and evaluated in nine countries in Equatorial Africa over an 18-month on-the-spot study by a team of two agricultural engineers, one agricultural economist, and one soil scientist-agronomist in 1966–1968. Key points pertaining to tillage systems are enumerated here:

1) In areas with wet and dry seasons as well as in areas where two or more crops are grown each year, timeliness of tillage is often the principal limiting factor in success or failure.

2) Mechanized tillage always requires larger fields and more level land areas than for animal-drawn and hand-powered tillage.

3) Mechanized tillage pays best on very fertile, level soils such as on deep Vertisols.

4) Thousands of hectares of Vertisols have lain idle in tall grasses and scattered trees until tractor mechanization became a reality. The reason is because the moisture content during which Vertisols can be tilled is very narrow; thus, demanding rapid completion of all tillage and planting operations. After a rain, proper moisture content for tillage may last for only a few days. Vertisols are very high in clay and are therefore too "boggy" when wet and too cloddy when dry within a time span of perhaps a week.

5) The size of the farm to be managed is determined largely by the area that can be kept weeded. For example, in Tanzania a farmer with only hand-powered tools can keep merely 2.5 hectares of crops weeded. With animal-powered tillage, a farmer can till about 10 hectares, and with a tractor, about 50 hectares.

6) For tillage operations, the common Equatorial African method of driving oxen (bullocks) with two men, whip, and voice control could be

improved by adopting the Indian technique of using nose ropes, lines, and one man.

7) Chemical herbicides are much too expensive for the average farmer in Equatorial Africa.

8) Animal-powered tillage is especially suited to the higher elevations where trypanosomiasis, carried by the tsetse fly, will not kill the animals.

9) Oxisols, Ultisols, and many Alfisols in Equatorial Africa are characterized by low structural stability and resultant surface crust formation, very low natural fertility, horizons compacted by crystallization of iron and aluminum, low available water-holding capacity, low organic matter, and extreme variability due to land clearing, brush burning, termite mounds, and differential erosion. Minimum tillage with organic residue mulching is a successful soil management technique (see Section 6: 8).

6: 10 SOIL CAPABILITIES FOR MECHANIZED TILLAGE (Donahue, 1970 and Obeng, 1968)

Although soils vary greatly, even within a one-hectare field, soil scientists are making soil survey maps that are valuable to every user of soil, including people who must decide what tillage system to use.

Interpretive use has been made of soil surveys in Ghana, western Africa, to delineate areas on a map suitable for tractor tillage, animal tillage, hand tillage or no tillage. The legend is in the following three categories:

A) Areas where more than 50 percent of the soils are capable of being cultivated *continuously* with any kind of power, hand, animal or tractor.

B) Areas where more than 50 percent of the soils are capable of being cultivated *intermittently* by hand-power or animal-power, in a system of shifting cultivation.

C) Areas where more than 50 percent of the soils are *not capable of being cultivated* except in small isolated patches because the soil is either too shallow, stony, gravelly, slowly permeable, or is subject to crystallization of plinthite into iron and/or aluminum pans (laterite) (Fig. 6.2).

Legend of Fig. 6.2

A. Land where more than 50 percent of the soils are capable of being cultivated continuously with tractors, bullocks, or by hand with little or no soil deterioration hazard. Restrictive layer of laterite or ironpan, bedrock, stony or gravelly layer, or slowly permeable soil material may lie below 24 inches. Includes U.S. Soil Conservation Service Land Capability Classes I to IV (20 percent of Ghana).

B. Land where more than 50 percent of the soils are capable of being cultivated intermittently by bullocks or by hand with a system of bush fallow. *Not capable of being farmed by tractors because of soil hazards.* Restrictive layer of laterite or ironpan, bedrock, stony or gravelly layer, or slowly permeable soil material may lie between 12 and 24 inches. Includes U.S. Soil Conservation Service Land Capability Classes V and VI (33 percent of Ghana).

C. Land where more than 50 percent of the soils are *not* capable of being cultivated except in isolated patches because the soil is *too shallow* (less

Fig. 6.2. Soil capability for mechanized cultivation in Ghana (Henry B. Obeng, 1968).

than 12 inches) to laterite or ironpan, bedrock, stony or gravelly layer or slowly permeable soil material; or *too steep* or rolling in topography. Includes U.S. Soil Conservation Service Land Capability Classes VII and VIII (47 percent of Ghana).

Note: As reported in: R.L. Donahue, 1970.

6: 11 BURNING TO INCREASE TILTH OF VERTISOLS (Donahue, 1972)

In central eastern Africa, Vertisols occupy 44.7 million hectares of fairly level, productive, black clay soils. Hand-powered and animal-powered tillage are the dominant systems because very few tractors exist. With such primitive power sources, killing weeds and preparing proper tilth for a seedbed is next to impossible. Therefore, farmers have resorted to burning the soil to achieve what tillage cannot do.

Traditional agriculture on Vertisols in Ethiopia consists of cropping them until yields decline because of weeds, insects, diseases, and/or poor tilth. Fields are then abandoned for five to fifteen years during which time wild grasses, weeds, and a few woody plants occupy the soils. Then the fields are plowed with a local, narrow-shovel plow. The sod pieces are picked up by hand and placed in piles perhaps a meter in diameter and 25 to 50 cm high in the middle. The sod pieces are allowed to dry for a few weeks, after which dry cattle manure is put in a depression in the middle of each pile. The cattle manure is lighted and the sod pieces are moved into the hottest part of the fire as burning continues.

After the fires have cooled, the residues are spread over the field. These residues are free of weed seeds, in good tilth, and have 122 percent more available phosphorus than the unburned soil. Furthermore, the black clay soil has turned reddish brown and has the apparent texture of a loamy sand. Burning changes the clay particles into fine water-stable aggregates the size of sand grains.

After burning, weeds are more easily controlled and desirable tilth for a satisfactory seedbed is more readily achieved. The soil is cropped for three to five years until yields decline, then the cycle is repeated.

6: 12 SUMMARY

Tillage has traditionally been used to prepare a mellow, weed-free seedbed, incorporate lime and fertilizer, and to control certain insects and diseases. Excessive tillage, however, destroys water-stable peds, decreases humus by increasing microbial decomposition, and causes compacted soil layers such as tillage pans and surface crusts. The logical conclusion is that tillage should be reduced to a minimum and the application of manures, sewage sludges, and plant residues should be increased to the maximum. Successful minimum tillage systems have been developed for most upland crops as well as for rice. Herbicides have replaced some tillage and thus can be credited with preventing physical soil deterioration.

CITED REFERENCES

Arakeri, H.R., G.V. Cholam, P. Satyanarayana and R.L. Donahue. "Soil Management in India." Asia Publishing House, London. 1st Edition, 1959, pages 279–283.

Bornemisza, E. and A. Alvarado. "Soil Management in Tropical America." Soil Science Dept., North Carolina State University, Raleigh, North Carolina, 1975.

De Datta, S.K., F.R. Bolton and W.L. Lin. "Prospects for Using Minimum Tillage in Tropical Low Land Rice." Weed Research. Vol. 19, 1979, pages 9–15.

De Datta, S.K. "Principles and Practices of Rice Production." John Wiley & Sons, New York, 1981, pages 259–296.

Donahue, R.L. "Ethiopia: Taxonomy, Cartography, and Ecology of Soils." African Studies Center in cooperation with the Inst. of International Agriculture, Michigan State University, East Lansing, Michigan, 1972.

Donahue, R.L. "Soils of Equatorial Africa and Their Relevance to Rational Agricultural Development." Institute of International Agriculture, Michigan State University, East Lansing, Michigan, 1970.

Donahue, R.L., R.H. Follett and R.W. Tulloch. "Our Soils and Their Management." 5th Edition, 1983. Interstate Printers and Publishers, Danville, Illinois.

Gautaman, K.C. and S. Sankaran. "Effect of Minimum Tillage in Deccan Hybrid Maize." Madras Agri. Jour., Vol. 63, 1976, pages 445–448.

International Crops Research Institute for the Semiarid Tropics. "ICRISAT Annual Report, 1976–1977." Hyderabad, Andhra Pradesh, India.

Khan, S.A., A.S. Roy and B.N. Chatterjee. "Note on Growing Winter Maize Under Minimum Tillage After Transplanted Rice." Ind. Jour. Agri. Sci., Vol. 51, 1981, pages 54–55.

Kline, C.K., D.A.G. Green, R.L. Donahue and B.A. Stout. "Agricultural Mechanization in Equatorial Africa." Research Report No. 6, Inst. of International Agriculture, Michigan State Univ., East Lansing, Mich., 1969.

National Commission on Agriculture, 1976. Part V, Resource Development, New Delhi, India.

Obeng, Henry B. "Land Capability Classification of the Soils of Ghana Under Practices of Mechanised and Hand Cultivation for Crop and Livestock Production." Transactions of the 9th Intern. Congress of Soil Science, Adelaide, Australia, 1968, pages 215–223.

Sandhu, H.S. and S.S. Brar. "Maize-wheat Cropping in Light, Medium Soils Possible with Minimum Tillage." Progressive Farming. Punjab Agricultural University, 1979, pages 35–36.

Singh A., V.M. Bhan and K.N. Singh. "Possibilities of Minimum Tillage Practices in Maize-Wheat Rotation." Ind. Jour. Agri. Sci., Vol. 41, 1971, pages 539–545.

ADDITIONAL REFERENCES

Aiyer, A.K. Yegna Narayan "Principles of Crop Husbandry in India." Bangalore Printing and Publishing Co., Ltd., Bangalore City, Mysore State, India, 1957.

Arakeri, H.R., G.V. Chalam, P. Satyanarayana, and R.L. Donahue. "Soil Management in India." Asia Publishing House, London, 2nd Edition, 1962.

Donahue, L. Roy and James E. Christiansen, "Exploring Agriculture: An Introduction to Food and Agriculture." 6th Edition, 1984. Prentice-Hall, Inc., Englewood Cliffs, New Jersey.

Follett, R.H., Larry S. Murphy, and R.L. Donahue. "Fertilizers and Soil Amendments." Prentice-Hall, Inc., 1981.

Green, David A.G. "Agricultural Mechanization in Ethiopia: An Economic Analysis of Four Case Studies." Research Report No. 10, Inst. of International Agriculture, Michigan State University, East Lansing, Michigan, 1971.

Imperial Chemical Industries. Plant Protection Division. "Outlook on Agriculture". Vol. 8, Special Number 1975, England.

Moormann, Frans R. and Nico van Breemen. "Rice: Soil, Water, Land." International Rice Research Institute, Los Baños, Philippines, 1978.

Khan, A.R. "The Art and Science of Tillage." Published by author 1974, India.

National Academy of Sciences. "Soils of the Humid Tropics." Washington D.C., 1972.

Roy, B., D.L. Jindal and K.L. Vyas, "No-Tillage Wheat Production in Punjab". Ind. Jour. Weed Sci., Vol. 13, 1981, pages 161–171.

Shanmugham, C.R. "Farm Machinery and Energy Research in India." Central Institute of Agricultural Engineering, Bhopal, India.

Thorne, D. Wynne and Marlowe D. Thorne. "Soil, Water and Crop Production." Avi Pub. Co., Inc. Westport, Conn., 1979.

Troeh, Frederick R., J. Arthur Hobbs, and R.L. Donahue. "Soil and Water Conservation for Productivity and Environmental Protection." Prentice-Hall, Inc., Englewood Cliffs, New Jersey, 1980, pages 274–319.

United States Department of Agriculture. "Gardening for Food and Fun." The Yearbook of Agriculture, 1977, Washington, D.C.

United States Department of Agriculture. "Soil: The Yearbook of Agriculture", 1957, Washington D.C.

CHAPTER 7

Fertilizers and Organic Amendments

7:1 INTRODUCTION

Fertilizers and soil amendments are used in every country of the world to increase production. Of special concern is food production. Most countries want either to be self-sufficient in food production or to have an industrial base that permits them to buy adequate food.

The world-wide race between food and fecundity is never pleasant to face because it is so tenuous. Some countries are only one failed monsoon rain away from starvation. Efficient use of fertilizers and soil amendments makes it possible to produce enough food in many countries. Per hectare consumption of plant nutrients is shown in Fig. 7.1.

7:2 CHEMICAL FERTILIZERS

Justus von Liebig (1803–1873) proposed the thesis that plants can be analyzed and the nutrients so found were the ones necessary and in the right proportion to apply as a fertilizer for maximum growth. This has since been proved fallacious, because the following assumptions are false:

1) The soil is an inert body and does not supply essential plant nutrients by the mineralization of soil organic matter and the weathering of soil minerals.

2) All of the minerals in the plant ash, when applied to the soil, would be available to the next plant.

3) The presence of an element in plant ash means that that element is essential.

Even though it has been more than 100 years since Liebig proposed his theories, many people, including some otherwise well-educated scientists, continue to believe in his proposals. For example, many scientists use data on the nutrients removed by a crop with a specified yield to determine what kinds and amounts of chemical fertilizers to apply. This is a serious fallacy. The technique is wrong because:

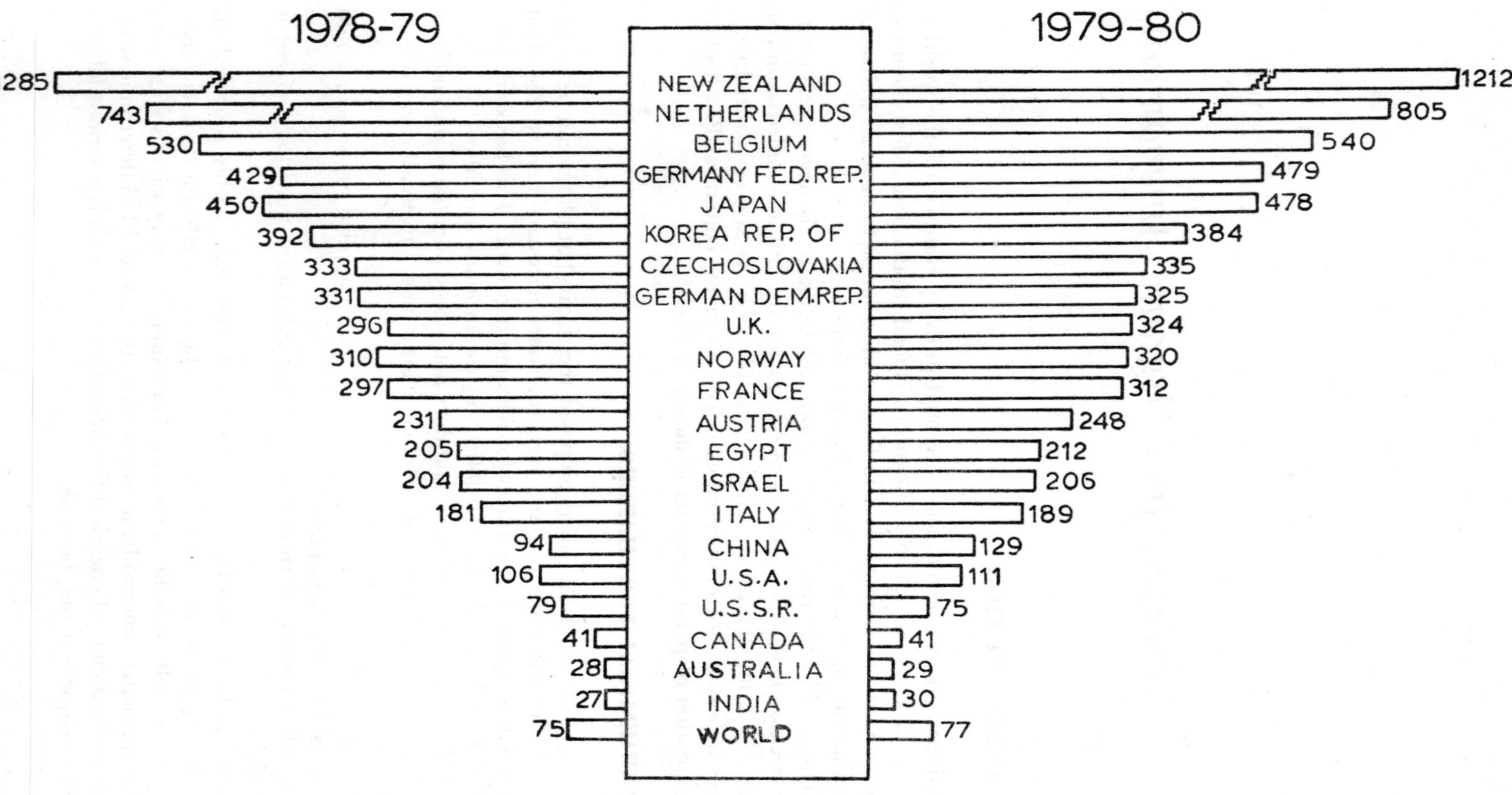

Fig. 7.1. Consumption of fertilizers in some of the countries in the world (kg per hectare of arable land).
Source: "Fertilizer Statistics", Fertilizer Assn. of India, New Delhi, 1981, page III–31.

1) In some soils there is enough of certain plant nutrients that become available each year to produce maximum crops for many years. This is true of calcium in Vertisols.

2) Luxury consumption is ignored. Some plants in some soils absorb more of some nutrients than they need simply because it is available. This is true especially of nitrates and potassium.

3) Most plants absorb nutrients which they do not need. This is true for sodium, lithium, chromium, and strontium.

4) Plant absorption is never 100 percent of any nutrient applied. The usual absorption efficiency of chemical fertilizers is:

N — 30 to 70%
P — 20 to 30%
K — 50 to 80%

5) The ratio of the essential elements in the plant are seldom the same as those in the soil solution or as those in applied fertilizer.

6) Soil colloids adsorb divalent calcium and magnesium more strongly than monovalent potassium and ammonium. For this reason both potassium and ammonium will be more readily absorbed by plants; thus, decreasing absorption of calcium and magnesium. When the plant is a forage crop, the magnesium percentage may be low, causing hypomagnesemia (grass tetany) in livestock.

7: 2.1 Determining Fertilizer Needs

Various methods have been employed to determine the deficiency of nutrient elements in the soil. One of the earlier methods was complete chemical analysis of soil. This method proved wanting as mentioned earlier. Deficiency symptoms of plants are frequently helpful in diagnosing the cause of poor growth. Simple diagnostic techniques were developed by understanding the symptoms the plants develop when grown in soils deficient in different nutrient elements. The defect in this method is that the symptoms appear only when the supply is very low and late in the season. Simple tissue tests using appropriate chemicals were also developed and employed. Tissue tests indicate a nutrient deficiency before the leaves show starvation symptoms. In both the cases it is difficult to take remedial measures in the same season. Pot experiments were conducted to know the response to different fertilizer elements at varying rates. This method also proved less than adequate for practical purposes.

Field plot research on each major crop on all major soils, varying fertilizer kinds and amounts, seems to be the ideal way to determine fertilizer needs. However, such research would be too costly. Most countries use the next best approach: Field fertilizer trials with the major soils and crops near the center of the principal producing areas, supplemented with laboratory chemical soil tests correlated with field plot results.

One more refinement is now being proposed: On a world-wide basis, select the principal soils (based on soil taxonomy and soil survey), and conduct exhaustive fertilizer field trials with the major crops (Moore, 1978).

The field trials can then be correlated with laboratory chemical tests for quickly determining fertilizer needs. India is an outstanding example of this work.

7: 2.2 Soil Testing: Indian Example

The use of fertilizers picked up momentum during the 1950s. This necessitated developing and recommending appropriate fertilizer application schedule for different crops in a rational manner. Fertilizer trials were started on farmers' fields to achieve this objective. Steps were taken simultaneously to expand soil testing facilities. By the end of 1958 only twenty laboratories were functioning in the country. At present there are several laboratories in every state. Model agronomic trials are being conducted on experimental bases to get indication of responses of different crops under varying agro-climatic conditions. The indicated levels are tested on farmers' fields. Soil test-crops response studies as well as experiments on micronutrient requirements are being carried out through a well-organized coordinated program through state and central research organizations. As a result practical recommendations are emerging continuously for use by farmers.

In one year more than a 100 percent increase in paddy yields per hectare has been reported from the Stage II villages in Raipur District, Madhya Pradesh, India, as a result of judicious and intensive use of fertilizers on the basis of field-to-field soil test information (Tamboli and Misra, 1965).* During 1964–65, three villages were selected under the Intensive Agricultural District Program (I.A.D.P.). This program envisaged testing of soils from every field in these villages, and the formulation of individual fertilizer recommendations for each field as a component of the recommended package of practices. (Before I.A.D.P. there was only one fertilizer recommendation for rice in all of the district.)

A majority of the cultivators followed these fertilizer recommendations and as a result there was nearly an eight-fold increase in the consumption of fertilizers in the villages; and the paddy (unhulled rice) yields were more than doubled. In actual figures the average fertilizer consumption for the three villages rose from 9 kg per hectare in 1963–64 to 72 kg per hectare in

*(a) Raipur district is one of the original seven in the Intensive Agricultural District Program (I.A.D.P.) started in cooperation with the Ford Foundation in early 1960.
(b) The assumed values for fertilizer were Rs. 1.45 (U.S.$ 0.30) per kg each for N and P_2O_5; and for paddy Rs. 40 (U.S.$ 8.40) per quintal.
(c) As quoted from Donahue, 1967.

1964–65; and the average paddy yield for the three villages increased from 1,674 kg per hectare in 1963–64 to 3,654 kg per hectare in 1964–65.

Thus for an increase of 63 kg per hectare in fertilizer use there was an increase of 1,880 kg per hectare of paddy—which means that when soil tests were used, every rupee invested in fertilizers (along with other improved practices) gave a return of Rs. 8.25 in terms of additional paddy yields (Table 7.1).

Table 7.1. Fertilizer consumption and paddy yields in Stage II villages under Raipur I.A.D.P. (kilograms per hectare)

Village	Average dose of N+ P_2O_5 used		Average paddy yields		Increase in yield
	1963–64 (Pre-Stage II)	1964–65 (Stage II)	1963–64 (Pre-Stage II)	1964–65 (Stage II)	percent
Khursenga	4.4+5.6	36+44	1,644	3,654	122
Pouni	6+5.5	35+43	1,918	3,837	100
Deopur	2.2+3.3	23+26	1,461	3,471	138

In other areas of the district too, it has been proved that as compared to the generalized fertilizer recommendation for the area, application of fertilizers on the basis of a soil test not only gives increased production, but also results in *more net profit to the farmer*. The results of two-plot trials on

Table 7.2. Soil tests resulted in Rs. 34 to Rs. 390 more profit per hectare for paddy compared with fertilizer applied according to the generalized district recommendation (Raipur District, M.P.)

Block	Village	Fertilizer used ($N+P_2O_5+K_2O$) kg/hectare		Yield of paddy kg/hectare		*Profit:* Soil test over generalized Rs/hectare
		Generalized	Soil Test	Generalized	Soil Test	
Dhartary	Bijnapuri	22+22+0	33+ 0+0	2,700	3,055	123
Dhamtari	Dahi	22+22+0	33+ 0+0	2,725	3,198	155
Magarlodh	Billora	22+22+0	33+33+0	1,875	3,125	390
,,	Bhaisnumdi	22+22+0	17+22+17	5,100	5,320	93
,,	Chhati	22+22+0	22+ 0+0	2,425	2,450	34
,,	Kareli	22+22+0	33+17+0	3,080	3,450	110
Mahasamand	Sorid	22+22+0	44+44+0	2,850	3,250	65
,,	,,	22+22+0	44+44+0	2,660	3,225	37

paddy conducted in the district, are given in Table 7.2. In these trials, one plot received fertilizer according to the generalized district recommendation and the other plot received fertilizers on the basis of a soil test for that plot. Such trials were conducted in many districts in the country as a part of extension programs to convince farmers as to why they should get their soil tested. Facilities for soil testing have been expanded considerably during the last 25 years in India.

Soil tests have thus helped in one or more of these three ways:

1) To reduce the total cost of fertilizers without affecting the yield; and thus to increase net profit.

2) To recommend fertilizers at the same total cost but to readjust the proportion of N, P_2O_5, and K_2O on the basis of the level of available nutrients supplied by the soil and thus to increase yields and net profit.

3) To recommend more total fertilizers which results in additional cost, but also result in much higher yields and more net profit.

7: 2.3 Nitrogen Fertilizers

World-wide, nitrogen is usually the first nutrient limiting plant production. There are at least two valid reasons for this fact: Percentage composition of all crop plants is higher in nitrogen (1–3 percent) than for any other fertilizer element and the principal storage in the soil is the small amount of organic matter present. Tropical soils are usually poor in organic matter and nitrogen content. The total nitrogen content varies from 0.01 to 1.0 percent in Indian soils (Das and Chatterjee, 1982). Most field crops with average yields will have absorbed from 100 to 200 kg/ha of nitrogen. Furthermore, upon decomposition (mineralization) the protein nitrogen changes to ammonium and then to nitrate nitrogen. In the nitrate form, unless absorbed rather quickly by plants, percolating waters will move the nitrates downward, and surplus soil water encourages gaseous loss of nitrogen by denitrification.

The principal nitrogenous fertilizer of the world is urea; this and others are detailed in Table 7.3.

Table 7.3. Sources of nitrogen fertilizer, grade, chemical and physical form (Walsh, 1973)

Fertilizer	Grade (N-P_2O_5-K_2O) (%)	Physical form
Anhydrous ammonia (NH_3)	82–0–0	High pressure liquid
Aqua ammonia (NH_3+H_2O)	20–0–0 to 24–0–0	Low pressure liquid

Low pressure N solutions ($NH_4NO_3+NH_3+H_2O$)	37–0–0 to 41–0–0	Low pressure liquid
Pressureless N solutions (NH_4NO_3+urea+H_2O)	28–0–0 to 32–0–0	Pressureless liquid
Ammonium nitrate (NH_4NO_3)	33–0–0	Dry prills
Ammonium sulfate $(NH_4)_2SO_4$	20–0–0	Dry granules
Urea ($NH_2 \cdot CO \cdot NH_2$)	45–0–0	Dry prills
Diammonium phosphate $(NH_4)_2HPO_4$	18–46–0	Dry granules
Potassium nitrate (KNO_3)	13–0–44	Dry granules
Ammonium phosphate solutions	10–34–0 11–37–0	Pressureless liquid

7: 2.4 Phosphorus Fertilizers

When phosphorus fertilizers are applied to a soil, the average amount absorbed by plants is only 20 to 30 percent of that applied. There are several reasons for this low efficiency. There is no mechanism in soils to hold phosphorus in an available form; since phosphorus is an anion and soils have very little anion exchange. However, mineralization of organic matter releases small amounts of available phosphorus.

Soils below about pH 6.5 have large amounts of soluble iron and alu-

Table 7.4. Common phosphorus (P) fertilizers (Donahue, Follet, Tulloch, 1983)

Name of fertilizer	Approximate chemical formula	Grade	
		Oxide basis (N-P_2O_5-K_2O) (%)	Elemental basis (N-P-K) (%)
Ordinary superphosphate	$Ca(H_2PO_4)_2 + CaSO_4$	0–20–0	0–8.8–0
Triple superphosphate	$Ca(H_2PO_4)_2$	0–45–0	0–20.8–0
Monoammonium phosphate	$NH_4H_2PO_4$	11–48–0	11–21.1–0
Diammonium phosphate	$(NH_4)_2HPO_4$	18–46–0	18–20.2–0
Ammonium polyphosphate:	$NH_4H_2PO_4 + (NH_4)_3HP_2O_7$		
Liquid form		10–34–0	10–15–0
Dry form		15–62–0	15–27.3–0

minum which readily combine with phosphorus to produce compounds of low solubility. In addition, soil pH's above 6.5 have highly soluble calcium to combine with phosphorus to make slowly soluble tricalcium phosphate. The amount of phosphorus absorbed by average yields of field crops is about 25 kg/ha; and their percentage composition is 0.1 to 1 percent.

The principal phosphorus fertilizers are presented in Table 7.4.

7: 2.5 Potassium Fertilizers

The *total* amount of potassium in most soils of temperate regions averages about 2 percent, principally as a component of such feldspar minerals as orthoclase ($KAl\ Si_3O_8$). In Oxisols and Ultisols, however, total potassium is very low because it has leached away. This means that in such soils available potassium is also in low supply. For example, in the tropical State of Kerala, potassium is often the first limiting element for most crops. The composition of most crops is between 0.3 and 6.0 percent potassium.

The principal source of potassium fertilizer is potassium chloride; this and others are presented in Table 7.5.

Table 7.5. Principal potassium (K) fertilizers (Donahue, Follett, Tulloch, 1983)

Name of fertilizer	Chemical formula	Grade	
		Oxide basis $N\text{-}P_2O_5\text{-}K_2O$ (%)	Elemental basis N-P-K (%)
Potassium chloride (muriate of potash)	KCl	0–0–60	0–0–49.8
Potassium sulfate	K_2SO_4	0–0–50	0–0–41.5 + 17.6% sulfur
Potassium-magnesium sulfate	$K_2SO_4 \cdot 2MgSO_4$	0–0–22	0–0–18.3 + 22.7% sulfur + 11.2% magnesium
Potassium nitrate	KNO_3	13–0–44	13–0–36.5
Potassium polyphosphate		20–40 K_2O+ 25–50% P_2O_5	16.6–33.2 K+ 11.22% P

7: 2.6 Secondary Plant Nutrients

The secondary plant nutrients are calcium, magnesium, and sulfur.

Calcium is abundant in most soils of temperate regions and in Vertisols in semitropical areas but low in Oxisols and Ultisols. The total CaO content of acid soils in India varies from less than 0.1 to about 1 percent although it may not exceed 0.5 percent in soils with pH ranging from 5 to 6 (Deo and Kumar, 1982). Adequate but not excess calcium mobilizes nitrogen, phosphorus, and molybdenum. Common sources of calcium are given in Table 7.6.

Table 7.6. Common sources of calcium (Ca) (Donahue, Follett, Tulloch, 1983)

Carrier	Percent calcium (Ca)
Slaked lime, $Ca(OH)_2$	54
Calcite, $CaCO_3$	40
Ground calcic limestone, 90% pure	36
Dolomite, $(CaCO_3+MgCO_3)$	22
Gypsum, $CaSO_4$	22
Ordinary superphosphate, 0–20–0	20
Triple superphosphate, 0–46–0	14

Most crops average 0.1 to 4 percent calcium. Magnesium is a constituent of chlorophyll and is often deficient where soils have developed from granite or other rocks low in magnesium or in highly-leached soils such as Oxisols and Ultisols. Low magnesium in forage for beef cattle, dairy cattle, and sheep may cause grass tetany (hypomagnesemia). Magnesium in crops is 0.05 to 1.5 percent. The most common sources of magnesium fertilizer are set forth in Table 7.7.

Table 7.7. Common sources of magnesium (Mg) (Donahue, Follett, Tulloch, 1983)

Carrier	Percent magnesium (Mg)
Dolomitic limestone	Variable
Dolomite, $(CaCO_3+MgCO_3)$	8 to 20
Epsom salt $(MgSO_4 \cdot 7H_2O)$	10
Kieserite $(MgSO_4 \cdot H_2O)$	18
Potassium magnesium sulfate $(K_2SO_4 \cdot 2MgSO_4)$	11

Sulfur reserves in the soil are nearly all in organic matter. Only upon mineralization does the sulfur become available to plants as a sulfate (SO_4^{2-}). In this form, however, it is leachable. Sulfur composition in most crops is between 0.05 and 1.5 percent. Common sources of sulfur as a fertilizer are given, by their solubility classes, in Table 7.8.

Table 7.8. Common sources of sulfur (S) (Donahue, Follett, Tulloch, 1983)

Name of fertilizer	Chemical formula	Grade $N\text{-}P_2O_5\text{-}K_2O$	Percent sulfur (S)
Very Soluble			
Ammonium sulfate	$(NH_4)_2SO_4$	21–0–0	24
Potassium sulfate	K_2SO_4	0–0–50	18
Potassium-magnesium-sulfate	$K_2SO_4 \cdot 2MgSO_4$	0–0–22	23
Magnesium sulfate (Epsom salt)	$MgSO_4$	0–0–0	14
Ordinary superphosphate	$Ca(H_2PO_4)_2 + CaSO_4$	0–20–0	14
Slightly Soluble			
Calcium sulfate (Gypsum)	$CaSO_4$	0–0–0	17
Insoluble			
Elemental sulfur	S	0–0 0	88–100

7: 2.7 Micronutrients

Micronutrients essential for plants include iron, zinc, copper, manganese, boron, molybdenum, and chlorine.

Iron is usually abundant in acid soils but deficient in alkaline soils because of its low solubility. On a field scale, iron sulfate or iron chelates are usually too expensive to use as a soil-applied fertilizer but feasible as a foliar spray. Heavy applications of animal manures or sewage sludges usually correct iron deficiency. Plants average 10 to 1,000 ppm of iron.

Zinc deficiency is common on alkaline soils low in organic matter. Furthermore, heavy phosphorus applications may induce zinc deficiency. From 5.0 to 100 ppm is the average zinc composition of crop plants. Manures, sewage sludges, or the fertilizers listed in Table 7.9 have been used successfully to correct zinc deficiency.

Table 7.9. Zinc (Zn) sources (Donahue, Follett, Tulloch, 1983)

Sources	Formula (Form)	Percent zinc (Zn)
Zinc sulfate	$ZnSO_4 \cdot H_2O$	36
Zinc oxide	ZnO	78
Zinc carbonate	$ZnCO_3$	56
Zinc chelate	$Na_2ZnEDTA$	14

Copper deficiencies are common in sandy soils and in Histosols. Also copper toxicities may occur when the available copper exceeds 30 kg/ha. Most crops average 2 to 50 ppm of copper. Deficiencies may be corrected by soil or foliar application of the fertilizers displayed in Table 7.10.

Table 7.10. Fertilizer sources of copper (Cu) (Donahue, Follett, Tulloch, 1983)

Source	Formula (Form)	Percent copper (Cu)
Copper sulfate	$CuSO_4 \cdot 3\ Cu(OH)_2$	13–53
Cuprous oxide	Cu_2O	89
Cupric oxide	CuO	75
Copper acetate	$Cu(C_2H_3O_2)_2 \cdot H_2O$	32
Copper oxalate	$CuC_2O_4 \cdot \frac{1}{2}H_2O$	40
Copper ammonium phosphate	$Cu(NH_4)PO_4 \cdot H_2O$	32
Copper chelates	$Na_2CuEDTA$	13

Manganese deficiencies occur most often on well-drained, humid-region, sandy, calcareous, or overlimed soils. Crops requiring more manganese are the small grains, soybeans, and sweet potatoes. Deficiency is corrected most often with manganese sulfate used as a soil or foliage application. Manganese in crops averages 5 to 500 ppm. Common manganese fertilizers are shown in Table 7.11.

Table 7.11. Commonly used manganese (Mn) fertilizers (Donahue, Follett, Tulloch, 1983)

Source	Formula or abbreviation	Percent manganese (Mn)
Manganese sulfate	$MnSO_4.4H_2O$	24
Manganous oxide	MnO	68–70
Manganese carbonate	$MnCO_3$	31
Manganese chloride	$MnCl_2$	17
Manganese chelate	MnEDTA	12
Manganese frits	Variable	10–25
Manganese polyflavonoid	MnPF	8

Boron in soils occurs mostly as water-soluble and therefore easily-leached forms. In humid-region soils boron may be deficient but in soils and waters of arid regions, boron may be toxic to plants. There is a narrow range between adequacy and toxicity. Adequate for alfalfa, sugar beets, peanuts, and cotton may mean toxic for corn and beans. Only by soil and irrigation water tests can the proper level of boron be maintained. When boron is needed, amounts as small as 0.2 kg/ha may be sufficient. Most crop plants contain from 3 to 60 ppm of boron. Fertilizer sources of boron are itemized in Table 7.12.

Table 7.12. Fertilizer sources of boron (B) (Donahue, Follett, Tulloch, 1983)

Fertilizer	Formula	Percent boron (B)
Boron frits	Variable	10–17
Borax	$Na_2B_4O_7 \cdot 10\ H_2O$	11
Boric Acid	H_3BO_3	17
Sodium pentaborate	$Na_2B_{10}O_{16} \cdot 10\ H_2O$	18
Sodium tetraborate		
Fertilizer borate —46	$Na_2B_4O_7 \cdot 5\ H_2O$	14
Fertilizer borate —65	$Na_2B_4O_7$	20
Solubor	$Na_2B_{10}O_{16} \cdot 10\ H_2O$	20

Molybdenum deficiency occurs in leached, humid-region, acid soils. Liming alone often corrects the deficiency. The four common sources of molybdenum fertilizer are given in Table 7.13. Methods of application include as little as 60 grams/ha applied as a seed treatment, foliar spray, or to the soil. From 0.01 to 10 ppm is the usual molybdenum content of most crop plants. Legume bacteria have a high molybdenum requirement.

Table 7.13. Molybdenum (Mo) sources (Donahue, Follett, Tulloch, 1983)

Source	Formula	Percent molybdenum (Mo)
Ammonium molybdate	$(NH_4)_6Mo_7O_{24} \cdot 2\ H_2O$	54
Molybdenum trioxide	MoO_3	66
Molybdenum frits	Variable	30
Sodium molybdate	$Na_2MoO_4 \cdot 2\ H_2O$	39

Chlorine is never intentionally applied as a fertilizer because it occurs in adequate amounts in fertilizers and in soils.

7: 3 FERTILIZER FORMULATIONS

A fertilizer formulation is the act of or result of mixing specific fertilizer materials of known physical and chemical composition to produce a predictable fertilizer containing two or more plant nutrients. A formulation may be *dry* or *fluid.* Nearly all dry formulations in recent years are either granulated, prilled, crystallized, or flaked. Earlier, mixed fertilizers of desired analysis were prepared by farmers themselves or readymade mixtures were purchased in the market. With the availability of complex fertilizers physically mixed fertilizers are not in use any more. Fluid fertilizers may be clear liquids (true solutions) or suspensions (supersaturated solutions or colloidal suspensions). Fluid fertilizers are not marketed in India at present.

7: 3.1 Dry Formulations

Dry formulations are mixed dry or in a slurry and then granulated, prilled, crystallized, or flaked as they dry.

Chemical and physical compatibility of dry formulations are crucial for a successful finished product. The formulation must have high critical relative humidity (be dry enough to spread at the ambient humidity), be compatible in size of granules (to reduce segregation), and the granules must be firm (nondusty). Data from India on the chemical compatibility of 17 fertilizers is presented in Fig. 7.2. To interpret this chart, look at line 1, ending with 1. Calcium nitrate. Block number 8 is designated as "fertilizers which cannot be mixed." Number 8 is urea. This means do not mix urea with calcium nitrate. Also on Line 1, numbers 11 (superphosphate), 12 (triple superphosphate), and 15 (muriate of potash) should not be dry mixed with calcium nitrate. A similar fertilizer compatibility chart for the principal fertilizers used in the United States is displayed in Fig. 7.3. The principal reason for fertilizer incompatibility is the fact that the mixture is deliquescent, i.e., it stays damp at commonly-encountered relative humidities (Fig. 7.3). For example, in Fig. 7.4, a mixture of calcium nitrate and potassium chloride (muriate of potash) has a critical relative humidity of less than 22 percent. This means that such a mixture will remain "tacky" and not be dry enough to spread until the relative humidity of the air is less than 22 percent (near-desert conditions). And seldom do the fertilizer-using areas of the world have air this dry, especially at fertilizer-applying time.

Physical compatibility means that the sizes of the granules of the fertilizers to be dry-mixed must be similar to avoid segregation. When a large-granule fertilizer is mixed with small granules, intimate and stable mixing is not possible. Any agitation after mixing such as rail or truck hauling will force the larger granules to the top and the nutrients will be applied unevenly. Uneven spreading also results when one fertilizer is dusty and is blown away as it is applied.

Because of its lower cost, there is always a tendency to use urea as the principal source of nitrogen in dry formulations. However, these precautions must be taken (Garn, 1973; Hignett, 1967):

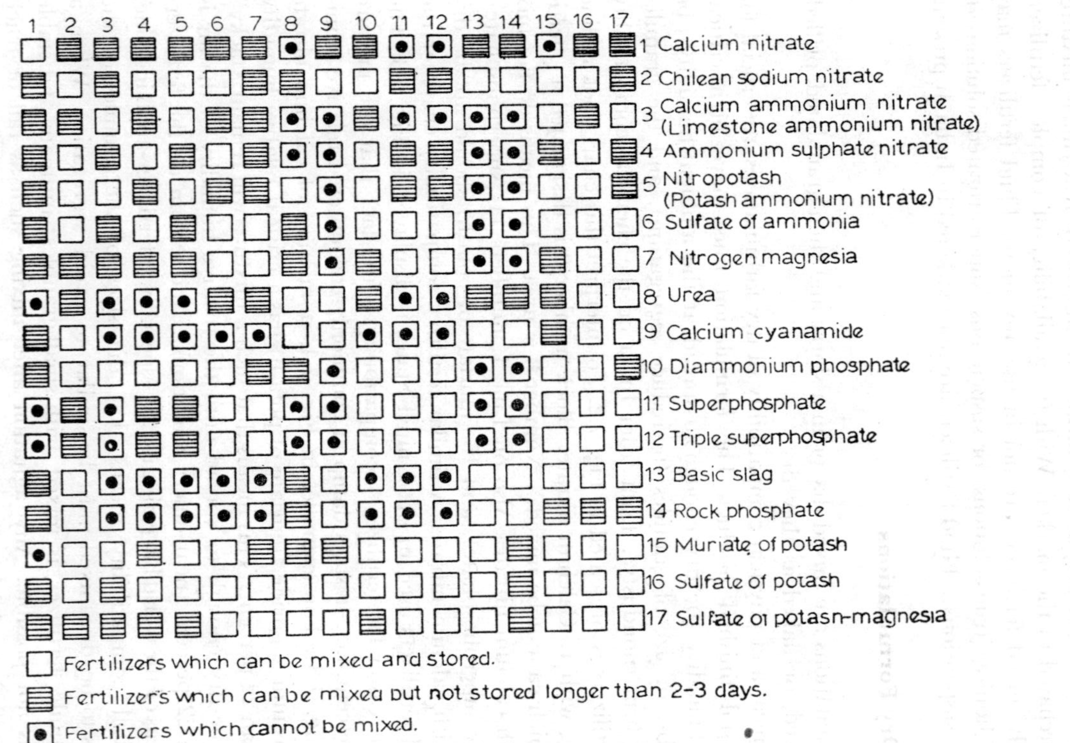

Fig. 7.2. Guide for dry mixing and storing fertilizers used in India and in several other countries of the world. Please note that many of the fertilizer materials are different from those used in the United States. (Adapted from: D. Raghavan, P. Kachroo, and R. R. Lokeshwar, editors. "Handbook of Manures and Fertilizers". Indian Council of Agricultural Research, New Delhi, India, 1964, page 129.)

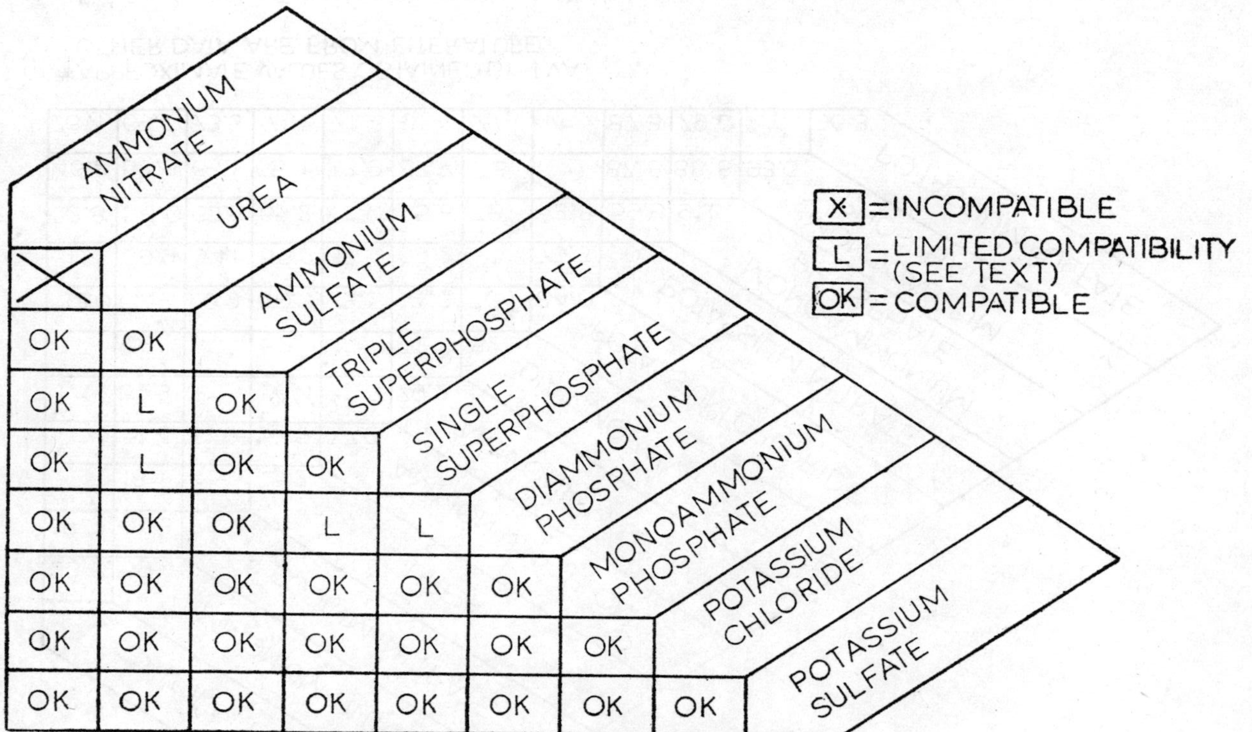

Fig. 7.3. Relative chemical compatibility of the principal fertilizer materials used in the United States for making formulations. (*Source:* National Fertilizer Development Center, TVA.)

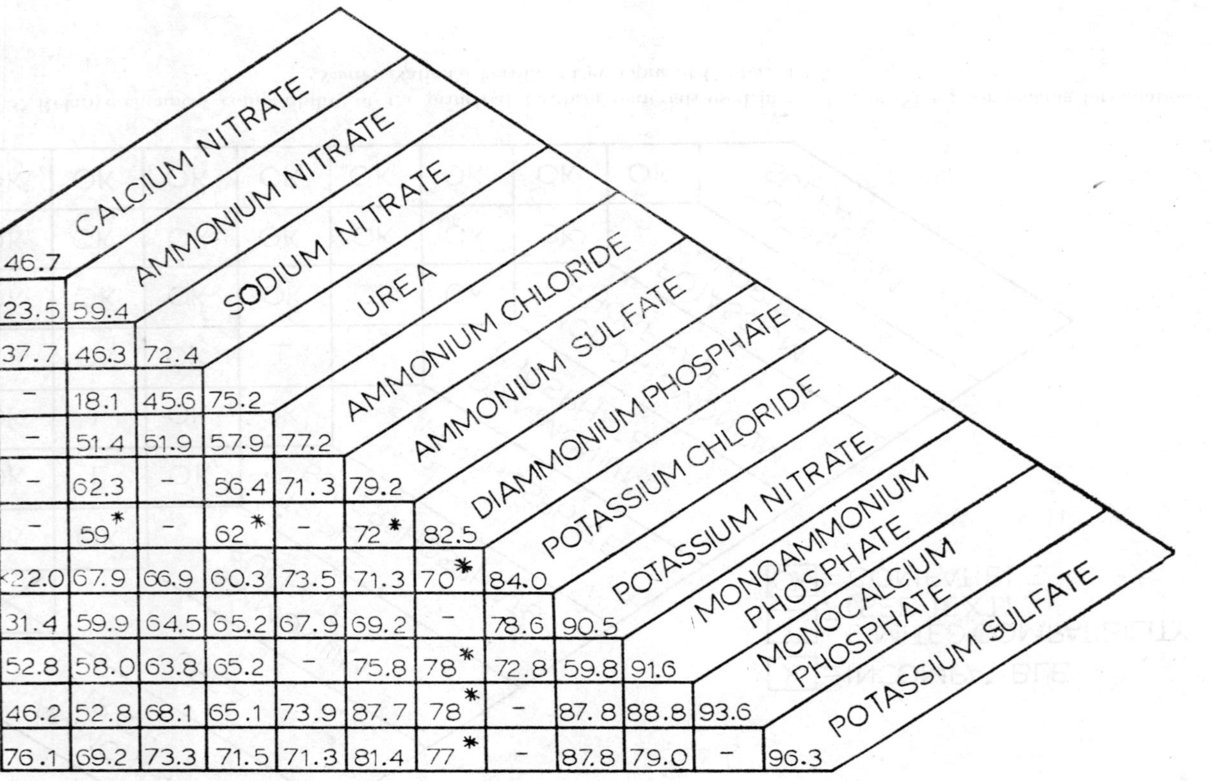

	Calcium nitrate	Ammonium nitrate	Sodium nitrate	Urea	Ammonium chloride	Ammonium sulfate	Diammonium phosphate	Potassium chloride	Potassium nitrate	Monoammonium phosphate	Monocalcium phosphate	Potassium sulfate
Calcium nitrate	46.7											
Ammonium nitrate	23.5	59.4										
Sodium nitrate	37.7	46.3	72.4									
Urea	–	18.1	45.6	75.2								
Ammonium chloride	–	51.4	51.9	57.9	77.2							
Ammonium sulfate	–	62.3	–	56.4	71.3	79.2						
Diammonium phosphate	–	59*	–	62*	–	72*	82.5					
Potassium chloride	<22.0	67.9	66.9	60.3	73.5	71.3	70*	84.0				
Potassium nitrate	31.4	59.9	64.5	65.2	67.9	69.2	–	78.6	90.5			
Monoammonium phosphate	52.8	58.0	63.8	65.2	–	75.8	78*	72.8	59.8	91.6		
Monocalcium phosphate	46.2	52.8	68.1	65.1	73.9	87.7	78*	–	87.8	88.8	93.6	
Potassium sulfate	76.1	69.2	73.3	71.5	71.3	81.4	77*	–	87.8	79.0	–	96.3

*APPROXIMATE VALUES OBTAINED BY TVA.
OTHER DATA ARE FROM LITERATURE.

Fig. 7.4. Critical relative humidity at 30°C (86°F) of fertilizer materials commonly used in dry formulations. (*Source:* National Fertilizer Development Center, Tennessee Valley Authority.)

1) When urea is to be mixed with a phosphorus fertilizer, use monoammonium phosphate, diammonium phosphate, ammoniated normal superphosphate or ammoniated triple superphosphate. Other mixtures of urea and phosphorus are too hygroscopic.

2) Do not mix urea and ammonium nitrate—such a mixture will liquefy.

3) Store urea at a temperature range of 21 to 30°C. At a temperature of 43°C, urea hydrolyzes and is lost as a gas at the rate of about 5 percent of the N a month.

4) Most urea is either prilled or pelleted in sizes too small to form a stable dry formulation with most other fertilizers. In recent years, a granular urea has become available which does mix well.

5) Dry urea formulations should be spread the same day they are mixed. High humidity at night may make the formulation too wet to apply.

6) Do not blend urea with any other fertilizer at or near the critical relative humidity of urea (75.2 percent at 30°C; see Fig. 7.4)

7) Incorporate urea and dry formulations with urea into the soil as it is being applied. Especially when applied on grass or bare alkaline soil at high temperatures, urea is hydrolyzed into ammonia and carbon dioxide, which are lost as gases to the atmosphere.

8) Urea and dry formulations containing urea should not be placed near seed or germinating seedlings because of the hazard of salt injury (desiccation by plasmolysis).

7: 3.2 Fluid Formulations

Fluid formulations may be solutions (clear liquids) or suspensions (salt suspensions, colloidal suspensions, or thin slurries). The principal true solutions are anhydrous ammonia (a liquid under pressure), aqua ammonia (anhydrous ammonia plus water), nitrogen solutions (dissolved solids or solids plus ammonia) and solutions of dissolved mixed fertilizers. Anhydrous ammonia is in use on a large scale in the U.S.A. and some west European countries. Although it is one of the cheapest nitrogenous fertilizers, it has not become popular in other countries mainly because of difficulties in establishing infrastructure in marketing.

Suspensions have become popular because they can be formulated to about twice the concentration of true solutions. Suspensions often consist of true solutions plus additional fertilizer salts to make a supersaturated suspension plus a suspending agent of 1 to 3 percent such as bentonite clay or attapulgite clay. Examples of high-grade suspensions include 15–15–15, 10–20–20, 7–21–21, and 3–10–30. Micronutrients and/or pesticides are frequently added to suspensions to reduce their cost of application and to obtain uniform coverage.

7: 4 ORGANIC AMENDMENTS

Cultivated soils in the tropics are normally low in organic matter, except in heavy rainfall areas they are enriched continuously from washings from surrounding forests. It should therefore be considered a crime if any material that can be used for increasing soil organic matter is just burnt. It is a wise policy to preserve carefully all the available plant and animal waste material for use as organic amendments. In India considerable attention has been paid for many years to develop and propagate appropriate methods to utilize various kinds of crop and animal residues to enrich soils.

7: 4.1 Organic Farming

The use of organic amendments was given a world-wide boost when Sir Albert Howard experimented with the Indore process of making compost during 1924 to 1931 (Howard, 1938, 1945, and 1972).

Human, animal, and plant residues in and around Indore, Madhya Pradesh, India, were composted. This compost was used to produce crops at a time when commercial fertilizers were not readily available. This composting process was later to be known in world literature as the "Indore Process". Humus from composted plant *and* animal residues were claimed to be superior to that made from either alone.

Plants receiving the Indore Process humus were attested to be insect- and disease-resistant and to impart disease resistance to people and livestock eating those plants. This tenet is succinctly stated on page 115 of Balfour, 1975, as follows:

> "That if the fertility of the soil is built up with adequate supplies of humus, crops do not suffer from diseases and do not require poison sprays to control parasites; that animals fed on these plants develop a high degree of disease resistance, and that man, nurtured with such plants and animals can reach a standard of health, and a power of resisting disease and infection, from whatever cause, greatly in advance of anything ordinarily found in this country."

Also on page 136 of Balfour, 1975, is this statement regarding the experience of Albert Howard when he was at Pune, India:

> " . . . Howard found that his oxen in India, fed on compost-grown food, failed to contract foot-and-mouth disease even when 'rubbing noses' with infected animals."

No one doubts the benefits of using plant and animal residues to increase crop yields. What all agricultural scientists believe can be summarized as stated on page 91 of the publication on organic farming from the U.S. Department of Agriculture, 1980, as follows:

"There is evidence that higher crop yields are possible when organic wastes and residues are applied in combination with chemical fertilizers than when either one is applied alone."

Starting in 1843, the Rothamsted Experiment Station near London, England, has compared plots of wheat yields with these variables: manure versus complete fertilizer versus no manure and no fertilizer. The wheat yields were 2,146, 2,287, and 847 kg/ha, respectively. Yield of wheat on manured plots were thus 94 percent as much as on those receiving complete fertilizer and 253 percent more than on plots with no manure and no fertilizer (Millar, 1955).

As early as the 1880's, research was being conducted in the United States with manures; as reported by King in 1911: "It is a fact long ago observed that increasing the organic matter in the soil increases its water-holding power..." After three years of research, King reported... "A total difference in favor of the manured ground amounting to 34.41 tons per acre" (77.15 mt/ha) of available soil water.

With more science and less emotion, the organic technique of plant production usually means the maximum use of plant and animal residues, no chemical fertilizers, no insecticides, no fungicides, and no herbicides. To reduce the chances of failure of the all-organic-no-chemical techniques, select insect and disease-resistant varieties; rotate crops to break the cycle of soil-borne insects, diseases, and weeds; and use as much and as many plant and animal amendments as feasible, preferably as a surface mulch.

Organic mulches make ideal surface covers to protect the soil against erosive raindrops, equalize soil temperature, reduce loss of water by surface evaporation, reduce weed emergence, eliminate mud after rains, add nutrients for growing plants, and encourage earthworms and other desirable soil fauna.

A practical solution to the organic controversy is to practice organic gardening *between* the rows and organic and chemical gardening *in* the rows.

7: 4.2 Plant and Animal Residues

Promoters of organic gardening and farming usually encourage the use of organic residues by implying that any kind can be used and in any amount. However, a little science can eliminate big failures.

Do not use organic materials that contain seeds of serious weeds, diseases, insects, or toxic materials; or materials with a large amount of carbon in relation to its nitrogen content. Serious weed pests include quackgrass and bermudagrass seeds, stolons, and rhizomes. Parthenium weed residue leaves toxic effects on many crop plants. Diseases can be avoided by never using sickly plants. Avoid nematodes (swellings on roots—but not to be confused with beneficial legume root nodules of *Rhizobium*). Do not use sawdust, wood chips, or any other wood products from toxic walnut (*Juglans* species) or toxic red cedar (*Juniperus* species). Use only *old hardwood* sawdust. Always use organic residues with a carbon to nitrogen ratio of 30:1 or narrower, unless a quick-acting high-nitrogen fertilizer is added to hasten decomposition. Such high-nitrogen materials of organic origin include sewage sludge, dried blood, guano, tankage, and nonedible oilseed meal. However, much cheaper materials (except possibly sewage sludge) include commercial fertilizer nitrogen such as urea or ammonium nitrate (Table 7.14).

Table 7.14. Average composition of principal commercial organic amendments*
(McCall, 1975 and Ohio State University, 1973)

Amendment	Percent plant nutrient		
	Total nitrogen (N)	Available phosphoric acid (P_2O_5)	Water-soluble potash (K_2O)
1	2	3	4
Castor Pomace	5.2	1.8	1.1
Cotton Bolls	1.0	0.23	4.0
Cottonseed Meal	6.0	2.5	1.4
Dried Blood	12.0	1.5	0.8
Dried Manures			
Dairy	0.7	0.3	0.6
Goat	2.7	1.7	2.8
Horse	0.7	0.3	0.5
Pig	1.0	0.7	0.8
Poultry	4.0	3.2	1.3
Rabbit	2.0	1.3	1.2
Sheep	2.0	1.0	2.5
Steer	2.0	0.5	1.9
Fish Scrap	6–10	6–7	0–1
Guano, Bat	13.0	5.0	2.0
Guano, Peruvian	12–13	8–11	2–4
Hoof and Horn Meal	11–15	2.0	—
Linseed Meal	5.5	2.0	1.5
Night Soil (China) (Hauck, 1977)	0.6	0.2	0.3
Night Soil (Japan) (Eqawa, 1975)	0.6	0.13	0.27
Peanut Hulls	0.4	—	—

Tabla 7.14 (*Contd.*)

1	2	3	4
Peat/Muck	2.3	0.5	0.7
Raw Bonemeal	4.2	18.5	—
Sawdust and Wood Chips (hardwood)	0.2	0.05	0.2
Seaweed (Kelp)	0.6	0.0	1.32
Sewage Sludge			
Activated (aerobic)	5–6	3.4	0.3
Digested (anaerobic)	2–3	1.4	0.8
Soybean Meal	5–6	2.0	1.4
Streamed Bonemeal	2.2	27.0	—
Staw (Grain)	0.6	0.23	1.1
Tankage			
Animal	7–12	1–10	1–2
Garbage	2.5–3.3	1.5	1.5
Process	6–9	1–6	0.8
Tobacco Residues	1.5	0.46	5.0
Wood Ash (hardwood)	0.0	7	20

*The percentages given in this table are average figures or indicate a range in composition. When obtaining fertilizer materials, always purchase according to the guaranteed analysis of the material. Most of the natural organic materials contain traces of one or more of the micronutrients; however, these are not generally guaranteed.

**Commercially dried. All manure is highly variable in composition. It should be purchased only on the basis of a guarantee.

When an organic amendment with a wide C:N ratio is added to the soil, soil bacteria will utilize the scarce nitrogen and the plentiful carbon to grow and reproduce, thus crop plants will starve for nitrogen.

Amounts of readily-soluble/quick-acting nitrogen to use on sawdust or other wood products with a ratio of 250 parts organic carbon to one part total nitrogen would be one kilogram of actual nitrogen (N) for each 50 kilograms of wood products. For small grain straw with a carbon: nitrogen ratio of 80:1, use one kilogram of soluble N per 16 kilograms of straw (Harkin, 1969).

7: 4.3 Farmyard Manure

Farm animals excrete dung and urine which are rich in plant nutrients. Good quantity of straw and other plant material becomes available to farmers in some seasons. Dung, urine and plant residues can be either incorporated directly in soil or systematically mixed and preserved in pits or heaps until converted into compost through a decomposition process. The final produce is known popularly as farmyard compost. It may contain about 1 percent of nitrogen (N), 0.5 percent of phosphorus (P_2O_5) and 1 percent potassium (K_2O) depending upon the type and age of animals, the way they are fed, the quantity and quality of plant material mixed and the care taken in collecting, preserving and handling of material.

Present recommended methods of preservation in India are:

1) Spread sufficient litter as bedding for animals to facilitate absorption of urine.

2) Use all cow dung without diverting any for the preparation of cow dung cake for fuel.

3) Conserve and mix all urine with dung and straw.

4) The pit should be one meter in depth, two meters in width and of any convenient length. Floor should be sloping in one direction.

5) Fill the pit systematically layer by layer each layer being 20–30 cm in height and cover each day's layer with a thin layer of soil. Enrichment with phosphatic fertilizer is advisable.

6) Excess water should not get into the pits. Where this is difficult to avoid it is better to adopt the heap method.

7: 4.4 Composts

All the available plant residues can be collected and converted into good compost by adopting various methods recommended depending upon the kind of material needed for the purpose. Methods have been developed for converting urban or rural refuse or even hard and wax covered material like sugar cane trash into compost which is almost as rich as farmyard manure. In general for getting good quality compost the following conditions should be satisfied:

1) The manure be heaped above the ground or filled in pits of proper size in a systematic manner and should be kept fairly moist but not saturated with water.

2) Appropriate temperature conditions should prevail for proper organic decomposition.

3) The needed status especially of major nutrients—N, P and K should be maintained through addition of animal wastes or fertilizers.

4) Proper inoculum of microorganisms in the form of decomposed compost or farmyard manure should be added.

7: 4.5 Green Manure

In tropical parts of the world it is a common practice to add leafy material to enrich the worn out soil. The material from certain kinds of trees especially those belonging to the legume family is preferred since it is rich in nitrogen. Raising of glyricidia, sannhemp, and dhaincha species of trees as plantations or growing them on the boundaries of fields is being recommended to increase the supply of green leafy material for manuring purpose. They contain about 3 percent N, 0.5 percent P_2O_5 and 3 percent K_2O.

It is also possible to raise a short season crop of suitable kind with a view to harvesting the green material at an appropriate stage incorporating it into the soil to increase its organic matter content. Such a practice known as green manuring can be adopted with advantage under specific situations. The crops grown for green manuring yield large quantities of non-woody green material in a short period of six to eight weeks. Instead of sacrificing the whole season for growing green manure crop it may be possible to raise an intercrop in broadly spread crops like maize, cotton, sugar cane etc.

Crops suitable for green manuring purposes are like cowpea, wild indigo and hemp.

The following aspects need to be borne in mind for ensuring maximum benefit:

1) Sow with higher seed rate and closer spacing than usual.
2) Apply phosphatic fertilizer and potassic also if necessary to get a good harvest.
3) Harvest and incorporate when the crop reaches growing stage.
4) Mix plant material with surface soil.
5) Green manuring is possible only when there is adequate moisture supply for decomposition and for growing the next crop.

7: 4.6 Sewage Sludge

On a dry weight basis, sewage sludge has the following average composition: (Halderson and Zenz, 1978) (Anonymous, 1975)

Essential Plant Nutrient	*Composition* (*Total*) (%)
Organic carbon	50
N	5.0
P_2O_5	6.8
K_2O	0.5
Ca	3.0
Mg	1.0
S	0.9
Fe	4.0
Zn	0.5
Cu	0.1
Mn	0.05
B	0.01

Sludges are also high in elements absorbed by plants but which are not essential for growth and reproduction. These include:

Nonessential Element	*Composition* (*Total*) (*ppm*)
Chromium (Cr)	3,000
Sodium (Na)	2,000
Lead (Pb)	1,000
Nickel (Ni)	400
Cadmium (Cd)	150

Please note that this composition is *total* and not *available.* However, decomposition (mineralization) is quite rapid. When the sludge is incorporated in a fine textured soil and under warm, humid conditions, about half of the nutrients may become available during the first year.

Use of 300 to 500 metric tons (dry weight basis) of sewage sludge per hectare per year on strongly acid mine spoils was reported to *raise* the soil pH from 2.5 to 6.0 and to enhance establishment of protective and productive vegetation. (Cunningham et al., 1975). Although no data on the subject are readily available, the authors assume that sludge applied to soils with a very high pH would *lower* the pH to permit more vegetation to grow.

Average composition of the principal commercial organic amendments are presented in Table 7.14 on pages 160 and 161.

7: 5 ENVIRONMENTAL CONCERNS

The principal hazards to the environment from using chemical fertilizers and organic amendments include nitrates in drinking water from fertilizers, manures, and sewage sludges; and heavy metals and pathogens from sewage sludges.

7: 5.1 Nitrates

Nitrates are so often in excess in the environment that they may be considered the number one fertilizer and organic residue pollutant. In surplus, nitrates may be absorbed by forage grasses in luxury consumption and thereby cause nitrate poisoning in livestock. Of less common occurrence, but no less serious, is a surplus of nitrates in drinking water for domestic animals and people.

Nitrates get into the water environment primarily from these five sources:

1) Chemical fertilizers containing nitrogen
2) Animal wastes (feces and urine)
3) City sewage and septic tank effluents
4) Municipal and factory wastes
5) Nitrification of organic matter in the soil

For humans, the U.S. Public Health Service has established 45 milligrams per liter [Mg/l equals parts per million (ppm)] of nitrate (NO_3^-) as the threshold of nitrate toxicity in drinking waters.

Cattle, horses, and sheep have a higher tolerance for nitrates than humans. Water with as high a concentration as 300 mg/l of nitrate (NO_3^-) is not harmful to cattle, horses, and sheep unless their forage contains more than 0.45 percent nitrate (NO_3^-) (dry weight basis). Swine and poultry have even a greater tolerance of nitrates (NO_3^-) in water and feed (Kerr, undated; anonymous, 1975; and Olson, et al., 1973).

In both humans and animals, water high in NO_3^- may produce these hazards:

1) *Methemoglobinemia.* This "blue baby" disease is caused by a reduction in the ability of the hemoglobin in red blood cells to transport oxygen. The symptoms are similar to poisoning by carbon monoxide (CO).

2) *Vitamin A utilization interference.* In suspected instances of nitrate poisoning, large doses of vitamin A are usually given to offset lack of storage in the liver.

3) *Antibody production impairment.* This hazard may result in an animal being more susceptible to pathogens (diseases).

4) *Abortion.* Abortion in cattle has been correlated with drinking water high in nitrates.

5) *Goiter-like condition.* Abnormal thyroid activity may occur due to the exclusion of the iodide anions from the thyroid glands by nitrate anions of similar size and charge.

The disease of infants commonly called "blue baby" but technically known as *methemoglobinemia,* has been associated with nitrate in drinking water, beginning in the United States in 1945. Since then, about 2,000 cases have been reported in North America and Europe and between 7 and 8 percent have died. Such a stage has not been reached in countries where fertilizer usage is at a low level. Babies less than three months of age appear most susceptible. Reporting of the disease is not mandatory, however, and some estimates place the incidence ten times more than the cases reported (Winton, et al., 1970).

The nitrate is itself not harmful in the usual amounts ingested. In the stomach of the infant, bacteria reduce the innocuous nitrate (NO_3^-) to harmful nitrite (NO_2^-). The nitrite then converts hemoglobin in the blood to methemoglobin and thus reduces the ability of the hemoglobin to carry oxygen throughout the body. The result is suffocation, as observed by a blue appearance of the skin.

Nitrates *are* a serious problem in heavily-populated, high-animal-density areas such as those in Connecticut, U.S.A. Waters from 160 Connecticut farm wells were sampled and analyzed for nitrates in 1971 and 1972 (Frink, 1973). The depth of each well was measured and data were recorded on whether each farm was predominantly a dairy or a poultry farm.

Valid conclusions:

1) Water in about 10 percent of the 160 farm wells contained 45 or more mg/l of nitrate and was therefore unfit for human consumption.

2) About half of the high-nitrate water was from dairy farms and half from poultry farms.

3) Wells on two poultry farms as deep as 107 meters (350 feet) contained an excessive amount of nitrates, although shallow wells were more often contaminated.

4) Nitrates in the well waters came from the decomposition of livestock and poultry manures.

Only by an on-site inspection of experts can the cause and proposed cures for high-nitrate waters be made. Technical agencies qualified to assist with a viable diagnosis and solution include the Department of Public Health, the County Extension Service, and the Soil Conservation Service.

Suggestions for reducing the hazard of nitrate pollution include:

1) Locate feedlots and manure piles in a different drainage basin from the well. Nitrates from decomposing animal manures pollute the ecological environment in the same way as excessive nitrate fertilizer applications.

2) Delay the use of nitrogen fertilizer until the crop is growing rapidly and its roots can absorb the nitrate as fast as they occur in the rhizosphere (root zone) and before they leach through it.

3) Use recommended rates of nitrogen fertilizers. In determining the amount of nitrogen fertilizer to apply, deduct the amount being added in the irrigation water, legumes, barnyard manure, sewage sludge, and from mineralization of soil organic matter.

7: 5.2 Heavy Metals

Sewage sludges are generally high in lead, zinc, copper, nickel, and cadmium. There is public concern that these heavy metals may accumulate in soils to levels toxic to crop plants, or enter the human and animal food chain and become toxic, or contaminate the water supply for people and animals. The subject is being researched in nearly every state in the United States and in almost all countries of the world. For this reason, only "safe" guidelines can be suggested. (Council for Agricultural Science and Technology, 1976; EPA, 1978; Ettlish, 1977; and Soil Conservation Society of America, 1976).

Because all of these heavy metals are cations, most soils and humus throughout the world will adsorb them up to their cation exchange capacity. However, of the five heavy metals, only zinc and copper are essential elements for plants. Furthermore, the more the exchangeable heavy metals on the exchange sites, the less the capacity for adsorbing essential calcium, magnesium, potassium, and ammonium.

Many researchers have proposed environmentally safe applications of heavy metals based on the cation exchange capacity of the soil on which sewage sludge is to be applied. On this basis, criteria for environmentally safe applications of the heavy metals are proposed in Table 7.15 (Knezek and Miller, 1976).

Table 7.15. Environmentally safe cumulative threshold levels of heavy metal toxicity induced by the application of sewage sludge to cropland soils with different cation exchange capacities (Knezek and Miller, 1976)

Heavy metal	Cation exchange capacity of soil (meq/100 g soil)		
	0–5 (usually sands)	5–15 (usually loams)	More than 15 (usually clays)
	Cumulative threshold level of toxicity of metal		
	kg/ha	kg/ha	kg/ha
Lead (Pb)	560	1,121	2,242
Zinc (Zn)	280	560	1,121
Copper (Cu)	140	280	560
Nickel (Ni)	56	112	224
Cadmium (Cd)	5.6	11.2	22.4

In India the state water pollution control boards and department of health service exercise control over disposal of industrial and municipal liquid waste.

7: 5.3 Pathogens

Sewage effluents may contain many pathogens for humans, but desiccation will in time kill most of them. The principal disease-producing organisms, the diseases they cause in people, and average survival time on various media are presented in Table 7.16.

7: 6 NITROGEN FIXATION BY SOIL MICROBES

With the increasing cost of petroleum and therefore of the nitrogen fertilizer made from it, there has been an intensification of interest in microbial nitrogen fixation from atmospheric dinitrogen (N_2).

Table 7.16. Major pathogens in sewages, the diseases implicated, and survival time on various media (Parsons et al., 1975)

Organism	Disease implicated	Media	Survival time
Ascaris ova	Intestinal worm	Soil fruits, vegetables	(up tp 7 years) 27–35 days
Coliforms	None (an indication of human/animal fecal contamination	Soil surface vegetables grasses, clovers	38 days 35 days 6-34 days
Entamoeba histolytica cysts	Amoebic dysentery	Soil vegetables water	6–8 days <1–3 days 8–40 days
Enteroviruses	Hepatitis	Soil vegetables	8 days 4–6 days
Hookworm larvae	Hookworm	Soil	42 days
Leptospira	Jaundice	Soil water sewage	15–43 days 5-32 days 30 days
Liver Fluke cysts	Liver worms	Dry hay moist hay	(few weeks) (>a year)
Polio virus	Poliomyelitis	Water at 20°C (68°F)	20 days
Salmonellae	Bacillary diarrhea	Soil vegetables, fruits grasses, clovers	15–>280 days 3–49 days 12–>42 days and over winter
Shigellae	Bacillary dysentery	Raw sewage on grasses vegetables water-containing humus	42 days 2–10 days 160 days
Streptococci	A genera with many pathogenic species	Soil	35–63 days
Streptococci, fecal	,, ,,	Soil	26–77 days
Tubercle bacilli	Tuberculosis	Soil	>180 days
Vibrio cholerae	Cholera	Vegetables, fruits Water, sewage	<1–29 days 5–32 days

In 1886, H. Hellriegel and H. Wilfarth demonstrated the fixation of atmospheric nitrogen by bacteria on the roots of legumes. Two years later Beijerinck isolated the bacteria and named it *Bacillus radicicola.* Later scientists changed the name to *Rhizobium.*

Research on nitrogen (N_2) fixation by microbes was given impetus in the late 1960's when the fact was discovered that the enzyme, *nitrogenase,* was an essential step in the process. Nitrogenase is capable of reducing acetylene (C_2H_4) to ethylene (C_2H_2). By the use of gas chromatography, this chemical reduction can be measured quickly, and as a consequence, research on N_2 fixation was accelerated. Although new N_2-fixing microbes are being discovered every year, as of 1978 the following ones were known to fix nitrogen (Alexander, 1977):

1) Symbiotic Legume Bacteria
   - a) *Rhizobium meliloti*—alfalfa and sweet clover
   - b) *Rhizobium trifolii*—true clovers
   - c) *Rhizobium leguminosarum*—peas
   - d) *Rhizobium phaseoli*—beans
   - e) *Rhizobium lupini*—lupines
   - f) *Rhizobium japonicum*—soybeans
2) Symbiotic Nonlegume Bacteria
   - a) Nodulated (Table 7.17)
   - b) Nonnodulated (Table 7.18)
3) Nonsymbiotic (freeliving) Nonphotosynthetic
   - a) Aerobic—*Azomonas*
     Azotobacter
     Beijerinckia
     Derxia
     Methylomonas
     Mycobacterium
   - b) Anaerobic—*Clostridium*
     Desulfotomaculum
     Desulfovibrio
   - c) Facultative aerobic/anaerobic—*Klebsiella*
     Enterobacter
     Bacillus polymyxa
4) Nonsymbiotic (freeliving) Photosynthetic
5) Symbiotic Blue-Green Algae
   - o *Anabaena azollae* with *Azolla pinnata* (water fern)
   - o *Nostoc* sp.
6) Nonsymbiotic (freeliving) Blue-Green Algae
   - o *Anabaena spiroides*
   - o *Anoboenopsis*

- *Aulosira fertilissima*
- *Calothrix*
- *Cylindrospermum*
- *Gloevcapsa*
- *Mastigocladus*
- *Nostoc*
- *Oscillatoria*
- *Phormidium*
- *Plectonema*
- *Schizothrix*
- *Tolypothrix*

7) Miscellaneous: One species of Actinomycete and several genera of fungi are capable of fixing atmospheric nitrogen, including *Aspergillus, Botrytis, Cladosporium, Mucor, Penicillium,* and *Phoma.*

Table 7.17. Nodulated, nonleguminous plants capable of fixing atmospheric nitrogen symbiotically with bacteria (Alexander, 1977; Cornell Univ., 1976)

Common name(s) of plant(s)/Number of species	Genus
Seed-Bearing Plant(s) (Angiosperms)	
Alder (30 species in U.S.)	*Alnus*
Beefwood, Australian pine, She oak, Horsetail tree (30 species in Australia and Pacific Islands)	*Casuarina*
Redroot (55 species in U.S.)	*Ceanothus*
Mountain mahogany (7 species in North America)	*Cercocarpus*
Sweetfern (1 species in U.S.)	*Comptonia*
(No common name) (Up to 30 species in tropics and subtropics)	*Coriaria*
(No common name) (15 species in tropics)	*Discaria*
Mountain avens (less than 10 species in northern hemisphere)	*Dryas*
Wild olive, Russian olive (40 species in world)	*Elaeagnus*
Sea buckthorn, Sallow thorn (2 species in world)	*Hippophae*
Sweet gale, wax myrtle, bayberry (50 species in world)	*Myrica*
Antelope bush (2 species in western North America)	*Purshia*
Buffaloberry, Soapberry (3 species in North America)	*Shepherdia*
Non-Seed-Bearing Plants (Gymnosperms)	
Brazilian pine, Monkey puzzle (15 species in tropics)	*Araucaria*
Cycad, Sago palm (20 species in old world tropics)	*Cycas*
Breadtree, prickly cycad (20 species in Africa)	*Encephalartos*
Ginkgo, Maidenhair tree (1 species hardy to Mid-U.S.)	*Ginkgo*
(No common name) (14 species in Australia)	*Macrozamia*
Podocarpus, Fernpine (75 species in highlands of southern hemisphere and Pacific region)	*Podocarpus*

Table 7.18. Nonnodulated, nonleguminous plants capable of fixing atmospheric nitrogen symbiotically with bacteria

Common name of plant	Symbiotic bacteria
Bermudagrass	Sp. not reported
Bluestem grasses	Sp. not reported
Corn	*Spirillum lipoferum*
Digitaris sp. (crabgrass)	*Spirillum lipoferum*
Goosegrass	Sp. not reported
Guineagrass	*Spirillum* sp.
Hyparrhenia sp.	Sp. not reported
Panic grass	Sp. not reported
Molassesgrass	*Spirillum* sp.
Pangolagrass	*Spirillum* sp.
Paspalum sp.	*Azotobacter paspali*
Pennisetum sp.	Sp. not reported
Rice (root and shoot)	*Anabaena, calothrix, nostoc* (IRRI, 1979)
Signalgrass	Sp. not reported
Sorghums	*Spirillum* sp.
Sugarcane	*Beijerinckia* sp.
Wheat	*Spirillum* sp.

Extensive work has been carried out in India to understand the various aspects of legume-*Rhizobium* symbiosis. Yield increases to the order of 10–76 percent of different grain legumes with *Rhizobium* inoculation have been reported (Subba Rao et al., 1982).

Further work on the following aspects is in progress:

1) Evolving of better strains and testing the same in different locations.

2) Survey of root nodulation habit.

3) Effect of soil conditions on root nodulation, and efficiency of nitrogen fixation and yield of treated crops.

4) Studies on physiology and enzymology.

In the U.S.S.R., *Azotobacter* inoculum applied on soils has been credited with significant increases in yields of wheat, oats, barley, corn, sugar beets and potatoes. The same techniques were used in India and the conclusions were:

1) *Azotobacter* does not fix atmospheric nitrogen under field conditions and cannot therefore substitute for chemical nitrogen fertilizer.

2) *Azotobacter* require adequate soil oxygen and plentiful soil organic matter—both of which are often inadequate in many soils of India (Goswami, 1976).

Gaur (1982) however has reported cases of beneficial effects on a number of crops like rice, cotton, sugarcane, maize, sorghum and wheat. Further research work is in progress in view of the obvious advantages especially in the cost factor (Venkatraman, 1982).

Spirillum. In Florida pearl millet and guineagrass were grown on a low-N, sand soil and inoculated with the symbiotic bacterium *Spirillum lipoferum.* The yields were compared with non-inoculated but N-fertilized plants. *Conclusion:* The symbiotic bacteria without N produced yields of pearl millet equal to those produced by 20 to 42 kg/ha of N. The corresponding increases of guineagrass yields from bacterial inoculation were equal to yields from 25 to 39 kg/ha of N (Smith, et al., 1976).

Azolla. This is a water fern that assimilates atmospheric nitrogen in association with nitrogen fixing blue-green algae. N content of Azolla is 4 to 5 percent on dry weight basis and 0.2 to 0.3 percent on fresh weight basis (Singh, P.K., 1982). It is a biological system proved beneficial for increasing rice yields at comparatively low cost. The system is used traditionally in Vietnam and in parts of China. After drying its culture has to be maintained alive throughout the year in nurseries either in shallow pots, trays or ponds. It can either be inoculated in fallow fields with enough standing water at the rate of 500–1000 kg/ha along with 4–8 kg of P_2O_5 per hectare or one week after transplanting rice, at the rate of 500 kg per hectare (Singh, P.K., 1982). Azolla cultures can be produced in nursery plots. To control the pest that infects the fern application of corbofuron is recommended. It is reported that it saves nitrogen fertilizer as much as 30 kg per hectare. Attempts are being made to popularize the technique in rice-growing areas in India.

Scientists at the International Rice Research Institute in the Philippines developed a plastic-bag technique for assaying N_2 atmospheric nitrogen fixation by blue-green algae under field conditions in wetland rice soils. One experiment was on bare soil (no rice plants) that compared no N fertilizer with 90 kg/ha of N fertilizer. The average rates of N_2 fixation during daylight hours of 0830 to 1130 were:

No N fertilizer —39 grams of N_2 per hectare per hour.

90 kg/ha of N fertilizer—26 grams of N_2 per hectare per hour.

Conclusion: N fertilizer depressed N_2 fixation by blue-green algae by one-third (IRRI, 1975).

Mycorrhizae. Mycorrhizae are symbiotic fungi that are ubiquitous in nature on common field crops and on woody plants. They are known to stimulate growth by increasing nutrient uptake, increasing resistance to drought, and increasing resistance to certain diseases. Many species exist but two types are recognized: endotrophic mycorrhizae (occurring inside root cells) and ectotrophic mycorrhizae (occurring around and outside of roots).

An example of endotrophic mycorrhizae in relation to fertilization and nutrition of peach nursery stock will be cited (Larue, et al., 1975). In California and in most other states, it is customary to fumigate nursery soils to kill plant pathogens. The fumigation, however, also kills beneficial microbes such as mycorrhizae. Research in 1975 on a fumigated soil compared inoculation with mycorrhizae and fertilization with phosphorus and zinc. The test crop was peach nursery stock. The *best* peach trees resulted from the inoculation with mycorrhizae alone. However, there was no statistically significant difference among most of these treatments: fertilizer alone, fertilizer plus mycorrhizae, and mycorrhizae alone. Plant zinc levels were significantly higher, with mycorrhizae alone.

Ectomycorrhizae on 11-year-old loblolly pine trees were depressed in numbers following fertilization with N only. Over a two-year period, the decrease in numbers of ectomycorrhizae were 14 percent following application of 56 kg/ha of N and 20 percent with 112 kg/ha of N. Nitrogen+P reduced numbers by 13 to 15 percent. Phosphorus alone and N+P+K had no significant effect on number (Menge, et al., 1977).

A summary statement from the U.S.D.A.—Agricultrual Research Service is as follows: "The relationship between the mycorrhizal fungi and the host plant is beneficial to both, and many researchers feel that the relationship is essential to the host plants' survival and well-being. Yet we currently suppress the mycorrhizae by overfertilization (USDA, 1976).

7: 7 FERTILIZER USE EFFICIENCY

Concern is being expressed all over the world about the fertilizer use efficiency. Efficient use results in increased profits to farmers and less pollution. The utilization efficiency under Indian conditions is stated to be quite low (Dhar, B.K., 1981). The utilization of nitrogen is reported to vary from 30–40 percent in case of lowland paddy and 50–60 percent in case of upland irrrigated crops. Nitrogen is lost through leaching and by conversion to gases which escape into atmosphere (Fig. 7.5). Phosphorus utilization is still lower as it is about 15–20 percent. In case of potassium 60–70 percent of applied fertilizer is not used by the crop to which it is applied. New kinds of slow release fertilizers are being recommended for better utilization of applied fertilizers (Rajendra Prasad, 1981).

7: 7.1 Measures to Increase Efficiency

Factors that affect utilization are many and include all aspects of soil, water and crop management in general. The important factors concerning use of fertilizers however, are the kinds of fertilizers and the time and method of application. The following measures would help to improve efficiency:

a) Choice of the right kind of fertilizer according to the soil properties and crop requirements.

b) Use of balanced fertilizers according to soil test results.

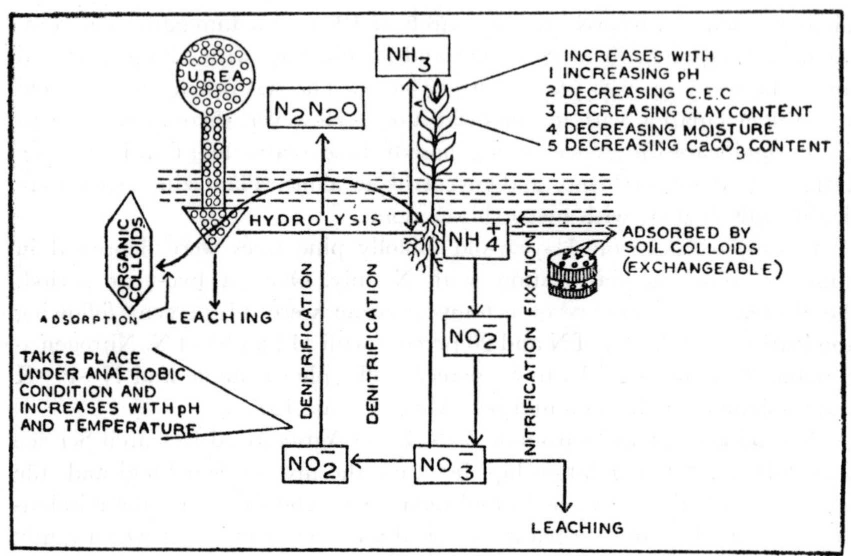

Fig. 7.5. Schematic presentation of urea transformation in soil.
Source: Mahapatra, I.C. "Nitrogen Losses in Wetland Rice in Soil." Ind. Farming, Vol. XXXI, No. 7, ICAR, New Delhi, pages 69–74.

c) Application at the proper time according to needs of crops and nutrient-release properties of fertilizers.

d) Placing the fertilizers at a specific place in the soil with reference to position of seeds at planting time and root growth at later stages and also according to mobility of fertilizers applied. Placement can best be done with suitable implements.

e) Use of slow-release fertilizers whenever found advantageous and available.

f) Use of soil amendments as corrective methods as and when required.

g) Ensure optimum growth of crop plants by all means possible.

7: 7.2 Fertilizer Festivals

In all countries of the world, the efficient use of fertilizers must be promoted to assure adequate food and fiber production. Although techniques of promotion differ, guidelines for success usually include these 12 characteristics (Hapgood, 1965):

1) Profitability
2) Novelty
3) Complementarity
4) Appeal

5) Compatibility
6) Simplicity
7) Availability
8) Immediate Applicability
9) Inexpensiveness
10) Low Risk
11) Short Pay-off Period
12) Expandability

Fertilizer use has been promoted in India with the aid of these 12 guideline characteristics and at times, with a special emphasis on the novelty and appeal of fertilizer festivals (Subramoney, 1976 and Anthraper, 1976).

Starting in South India in 1966, the fertilizer festival may begin with a parade led by a band and the village leaders. The parade would end at a mobile soil testing laboratory where local soil samples had previously been taken and tested. The concerned agricultural scientist would explain that fertilizers used properly may increase yields by about 50 percent, and profit by several hundred percent. Extension specialist would explain the results of previous fertilizer demonstrations in the village. Then leading farmers would relate their experiences with fertilizers.

The results of the soil tests would be explained as well as the procedure for analyzing additional soil samples. Some of the testing would be done while the villagers would watch. The relationship between soil testing, fertilizer recommendations, yield, and profit would be discussed (Motsara, 1976 and Muhr, et al., 1965).

The fertilizer festival would end by detailing how proper fertilizer use is only one of the essentials in a full "package of practices." Other essentials are tillage, variety, weed control, and timeliness of planting, harvesting, and selling.

7: 7.3 The Method Demonstration (Donahue, 1967)

In general it seems that the lower the educational level, the less a person believes the spoken or written word and the more he must be convinced by seeing field method demonstrations. The following verse, "The Method Demonstration", and the graph showing that 87 percent of the farmers interviewed in eastern Andhra Pradesh, India, preferred a field method demonstration to other sources of fertilizer information—both attest to this generalization (Fig. 7.6).

7: 8 INTERNATIONAL FERTILIZER DEVELOPMENT CENTER

In October of 1974 the International Fertilizer Development Center was established at Muscle Shoals, Alabama, U.S.A. Administered by a group of

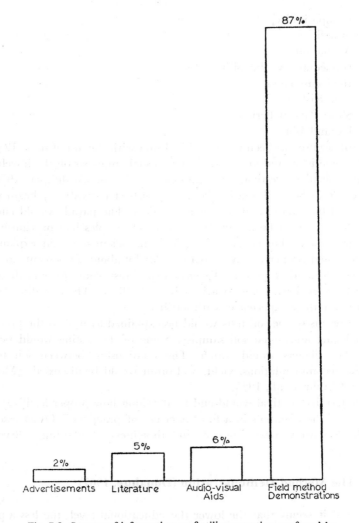

Fig. 7.6. Sources of information on fertilizer practices preferred by farmers in India.

fertilizer experts from many countries, the Center has these objectives:

1) Providing a world fertilizer information service.

2) Offering technical and administrative services to all countries.

3) Assisting countries in building fertilizer plants and in operating them efficiently.

4) Helping countries to more accurately determine the kinds and amounts of fertilizers needed for maximizing production.

5) Testing the efficiency of foreign sources of fertilizers.

THE METHOD DEMONSTRATION

(Author Unknown)

I'd rather see a lesson
Than hear one any day;
I'd rather you would walk with me
Than merely show the way.

The eye's a better teacher
And more willing than the ear,
And counsel is confusing
But examples always clear.

The best of all the teachers
Are those who live their creeds,
To see good put to action
Is what everybody needs.

I can soon learn to do it
If you'll let me see it done;
I can watch your hands in action
But your tongue too fast may run.

And the counsel you are giving
May be very fine and true,
But I'd rather get my lesson
By observing what you do.

7: 9 INTERNATIONAL RESEARCH ON SOILS OF THE TROPICS

There are now 12 agricultural research centers around the world but none centered on soil science (Table 7.19). One suggestion is to establish a research center by soil orders; e.g., one for Oxisols which occur only in the tropics. Two other centers may serve both tropics and subtropics with centers for Ultisols and Vertisols (Baird, 1978)

There is a proposal to establish a Central Soil Research Institute in India. This will be in addition to Advance Center for Black Soil Research functioning at Dharwad, Karnataka State and member of All India Coordinated Research Projects under the aegis of which research is being carried out at many places.

7: 10 SUMMARY

Chemical composition of a growing plant is not a valid criterion for determining its fertilizer needs. Field plot research is the most accurate technique; and this combined with laboratory soil testing has been the adopted pattern around the world. India has made extensive use of field plot work correlated with soil testing to achieve rational fertilizer recommendations.

Table 7.19. The twelve international centers sponsored by the Consultative Group on International Agricultural Research (CGIAR)

Center	Location	Research	Date of initiation
IRRI (International Rice Research Institute)	Los Baños, Philippines	Rice under irrigation; multiple cropping systems; upland rice	1959
CIMMYT (International Center for the Improvement of Maize and Wheat)	El Batan, Mexico	Wheat (also triticale, barley); maize and cold tolerant sorghum	1964
IITA (International Institute for Tropical Agriculture)	Ibadan, Nigeria	Farming systems; cereals (rice and maize as regional relay stations for IRRI and CIMMYT); grain legume (cowpeas, soybeans, lima beans, pigeon peas); root and tuber crops (cassava, sweet potatoes, yams)	1965
CIAT (International Center for Tropical Agriculture)	Palmira, Colombia	Beef; cassava; field beans; farming systems; swine (minor); maize and rice (regional relay stations to CIMMYT and IRRI)	1968
WARDA (West African Rice Development Association)	Monrovia, Liberia	Regional cooperative effort in adaptive rice research among 13 nations with IITA and IRRI support	1971
CIP (International Potato Center)	Lima, Peru	Potatoes (for both tropics and temperate regions)	1972
ICRISAT (International Crops Research Institute for the Semi-Arid Tropics)	Hyderabad, India	Sorghum; pearl millet; pigeon peas; chickpeas; farming system; groundnuts	1972

IBPGR (International Board for Plant Genetic Resources)	FAO, Rome, Italy	Conservation and utilization of plant genetic material with special reference to cereals	1973
ILRAD (International Laboratory for Research on Animal Diseases)	Nairobi, Kenya	Trypanosomiasis; theileriasis (mainly East Coast Fever)	1974
ILCA (International Livestock Center for Africa)	Addis Ababa, Ethiopia	Livestock production systems	1974
ICARDA (International Center for Agricultural Research in Dry Areas)	Lebanon with major stations in Iran and Syria	Farming systems including livestock with a focus on barley, wheat, broadbeans, lentils, and sheep	1976
International Food Policy Research Institute	Wash. D.C.	Research on food policy	1979

Urea is the principal nitrogenous fertilizer of the world. Many forms of phosphorus fertilizers exist, but most of them start with an ocean-laid rock phosphate. Potassium chloride is the principal potassium fertilizer.

Secondary nutrients are calcium and magnesium, originating primarily from limestones; sulfur is the third secondary nutrient. Micronutrients include iron, zinc, copper, manganese, boron, molybdenum, and chlorine.

Except for nitrogen, fertilizers are seldom applied as a single nutrient. Mixtures of two or more nutrients are usually known as formulations. These are usually dry or slurry mixes with carefully-determined ingredients. Others are fluids; some of which are true solutions and others are supersaturated solutions and colloidal suspensions. Fluid formulations are becoming increasingly popular, especially in developed countries.

Ingredients for dry mixes must be both chemically and physically compatible. Chemical compatibility usually means that the mixture is not deliquescent, i.e., it stays dry enough to spread at ambient relative humidities. Physical compatibility relates to size uniformity of granules to prevent segregation. Urea for use in dry and fluid mixes presents some of the most difficult problems of chemical and physical compatibility.

Organic amendments are used increasingly as substitutes for chemical fertilizers. Animal manures have been appreciated for use as a fertilizer since ancient times. Improved methods of preserving farmyard manure and of compost making are recommended in India. Green manuring is a useful practice for improving soil organic matter content. Sewage sludges have become more popular as soil amendments, as their volume has increased. However, many serious environmental concerns remain to be answered. These include nitrates in drinking waters, heavy metals in the food chain, and pathogens in the environment. Crop residues have been used in greater abundance in recent years.

Many microbes in nature, some free-living and some symbiotic, fix atmospheric dinitrogen (N_2). The *Rhizobium*-legume symbiotic relationship has been known since 1886, but new facts are still being discovered.

Efficient fertilizer use is being promoted by fertilizer festivals, method demonstrations, and by other suitable techniques.

In 1974, the International Fertilizer Development Center was established and in 1978 concentrated research on tropical soils was officially requested.

CITED REFERENCES

Alexander, Martin. "Introduction to Soil Microbiology." John Wiley & Sons, 1977, pages 297–299, 318–321.

Anonymous. "Forage Nitrate Poisoning." South Dakota State University and U.S. Dept. of Agriculture, FS–420, 1975, 4 pages.

Anonymous. "Utilization of Sewage Sludge on Agricultural Land." Univ. of Illinois Soil Management and Conservation Series No. SM–29, 1975, 7 pages.

Anthraper, Mathew. "Fertilizer Promotion: A Novel Approach." Fertilizer News, New Delhi, India, Nov., 1976, pages 3–5.

Baird, G.B. "Need for an International Research and Technology Transfer Network in Tropical Soils." *In* Leslie D. Swindale (ed.) "Soil-Resource Data for Agricultural Development." Hawaii Agr. Exp. Sta., 1978, pages 185–192.

Balfour, E.B. "The Living Soil and the Haughley Experiment." Universe Books, 1975, 383 pages.

Cornell University. "Hortus Third." Liberty Hyde Bailey Hortorium, Ithaca, New York, 1976.

Cunningham, R.S., C.K. Losche, and R.K. Holtje. "Water Quality Implications of Strip-Mined Reclamation by Wastewater Sludge." *In* Proc. 2nd National Conf. on Complete Water Reuse, 4–8 May, 1975. Amer. Inst. of Chem. Eng. and U.S. EPA, Chicago, Illinois.

Council for Agricultural Science and Technology. "Application of Sewage Sludge to Cropland: Appraisal of Potential Hazards of the Heavy Metals to Plants and Animals." U.S. Environmental Protection Agency, EPA–430/9–76–013, 1976.

Das, S.C. and R.K. Chatterjee. "Chemical Composition of Soils in India." Proceedings of 12th Int. Cong. Soil Sci. Part I. "Review of Soil Research in India" 1982, pages 83–109.

Deo, G. and Vinod Kumar. "Secondary Nutrients." Proc. 12th Int. Cong. Soil Sci. Part I. "Review of Soil Research in India" 1982, pages 342–360.

Dhar, B.K. "Fertilizer Consumption Trends and Nutrients for Increasing Fertilizer Use Efficiency." Ind. Farm. Vol. XXXI, No. 7, 1981, pages 3–12.

Donahue, R.L. "India and Its Food Problem." Unpublished manuscript, 1967, 96 pages.

Egawa, Tomoji. "Utilization of Organic Materials as Fertilizers in Japan." *In* "Organic Materials as Fertilizers." Food and Agriculture Organization Soils Bul. No. 27, 1975, pages 266–267.

Environmental Protection Agency. "Sludge Treatment and Disposal. Vol. 1. Sludge Treatment. Vol. 2. Sludge Disposal." U.S. EPA–625/4–78–012, 1978.

Ettlich, W.F. and A.E. Lewis. "A Study of Forced Aeration Composting of Wastewater Sludge." U.S. EPA–600/2–78–057, Cincinnati, Ohio, 1977.

Food and Agriculture Organization of the United Nations and International Atomic Energy Agency. "Soil Organic Matter Studies." STI/PUB No. 438, Vol. 1, 1977, 425 pages.

Frink, C.R. "Agricultural Waste Management." Connecticut Agr. Expt. Sta. Special Soils Bul. 34, 1973, 15 pages.

Garn, Robert. "Role of Urea in Bulk Blending." TVA Fertilizer Bulk Blending Conference, Aug. 1, 2, 1973, Louisville, Kentucky.

Gaur, A.C. "Organic Manures and Bio-Fertilizers." Proc. 12th Int. Cong. Soil Sci. Part I. "Review of Soil Research in India" 1982, pages 278–308.

Goswami, K.P. "Worth of Azotobacter as a Bacterial Fertilizer." Fertiliser News, Nov. 1976, pages 32–34. Fertiliser Assn. of India, New Delhi, India, 1976.

Halderson, James L. and David R. Zenz. "Use of Municipal Sewage Sludge in Reclamation of Soils." *In* "Reclamation of Drastically Disturbed Lands." Amer. Soc. of Agronomy, Crop Science Soc. of America, Soil Science Soc. of America, 1978, pages 355–377.

Hapgood, David, editor. "Policies for Promoting Agricultural Development." Mass. Inst. of Technology, 1965, pages 111–129.

Harkin, John M. "Uses for Sawdust, Shavings, and Waste Chips." U.S.D.A.—Forest Service Research Note FPL–0208, 1969.

Hauck, F.W., team leader. "China: Recycling of Organic Wastes in Agriculture." Food and Agriculture Organization of the United Nations. FAO Soils Bul. 40, 1977, page 27.

Hignett, Travis P. "The Use of Urea in Compound Fertilizers." Chemical Age of India, Vol. 18, No. 11, Nov. 1967, pages 800–809.

Howard, Albert. "An Agricultural Testament." Rodale Press, Emmaus, Pennsylvania, 1972.

Howard, Albert. "Farming and Gardening for Health or Disease." Faber and Faber, London, England, 1945.

Howard, Albert. "The Manufacture of Humus by the Indore Process." Journal of the Ministry of Agriculture, New Delhi, India, 1938.

International Rice Research Institute. "Annual Report for 1974." Los Baños, Philippines, 1975, pages 158, 159.

International Rice Research Institute. "Annual Report for 1979." Los Baños, Philippines, 1980, pages 290, 291.

Kerr, F. F. and John Hatch. "Nitrates in South Dakota Drinking Water." South Dakota State Univ. and U.S. Dept. of Agriculture, FS–604, 3 pages, undated.

King, F.H. "The Soil." The Macmillan Co., New York, 1911, page 288–290.

Knezek, Bernard D. and Robert H. Miller. "Application of Sludges and Wastewaters on Agricultural Land: A Planning and Educational Guide." North Central Regional Research Pub. No. 235, 1976 and U.S. EPA No. MCD–35, 1978.

Larue, J.H., W.D. McClellan, and W.L. Peacock. "Mycorrhizae and

Peach Nursery Nurtition." *In* California Agriculture, Vol. 29, No. 5, 1975, page 7.

McCall, Wade W. "Average Composition of Some Organic Fertilizer Materials." Univ of Hawaii General Home Garden Series No. 15, 1975.

Menge, J.A., L.F. Grand, and L.W. Haines. "The Effect of Fertilization on Growth and Mycorrhizae Numbers in 11-Year-Old Loblolly Pine Plantations." *In* "Forest Science," Vol. 23, No. 1, March, 1977.

Millar, C.E. "Soil Fertility." John Wiley & Sons, New York, 1955, page 399.

Moore, A.W. "Soil Survey, Soil Classification and Agricultural Information Transfer." *In* Leslie D. Swindale (ed.), "Soil-Resource Data for Agricultural Development." Hawaii Agr. Exp. Sta. 1978, pages 193–203.

Motsara, M.R. "Soil Testing in India: Retrospect and Prospect." Fertilizer News, New Delhi, India, Sept. 1976, pages 52–55.

Muhr, Gilbert R., N.P. Datta, H.S. Subramoney, V.K. Leley, and R.L. Donahue. "Soil Testing in India." U.S. Agency for International Development Mission to India, New Delhi, India, 2nd Edition, 120 pages, 1965.

Ohio State University. "Let's Take A Closer Look at Organic Gardening." Extension Bul. 555, 1973.

Olson, O.E. , R.J. Emerick, and L. Lubinus. "Nitrates in Livestock Waters." South Dakota State Univ. and U.S. Dept. of Agriculture, FS–603, 1973, 4 pages.

Parsons, D., C. Brownlee, D. Wetler, A. Maurer, E. Haughton, L. Kornder, and M. Selzak. "Health Aspects of Sewage Effluent Irrigation." Pollution Control Branch, British Columbia Water Resources Service, Dept. of Lands, Forests, and Water Resources, British Columbia, Canada, 1975.

Rajendra Prasad. "Slow Release Fertilizer and Nitrification Inhibitors for Increasing Fertilizer N Efficiency." Ind. Farm. Vol. XXXI, No. 7, 1981, pages 17–22.

Singh, P.K. "Azolla as an Organic Nitrogen Fertilizer for Medium and Low Land Rice." Proc. 12th Int. Cong. Soil Sci. Part I. "Review of Soil Research In India" 1982, pages 236–242.

Smith, Rex L., et al. "Nitrogen Fixation in Grasses Inoculated With *Spirillum lipoferum.*" Science, Vol. 193, 10 Sept. 1976, pages 1003–1005.

Soil Conservation Society of America. "Land Application of Waste Materials." Ankeny, Iowa, 1976, 313 pages.

Subba Rao, N.S., A.N. Sen and K.R. Dadarwal. "*Rhizobium* Research in India." Proc. 12th Int. Cong. Soil. Sci. Part I. "Review of Soil Research in India." 1982, pages 211–224.

Subramoney, H.S. "Maximizing Fertilizer Productivity Through Farmer Development." Fertilizer News, New Delhi, India, April, 1976, pages 17–19.

Tamboli, P.M. and V.K. Misra. "Increase in Crop Production Through Soil Testing in Raipur." Paper presented at the symposium on, "Soil Survey and Soil Testing for Increasing Agricultural Production." Raipur, Madhya Pradesh, India, 1965.

United States Department of Agriculture. "Agrisearch Notes." *In* "Agricultural Research," Vol. 25, No. 6, Dec., 1976, page 17.

United States Dept. of Agriculture. "Improving Soils With Organic Wastes." 1978, 157 pages.

United States Department of Agriculture. "Report and Recommendations on Organic Farming." 1980, 94 pages.

Venkatraman, G.S. "Non-symbiotic Nitrogen Fixation." Proc. Int. Cong. Soil Sci. Part I. "Review of Soil Research in India." 1982, pages 225–235.

Walsh, L.M. "Soil and Applied Nitrogen." Univ. of Wisconsin Extension Fact Sheet A 2519, 1973.

Winton, E.F., R.G. Tardiff, and L.J. McCabe. "Nitrates in Drinking Water." Paper presented at the Bureau of Water Hygiene Conference in Washington, D.C., June 23, 1970.

ADDITIONAL REFERENCES

Arakeri, H.R. "Indian Agriculture." Oxford & IBH Publishing Co., New Delhi, 1982.

Berger, Kermit C. "Introductory Soils." Macmillan Co., New York, 1965.

Donahue, R.L., R.H. Follett, and Rodney Tulloch. "Our Soils and Their Management." Interstate Printers and Publishers, Danville, Illinois, 5th Edition, 1983.

Donahue, R.L., Raymond W. Miller, and John C. Shickluna. "Soils: An Introduction to Soils and Plant Growth." Prentice-Hall, Inc., New Jersey, 5th Edition, 1983.

Follett, R.H., Larry S. Murphy, and R.L. Donahue. "Fertilizers and Soil Amendments." Prentice-Hall, Inc., New Jersey, 1981.

Khanna, S.S. and A.N. Pathak. "Phosphorus." Proc. Int. Cong. Soil Sci. Part I. "Review of Soil Research in India." 1982, pages 223–230.

Krishnamurthy, K.K. "Long Time Fertilizer Experiments." Proc. Int. Cong. Soil Sci. Part I. "Review of Soil Research in India." 1982, pages 453–463.

Rajendra Prasad and G. Thomas. "Nitrogen." Proc. 12th Int. Cong. Soil Sci. Part I. "Review of Soil Research in India." 1982, pages 309–322.

Randhava, N.S. and V.K. Nayyar. "Crop Responses of Applied Micronutrients." Proc. 12th Int. Cong. Soil Sci. Part I. "Review of Soil Research in India." 1982, pages 392–411.

Schaller, F.W. and P. Sutton (Eds.). "Reclamation of Drastically Disturbed Lands." Amer. Soc. of Agronomy, Crop Science Society of America. Soil Science Society of America, Madison, Wisconsin, 1978.

Sekhou, G.S. and A.B. Ghosh. "Potassium." Proc. Int. Cong. Soil Sci. Part I. "Review of Soil Research in India." 1982. pages 331–341.

Soundara Rao, W.V.B. "Bacterial Fertilizers." Indian Council of Agricultural Research, New Delhi, India, 1981.

Takker, P.N. "Micronutrients—Farms, Contents, Distribution in Profile, Indices of Availability and Soil Test Methods." Proc. 12th Int. Cong. Soil Sci. Part I. "Review of Soil Research in India." 1982, pages 361–391.

Tisdale, Samuel L. and Werner L. Nelson. "Soil Fertility and Fertilizers." Macmillan Pub. Co., Inc., New York, 1975.

CHAPTER 8

Soil and Water Conservation

8: 1 INTRODUCTION

A brief study of the increase in population of the world (Fig. 8.1) makes thinking and concerned people frightened. Yet a report on potentially arable soils in the tropics not now used for food production (Table 8.1)

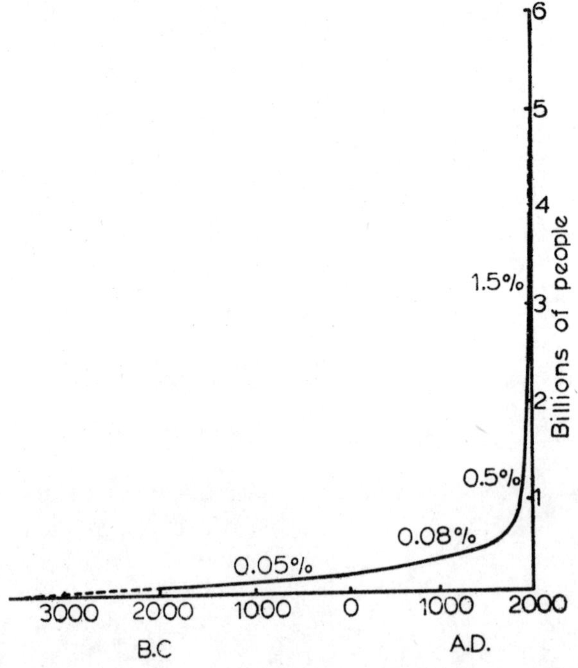

Fig. 8.1. The world population grew at a rate less than 0.1 percent per year until about 1600 A.D.; since then the growth rate has increased to about 1.5 percent per year. The numbers beside the population curve tell the approximate annual increase in population. (*Source:* President's Advisory Committee Panel on World Food Supply, 1967.)

Table 8.1. Kinds of soils in the tropics and their potential arability[a]

Soil classification	Moisture conditions (area in millions of hectares)						Potentially arable	
	Wet all months	Wet most months	Wet-dry	Dry most months	Semi-desert and desert	Total	Million hectares	Percentage of total
Light-colored, base-rich (mostly Aridisols)	4	7	98	378	211	698	134	19
Dark-colored, base-rich (mostly Vertisols, some Mollisols and Inceptisols)	23	56	119	93	2	293	140	48
Moderately weathered and leached (mostly Alfisols and Inceptisols)	4	34	90	75	6	209	77	37
Highly weathered and leached (mostly Ultisols and Oxisols)	931	1084	474	49	2	2540	1071	42
Shallow soils and deep sands (Entisols and shallow families of most soil orders)	81	105	170	153	336	845	77	9
Alluvium (mostly Entisols and Mollisols)	146	124	71	24	5	370	174	47
Total	1189	1410	1022	772	562	4955	1673	34

[a]Technology, farm inputs, relative prices, and irrigation water are assumed to be equal to those in the United States in 1967.

Source: President's Advisory Committee Panel on World Food Supply, 1967.

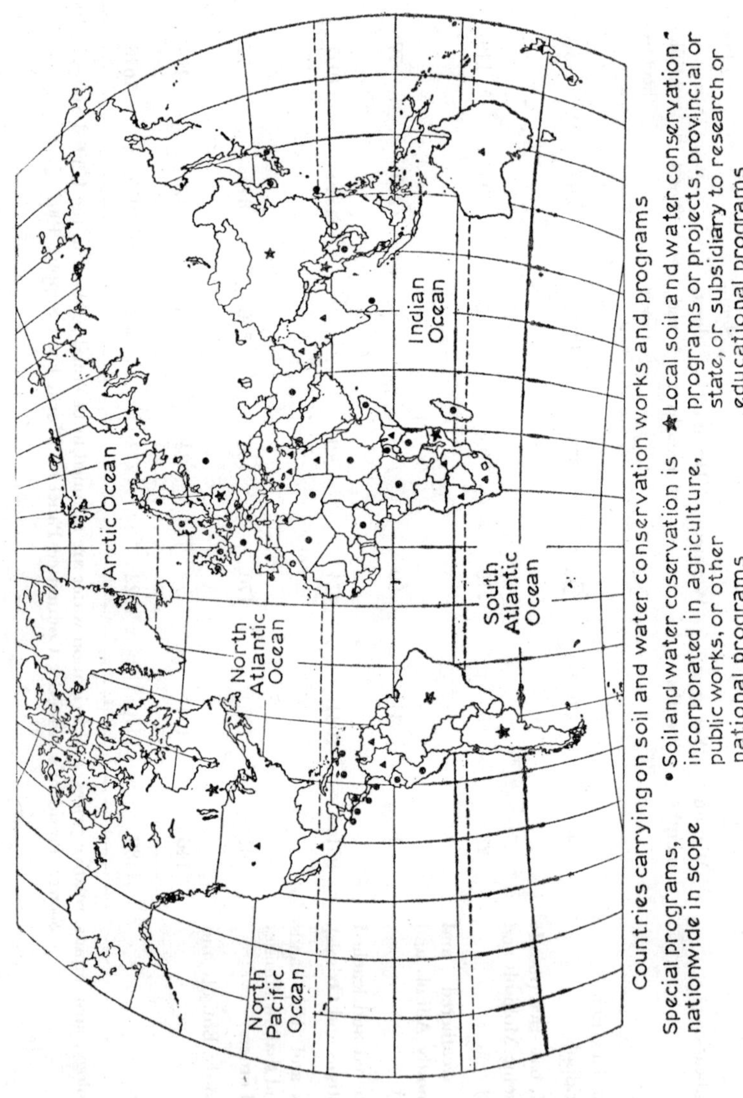

Fig. 8.2. Almost every country has some form of soil and water conservation program. Many of them have been inspired and assisted by the work in the United States. (*Courtesy*: USDA—Soil Conservation Service.)

gives hope. How a person interprets these facts depends on the world-wide experience and attitude of the person. A third segment of the people-food race is the well-organized international agricultural research stations network that is being developed in recent years (See Table 7.19 and Section 7.9).

When the people-food-agricultural research factors are considered together, the authors believe there is hope but no reason for relaxing efforts to promote family planning and food production. However, there is one big gap in the world efforts—there is not enough international emphasis on soil and water conservation.

The subject of soil erosion and its control received major attention in 1935 when the United States established the Soil Conservation Service. Since then, most countries of the world have developed a similar service, often with the help of the United States (Fig. 8.2).

However, even in the United States, erosion is now as serious as it was in 1935. As late as 1971, half of the soils of the United States were limited in their most productive use by erosion and sedimentation (Fig. 8.3). In the United States, nearly four billion metric tons of soil a year erode (Soil and Water Conservation News, 1981). The situation is as bad or even worse in many other countries.

It is the authors' opinion that people-food race cannot be won by people unless more emphasis is placed on world-wide research and application of soil and water conservation. Available and pertinent research and application have been obtained from the most recent literature on the subject of soil and water conservation. To this has been integrated the world-wide experience of the authors, as presented here.

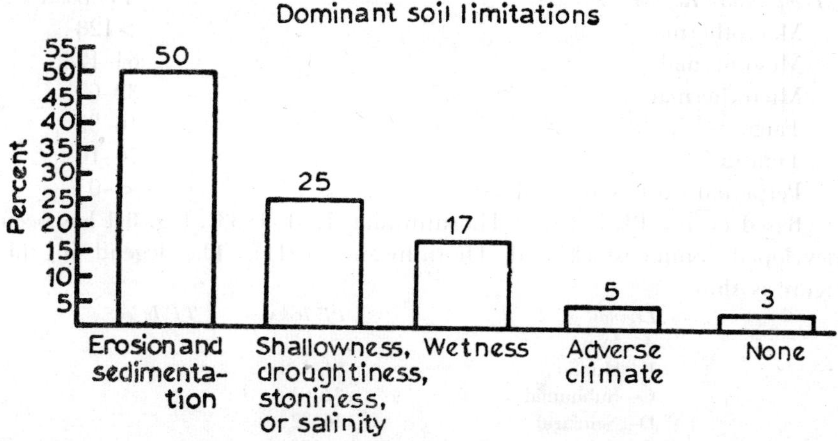

Fig. 8.3. Dominant limitations (subclasses) that restrict the suitability of soils of the United States for more intensive use. Erosion and sedimentation limit the most intensive use of half of the soils of the nation. (USDA—Soil Conservation Service, 1971.)

8: 2 WORLD CLIMATE

Weather is the state of the atmosphere at a given time and place, and climate is average weather. Elements of climate and weather include rainfall, snowfall, sleet, hail, glaze, dew, humidity, winds and temperature. Of these rainfall and temperature are usually the most important in determining vegetation, soils, agricultural use of land, and soil and water conservation.

Several scientists developed indices of precipitation (all forms of moisture reaching the earth) and temperature. Temperature data were used instead of evaporation because more temperature records are available. Furthermore, evaporation is a function of temperature. The best known of these indices is Thornthwaite's, who developed a monthly climatic precipitation/evaporation (*PE*) index, as follows:

$$PE \text{ (climate) index} = \frac{P}{T-10}\ 10/9$$

Where P = total monthly precipitation in inches.

T = mean monthly temperature in degrees Fahrenheit.

Each monthly *PE* index is added to obtain the yearly *PE* index.

Thornthwaite also developed a temperature efficiency (TE) index by this technique: He subtracted 32°F from each mean monthly temperature above 32°F (the temperature at which most plants start to grow). The 12 monthly figures are added to obtain "growing temperatures". Then the annual temperature is divided by four to obtain numbers in the same range as the PE index numbers. The TE indices are named and defined as follows:

Name of Temperature Region	*TE Index*
Macrothermal	>128
Mesothermal	64–128
Microthermal	32–64
Taiga	16–32
Tundra	0–16
Perpetual frost (snow and ice)	<-0

Based on the PE index of Thornthwaite (1931, 1933), Fig. 8.4 has been developed (Blumenstock and Thornthwaite, 1941). The legend in this figure is thus:

Legend	*PE Index*	*TE Index*
A—Wet	> 128	
B—Humid	64–128	
C—Subhumid	32–64	
D—Semiarid	16–32	
E—Arid	< 16	
D′—Taiga		16–32
E′—Tundra		0–16
F′—Perpetual frost		<0

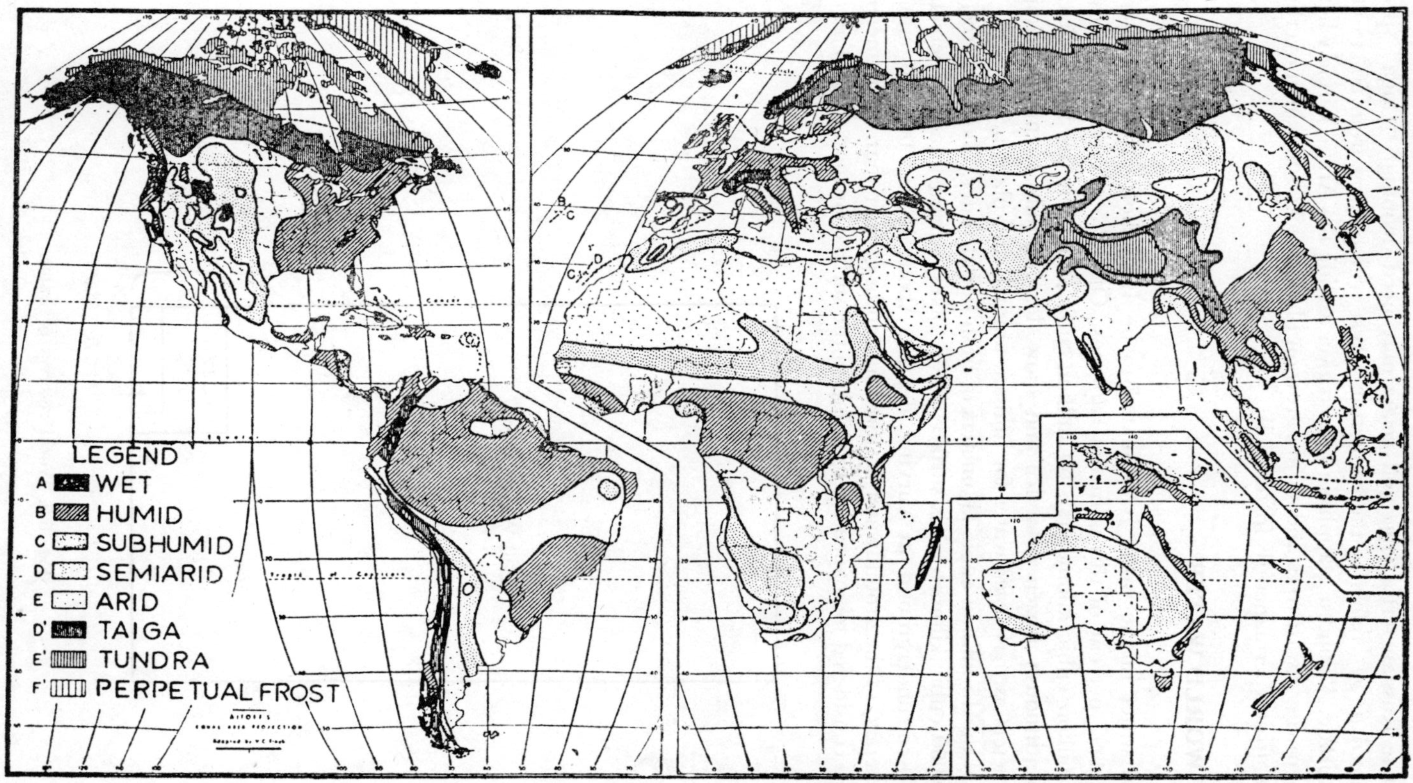

Fig. 8.4. Distribution of the principal climates of the earth.

The Russian terms *taiga* and *tundra* may need defining. "Taiga" (pronounced *tie ga*) refers to the coniferous forest region lying from 50° to 60° N latitude. "Tundra" applies to the region astride the Arctic Circle where low-growing dwarf trees and shrubs grow on black mucky soil which overlies permafrost (permanently frozen soil).

8: 3 WORLD WATER

Total water in the world is estimated to be 1.5 billion cubic kilometers. About 95 percent of this is in the *salty* seas. Of the 5 percent *fresh* water (75 million cubic kilometers), 60 million cubic kilometers are immobilized as continuously frozen polar ice and snow, leaving only 15 million cubic kilometers as *fresh liquid* water for human, animal, and plant needs.

Of the 15 million cubic kilometers of fresh liquid water, about 1 percent (150,000 cubic kilometers) is surface water (lakes, streams) and 99 percent is stored underground at varying depths. About half (7,000,000 cubic kilometers) of the groundwater is stored at depths greater than 1,000 meters and is considered too expensive to pump to the surface for most uses. There-

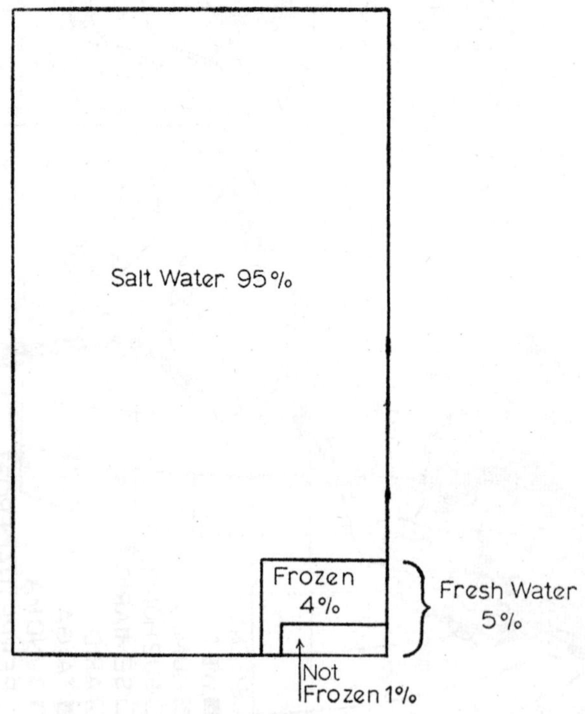

Fig. 8.5. World reserves of water.

fore, for all practical purposes, the 7 million cubic kilometers of fresh groundwater at reasonable depths plus the 150,000 cubic kilometers of surface water is the world's usable water (National Commission on Agriculture, 1976, Part V) (Figure 8.5).

Whereas, at any one time, only 150,000 cubic kilometers of *fresh liquid* water exist in lakes and streams of the world, each year 380,000 cubic kilometers of *fresh* water are in constant circulation. Note that in Fig. 8.6, 380,000 cubic kilometers of water each year (mostly fresh liquid) falls on land and oceans and the same amount is evaporated from the oceans and land.

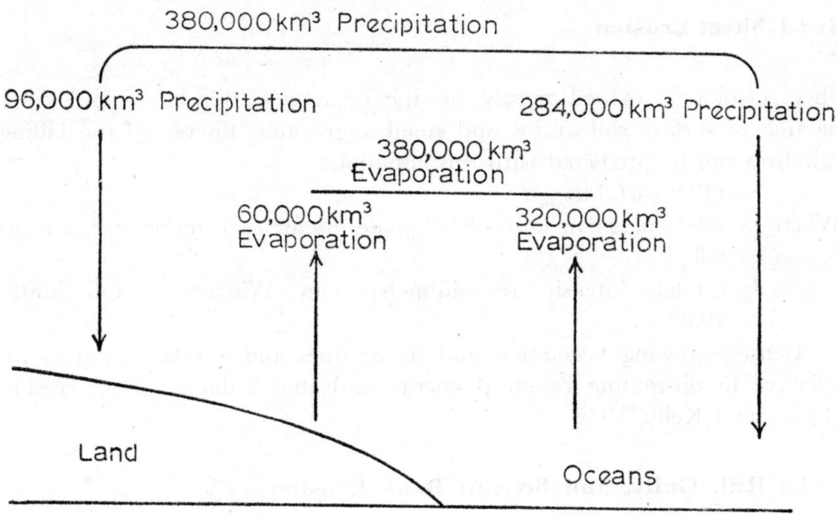

Fig. 8.6. World circulation of fresh water each year.

Note also that precipitation on land exceeds evaporation by 27 percent but over oceans evaporation exceeds precipitation by 13 percent. It is obvious that water vapor from the salty oceans is the source of the additional 27 percent of fresh-water precipitation over land (Lutgens and Tarbuck, 1979).

8: 4 WATER EROSION

The three phases of water erosion are detachment, transport, and deposition (sedimentation). On bare soil, particles are detached by raindrop splash, abrasion by moving soil particles, and by the force of runoff water. Stream banks are eroded by the latter two forces. Transport and deposition of soil particles are controlled by reducing the velocity of the water, the flowing dispersion medium.

Recognized types of water erosion are:

Sheet erosion, caused mostly by raindrop splash and secondarily by surface flow.

Rill erosion results when sediment-laden surface flow concentrates in many parallel channels.

Gully erosion is the result of continued rill erosion whereby a few rills "capture" the surface flow of other rills, thus destroying the usefulness of productive soils.

Stream bank erosion is caused by sediment-laden flowing water scouring the banks of the stream.

8: 4.1 Sheet Erosion

Sheet erosion is caused mostly by the detaching, splashing, and compacting of surface soil grains and small aggregates. Energy of the falling raindrop can be predicted with this equation:

$$e = 118.9 + 87.3 \log_{10} I$$

Where e = total energy in units of 10^3 joules/ha for each millimeter of rainfall.

I = rainfall intensity in millimeters/hour (Wischmeier and Smith, 1958).

Densely-growing vegetation and its residues and animal manures are effective in dissipating raindrop energy and thus reducing sheet erosion (Duley and Kelly, 1939).

8: 4.2 Rill, Gully, and Stream Bank Erosion

Flowing water laden with soil particles causes erosion in rills, gullies, and stream banks. When rainfall infiltrates the soil as fast as it is received, no surface flow results and therefore no erosion except from raindrop splash. With slower infiltration, rain water moves over the surface of a slope, transporting sediment. The less the infiltration, the more the surface flow and the greater the erosion. Water with no sediment has very little erosive action. For this reason, it is crucial to provide living or dead vegetation to break the velocity of the raindrop and thus cause more clean water to move into the soil and therefore less for overland flow. Water erosion can now be predicted with sufficient accuracy to permit the selection of management alternatives with low erosion potential.

8: 4.3 Water Erosion Prediction Equation

The Universal Soil Loss Equation was developed and reported by Wischmeier and Smith in 1965. It has been successfully used, with modifications, in all areas of the United States, Europe, Africa, and India. The equation is:

$$A = R \times K \times LS \times C \times P$$

Where, A = estimated average annual soil loss in metric tons/hectare.

R = rainfall and runoff factor in joules per hectare.

K = soil-erodibility factor, soil loss per unit of rainfall-erosivity. index from bare fallow soil on a 9 percent slope 22.1 meters long, in metric tons per joule.

LS = slope length and steepness factor, dimensionless.

C = cropping-management factor, dimensionless.

P = erosion-control-supporting-practice factor, dimensionless.

This equation can be used to predict long-term average annual sheet and rill erosion under specific land use and management practices.

Details on how to use this equation (for the first time converted to metric units) can be followed in the recent publication by Troeh, Hobbs, and Donahue, 1980.

8: 4.4 Water Erosion Control

The main objectives in controlling soil erosion caused by water are:

1) to reduce dispersion of soil particles,
2) to reduce surface runoff,
3) to put mechanical obstruction in the way of flowing water.

These objectives can be achieved by:

1) Bringing about improvement in physical condition of soil through proper manuring and cropping with a view to increasing water infiltration and holding capacity.

2) Ensuring good crop growth by adopting the recommended agronomic practices for each crop.

3) Practicing other conservation measures like contour bunding, terracing, contour trenching, contour cultivation, strip cropping, mulching, reclamation of gullies etc.

The problem of soil erosion can be tackled best on a catchment basis rather than on individual plots. In the words of Rama Rao (1974), "A true program should be to take into account each patch of land and the plant and animal that live on it, each stream or nala course that flows through it and in short each and every activity of the entire area."

The planning should include:

1) All measures like contour bunding, terracing, diversion channels and other agronomic measures like strip cropping, crop rotations, etc. on land under cultivation.

2) Structural or vegetative gully stabilization.

3) Structures like the use of spurs, revetments, checkdams, retaining walls, etc. to stabilise stream banks.

4) Structures for any combined purpose like irrigation and power to control flood.

5) Desilting basins to hold back sediment.

6) Erosion control measures on non-agricultural lands including highways, railway lines, and other waste lands.

8: 5 WIND EROSION

Wind erosion has the same three phases as water erosion: detachment of soil particles, their movement, and their deposition. Control of wind erosion is accomplished by reducing detachment and movement and increasing deposition. Detachment of soil can be reduced by compaction, aggregation, wetting, stabilizing with living or dead vegetation, and/or by a chemical means such as the use of organic polymers or asphalt emulsion.

Peds and clods larger than 1 mm in diameter are too large and have too much mass to be readily detached. Aggregates between 0.5 mm and 1 mm are too large to be wind-borne but can be moved along the soil surface by strong winds. This movement is known as *surface creep.* Individual soil grains and aggregated soil between 0.05 mm and 0.5 mm (very fine to medium sand, if individual soil particles) move by a series of rolls and leaps, known as *saltation.* Soil grains and aggregates smaller than 0.05 mm in diameter (silt and clay), once detached and suspended in the atmosphere (then known as dust) are usually kept aloft by air turbulence and may be moved long distances before being deposited.

Two such duststorms changed the history of soil and water conservation in the United States and probably in the world. On May 11, 1934 and March 6, 1935, dust clouds from the Great Plains 2,500 km to the west, deposited dust on the Congressmen and their desks in Washington, D.C. Before the Congress was a bill (with dust on it) proposed by Hugh Bennett to establish a permanent Soil Conservation Service from the temporary Soil Erosion Service. On March 25 and April 27, 1935, the bills were signed by President Franklin D. Roosevelt.

8: 5.1 Control of Wind Erosion

Principles of wind erosion control are:

1) Reduce wind velocity at ground level.

2) Remove sediment from the windstream.

3) Reduce the erodibility of the soil.

Practices of wind erosion control include:

1) Establishing ridges of soil from 5 to 10 cm high and at right angles to the direction of the prevailing wind at time of maximum wind erosion.

2) Planting dense vegetation on the eroding field at right angles to the most erosive winds.

3) Establishing a windbreak of vegetation or a structure on the windward side of an eroding field (Troeh, Hobbs, and Donahue, 1980).

8: 5.2 Wind Erosion Prediction Equation

An equation to predict wind erosion is necessary in scientific land-use management to determine "safe" use of soils in fields. For example, on a particular soil will there be less wind erosion with a wheat-summer fallow system, a grain sorghum-winter fallow system, or established permanent range grasses properly grazed.

Factors in the wind erosion prediction equation are as follows:

$$E = f(I', K', C', L', V)$$

Where E = predicted annual soil loss in mt/ha.

f = function of.

I' = soil-erodibility factor in mt/ha/year.

K' = soil ridge roughness factor.

C' = climate factor.

L' = width-of-field factor in meters.

V = vegetative-cover factor.

Although developed at Garden City, Kansas for the Great Plains of the United States, this equation can be modified and used in all countries of the world. (For practical details, consult Troeh, Hobbs, and Donahue, 1980.)

8: 6 PRECIPITATION IN INDIA

Precipitation in India is the result of a massive air movement that takes place during the warmer period of the year from the area south of the equator where the temperatures are lower and pressure is higher, towards the vast low pressure areas in central Asia and north India. Towards the end of May the large land mass gets heated and causes the warmed air to rise. As it rises it creates suction from all sides. Since India is to one side of the land mass, air is pulled across it in a northern direction (Fig. 8.7). As temperatures over the land mass start falling in winter, the cool air mass moves gradually in the reverse direction from October onwards (Fig. 8.8).

The movement of air masses and as such the rainfall over India is seasonal. Indians and Arabs knew about these rainy seasons as early as 326 B.C.

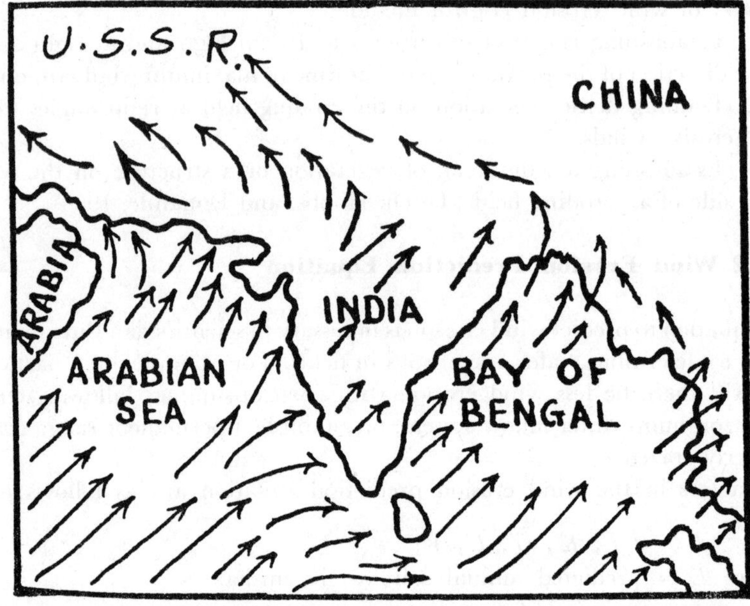

Fig. 8.7. Average wind currents over India in July during the southwest monsoon.

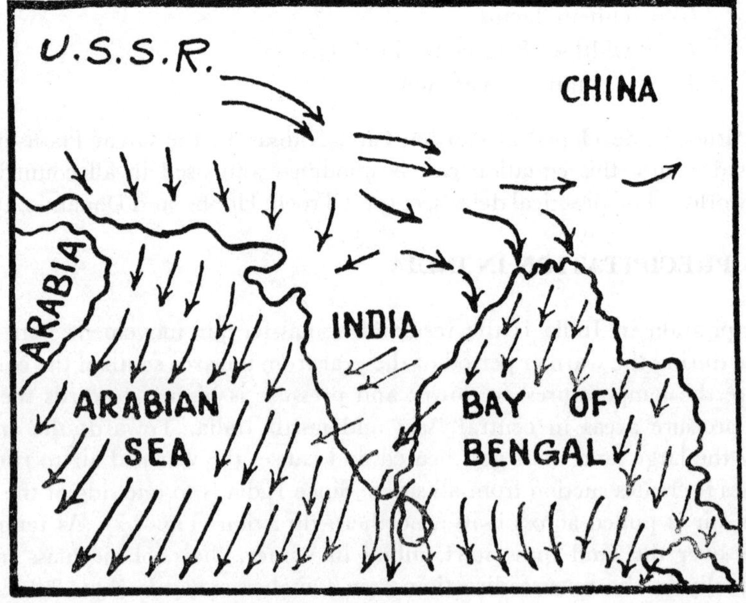

Fig. 8.8. Average wind current over India in January during the northeast monsoon.

and they are known as monsoons. The word 'monsoon' is derived from the Arabic word 'mausim' meaning wind. The season from June to September is referred to as the period of the southwest monsoon and from October to January as the northeast or retreating monsoon.

8: 7 FATE OF PRECIPITATION IN INDIA

On the average, India receives about 120 cm of precipitation a year, mostly as rainfall. On a volume basis, this is 400 million hectare-meters. The fate of this precipitation is estimated as follows:

Evaporation—18 percent
Surface runoff—29 percent
Soil infiltration—53 percent

(Fig. 8.9) (National Commission on Agriculture, 1976)

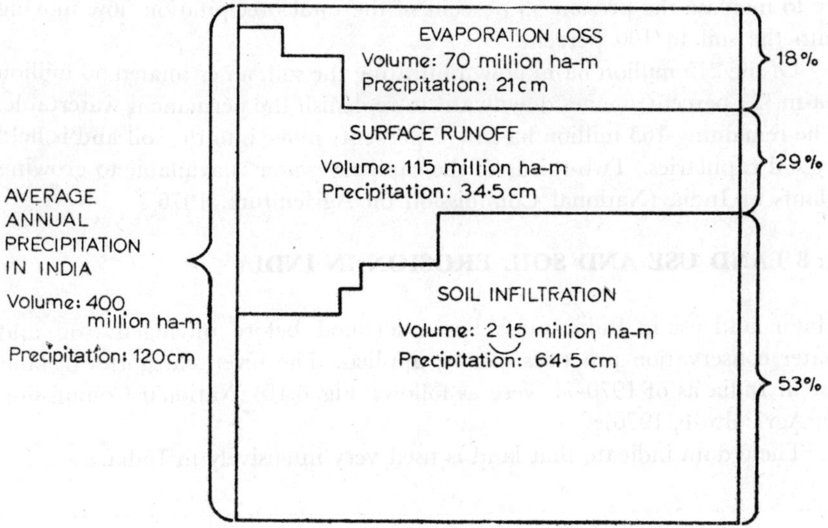

Fig. 8.9. Fate of precipitation in India. (National Commission on Agriculture, 1976.)

An average of 120 cm of precipitation a year in India's tropical and subtropical climate would be adequate for two or three rainfed crops each year if it were well-distributed. But over most of India, about 70 percent of the annual precipitation is received during a four-month period, June through September.

World-wide efforts have been made to increase the total amount of precipitation but successes have usually been offset by failures. The technique usually involves the introduction of frozen carbon dioxide or silver iodide into a "wet" cloud. The same technique has been used successfully to disperse fog around airports and to moderate hail, lightning, and hurricanes (Lutgens and Tarbuck, 1976).

For all practical purposes, the total amount of precipitation received is constant, and its wise management is the only way to increase production. Nothing can be done to reduce the 18 percent of total precipitation lost by evaporation, i.e., nothing economical. However, wise management can reduce the 29 percent lost by surface runoff. The establishment of terraces and bunds along with contour tillage can reduce runoff water and increase infiltration. Likewise, the growing of crops for as many months of the year as possible will reduce runoff losses by increasing infiltration.

The wisest management of soil and water is to encourage every drop of rainfall to move into the soil at the point where it strikes the earth. When this happens, evaporation will be at a minimum, there will be *no erosion,* and crop production will be at a maximum. The objective should therefore be to increase the present 53 percent of the total precipitation now moving into the soil to 100 percent.

Of the 215 million ha-m now infiltrating the soil, an estimated 50 million ha-m (23 percent) moves downward to replenish the permanent watertable. The remaining 165 million ha-m (77 percent) move into the soil and is held by soil capillaries. Two-thirds of the capillary water is available to growing plants in India (National Commission on Agriculture, 1976).

8: 8 LAND USE AND SOIL EROSION IN INDIA

Major land use in India must be understood before intelligent soil and water conservation practices can be applied. The seven categories of land use in India as of 1970-71 were as follows (Fig. 8.10) (National Commission on Agriculture, 1976):

These data indicate that land is used very intensively in India.

Land use	Hectarage (million hectares)	Percentage of total area
Cropped	165	50.3
Forests	66	20.1
Deserts, mountains	29	8.8
Culturable waste	16	4.9
Nonagricultural	16	4.9
Permanent pasture	13	4.0
Other	23	7.0
Total	328	100.0

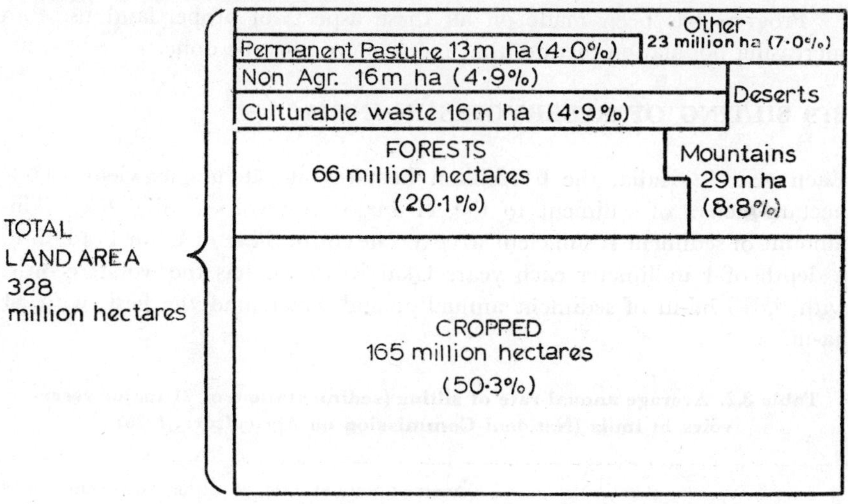

Fig. 8.10. Major land use in India, 1970-71 (National Commission on Agriculture, 1976) (*Note:* m=million).

Soil erosion is caused by water as well as wind in India. According to one estimate (Das & Mukherjee, 1980) it affects as much as 175 million hectares out of the total geographical area of 328 million hectares. It not only affects the productivity of land directly but it also results in silting up of reservoirs and tanks. Erosion by wind is predominant in the states of Rajasthan, Haryana, Gujarat and also in the coastal areas. It is estimated that an area of 32 million hectares including 7 million hectares under sand dunes is affected by wind erosion.

The entire rainfed cultivated land is subject to water erosion and in certain parts to wind erosion also. Areas, where paddy is cultivated and where irrigated crops are grown, are protected to a good extent in one way or the other. The remaining uncultivated areas excluding reserved forests are subjected to erosion hazards to varying degrees. Reserved forests being scientifically managed and well stocked can be said to be satisfactorily protected. Other kinds of forests (like the protected and unclassified) are also affected to a large extent by erosion.

Soil and water conservation problems in India are varied and complex. It, therefore, requires these intensive soil and water conservation techniques to be applied: vegetative and mechanical control of water erosion, wind erosion, sea-shore erosion; flood control structures; drainage and other control measures to reduce waterlogging; better irrigation methods; soil surveys to identify priority areas; soil testing to maintain or increase productivity; reclamation of saline and sodic soils; and viable alternatives to shifting cultivation.

Progress has been made on all these aspects of proper land use, but increasing population dictates that much more must be done.

8:9 SILTING OF RESERVOIRS IN INDIA

Each year in India, the 64 million hectares of catchments yield 29,085 hectare-meters of sediment to the 21 major reservoirs (Table 8.2). This amount of sediment is sufficient to cover the entire State of Uttar Pradesh to a depth of 1 millimeter each year. Ukai Reservoir has the worst records, with 6,848 ha-m of sediment annually; and Machkund the best, with 51 ha-m.

Table 8.2. Average annual rate of silting (sedimentation) of 21 major reservoirs in India (National Commission on Agriculture, 1976)

Reservoir	Average annual rate of silting (sedimentation)*	
	Total hectare-meters	Hectare-meters per 100 sq km of catchment
Ukai	6,848	14.29
Narmada	4,959	9.52
Bhakra Nangal	3,521	6.14
Hirakud	2,968	6.28
Tungabhadra	1,702	6.54
Nizamsagar	1,214	6.55
Beas, Unit II	987	14.29
Panchet	978	10.00
Matatilla	919	4.00
Gandhisagar	811	6.02
Mahi, Stage II	691	6.61
Maithon	685	13.10
Tawa	670	15.60
Ghod	553	15.24
Ramganga	546	18.19
Mayurakshi	294	16.43
Lower Bhawani	176	4.19
Kangsabati	142	9.65
Dhantiwad	130	5.95
Sivajisagar	119	15.24
Machkund	51	3.57
Total	29,085	
Average Annual	1,385	

**Note:* Includes annually deposited plus total suspended sediment.

On the basis of catchment area, Ramganga is the worst with 18.19 ha-m of sediment per 100 sq km of area; and again Machkund the least, with 3.57.

India has been working to reduce the sedimentation of the reservoirs by:

1) Making soil and land use surveys. In the catchment areas of the reservoirs, each soil mapping unit is interpreted into hydrologic groups (rainfall runoff potential), erosion-intensity units, sediment yield indices, irrigability classes, and paddy soil groups. These interpretive groupings are for the purpose of utilizing each soil mapping unit for its maximum production potential and at the same time reduce erosion losses to a minimum (Bali and Karale, 1978).

2) Establishing more weather stations and upgrading existing ones.

3) Promoting soil-conserving crops such as grasses and trees.

4) Promoting bunding.

5) Measuring sediment in rivers.

6) Conducting research on unsolved technical and human problems.

8: 10 INNOVATIVE SOIL AND WATER MANAGEMENT IN INDIA

Vertisols are black clay (cotton) soils developed on alkaline parent material in semiarid areas. They are very extensive, occupying 546,000 sq km in central India (Raychaudhuri, 1966).

Efficient management of Vertisols requires the application of new research technology. Traditional management consists of fallowing the soils during the four months of the monsoon rains, then planting a crop that matures on residual moisture (from field capacity to the wilting percentage).

New technology permits the growing of a crop during the monsoon rains and a second crop after the rains have ceased (ICRISAT, 1976-1977). The newer techniques, proved over a five-year period, include "dry planting" of sorghum, pigeonpea, and maize (corn) just prior to the onset of the monsoon rains. 'Dry planting" permits rapid crop establishment, no loss of soil water because of tillage incident to establishing a seedbed, and crop establishment ahead of insect and disease buildup.

A second innovation resulting from research on Vertisols is to replace traditional bunding with graded (150 cm) beds-and-furrows on a grade of 0.4 to 0.6 percent slopes draining into grassed waterways with runoff water collected in small tanks (ponds) and used for subsequent irrigation. Such a system reduces soil erosion, provides for a more uniform distribution of rain water, and greatly increases crop yields. By contrast, traditional bunding may decrease crop yields by impounding an excess of water above the bunds and reducing productivity of soil from areas where the soil was taken to build the bunds. The water balance in deep Vertisols is shown in Fig. 8.11.

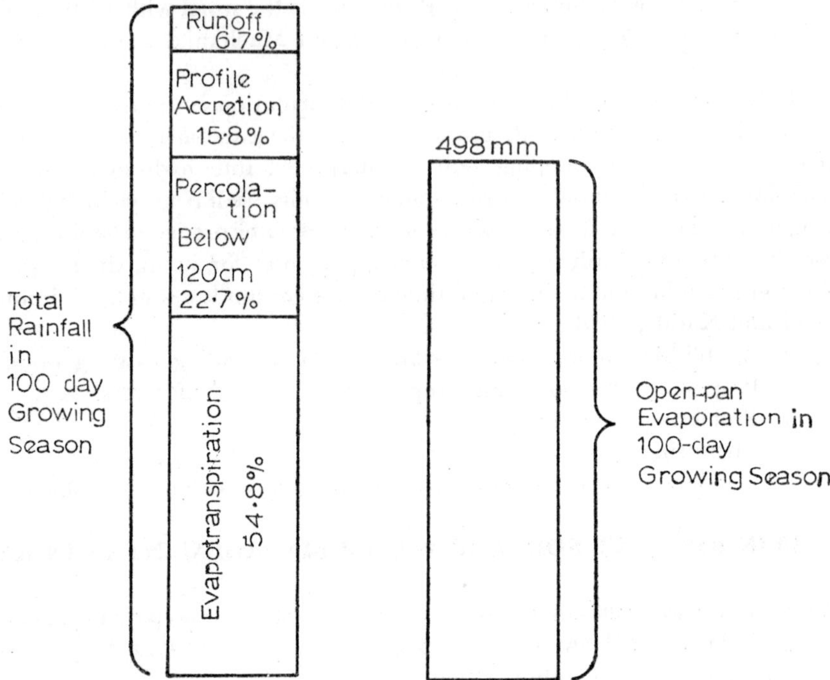

Fig. 8.11. Water balance in deep Vertisols in India (ICRISAT Annual Report, 1976-1977).

8:11 SUMMARY

Soil and water conservation is concerned with the wise use of these two essential resources for survival of civilization. Their wise use will determine whether future population can be adequately fed.

All countries of the world have serious erosion problems but most of them have not had a national erosion assessment. The last assessment in the United States indicated that erosion and sedimentation limited maximum potential use on half of all soils. This is especially serious, considering the fact that since 1935, millions of dollars each year have been spent on controlling erosion. It is hopeful that most countries of the world, including India, have a soil and water conservation program.

Although there is a world-wide water balance, i.e., the total amount of precipitation equals the total evaporation, it is little comfort when rains fail in certain areas and crops dry up and soils blow away or excess rains bring flood to drown both crops and people and erode soils.

The three phases of both water and wind erosion are detachment of soil particles, their transport, and their deposition. In water erosion, detachment of soil particles can be reduced by establishing and maintaining a living or dead vegetative cover to absorb the energy of the falling raindrop. In wind erosion, detachment can be reduced by soil compaction, aggregation, wetting, establishment of a living or dead vegetative cover, or stabilization with certain chemicals. Transport of soil particles by water or wind can be reduced, and thereby deposition hastened, by reducing the velocity of the water and of the surface wind by erecting barriers. Water and wind barriers on a field scale include densely growing crops, mulches, and manures. In addition, windbreaks are used for reducing wind velocity and thereby increasing deposition of wind-blown soil particles. Erosion problems are best tackled on a catchment basis rather than on individual plots.

There is an equation for estimating water erosion and one for estimating wind erosion. The estimates are valid for deciding what soil and water conservation practices should be adopted to achieve perpetual soil productivity.

Soil and water conservation is especially critical in India because of the spatial and temporal nature of rainfall. Spatially, annual rainfall varies from 10 to 1,000 centimeters; temporally, 70 percent of the annual rainfall occurs during a four-month period—June to September. Nevertheless, under these handicaps, India produces crops on more than half of its total land area. The problems of soil erosion in India are varied and complex needing urgent and increased attention.

CITED REFERENCES

Anonymous. "Improved Agronomic Practices In Dryland Crops in India." Indian Council of Agricultural Research. 1979.

Arakeri, H.R., G.V. Chalam, P. Satyanarayana, and R.L. Donahue. "Soil Management in India." Asia Publishing House, London, 2nd Edition, 1962.

Bali, Y.P. and R.L. Karale. "Soil-Survey Interpretations for Watershed Development." *In* Leslie D. Swindale (ed.), "Soil-Resource Data for Agricultural Development." Univ. of Hawaii, 1978, pages 73–84.

Blumenstock, David I. and C. Warren Thornthwaite. "Climate and the World Pattern." *In* U.S. Department of Agriculture, "Climate and Man." Yearbook of Agriculture, 1941, pages 98–127.

Das D.C. and B.K. Mukherjee. "National Perspective on Soil and Moisture Conservation." Agri. Eng. To-day. Vol. 4, No. 3, 1980, pages 11–17.

Das, D.C. "Influence of Current Land Use Policies on Some Watershed Problems." Paper presented in National Workshop on Westershed Management sponsored by GOI/UNESCO, Forest Research Institute, Dehra Dun, India, April 1981, (unpublished).

Duley, F.L. and L.L. Kelly. "Effect of Soil Type, Slope, and Surface

Conditions on Intake of Water." Nebraska Agr. Exp. Sta. Res. Bull. 112, 1939.

ICRISAT Annual Report, 1976–1977. International Crops Research Institute for the Semi-Arid Tropics, Hyderabad, India, pages 14-17.

Indian, Meteorological Department "Rainfall Atlas of India, "Meteorological Office, Pune, India, 1971.

Indian Meteorological Department "Tracks of Storms and Depressions in the Bay of Bengal and Arabian Sea 1877–1970." Meteorological Office, Pune, India, 1979.

Indian Oilseed Atlas, The Indian Central Oilseeds Committee, Hyderabad, Andhra Pradesh, 1958.

Lutgens, Frederick K. and Edward J. Tarbuck. "The Atmosphere: An Introduction to Meteorology." Prentice-Hall, Inc., 1979, 413 pages.

National Commission on Agriculture (India). "Report of the National Commission on Agriculture, Part IV. Climate and Agriculture." Govt. of India Press, New Delhi, India, 1976.

National Commission on Agriculture (India). "Report of the National Commission on Agriculture, Part V. Resource Development." Govt. of India Press, New Delhi, India, 1976.

Normand, C.W.B. "The Weather of India." The Indian Science Congress Assn., Calcutta, 1937, pages 1–6, 8, 10, 11, 1937.

President's Advisory Committee Panel on World Food Supply, The White House, Wash. D.C., 1967.

Rama Rao, M.S.V. "Soil Conservation in India." Indian Council of Agricultural Research, New Delhi, 1974.

Raychaudhuri, S.P. "Land and Soil." National Book Trust, New Delhi India, 1966.

Soil and Water Conservation News, USDA—Soil Conservation Service, Wash. D.C., 1981. (A monthly publication.)

Thornthwaite, C. Warren. "The Climates of the Earth." Geographic Review, Vol. 23, pages 433–440, 1933.

Thornthwaite, C. Warren. "The Climate of North America According to a New Classification." Geographic Review, Vol. 21, pages 633–655, 1931.

Troeh, Frederick R., J. Arthur Hobbs, and R.L. Donahue. "Soil and Water Conservation for Productivity and Environmental Protection." Prentice-Hall, Inc., Englewood Cliffs, New Jersey, 1980.

Wischmeier, W.H. and D.D. Smith. "Rainfall Energy and Its Relations to Soil Loss." Transactions American Geophysical Union, 39: 285–291, 1958.

Wischmeier, W.H. and D.D. Smith. "Predicting Rainfall—Erosion Losses from Cropland East of the Rocky Mountains." USDA—Agriculture Handbook, No. 282, 1965.

ADDITIONAL REFERENCES

Donahue, R.L, Raymond W. Miller, and John C. Shickluna. "Soils: An Introduction to Soils and Plant Growth." Prentice-Hall, Inc., 5th Edition, 1983.

Kamitbar, N.V., S.S. Sirur and D.H. Gokhale. "Dry Farming in India." Indian Council of Agricultural Research, 1960.

President's Science Advisory Committee. "The World Food Problem." The White House, 1967. Vol. I Summary, Vol. II and III, Report of the Panel on the World Food Supply.

Proceedings of the Symposium on "Problems of Indian Arid Zone, Jodhpur." Nov.-Dec. 1964. Ministry of Education, Government of India.

Seminar Proceedings on "Shifting Cultivation in North East India." North East India Council for Social Science Research, Shillong, Meghalaya, India, 1976.

Soil Science Society of America. "Soil Conditioners." SSSA Special Publication Series No. 7, Madison, Wisconsin, 1975.

Tamhane, R.V., D.P. Motiramani, Y.P. Bali, and R.L. Donahue. "Soils: Their Chemistry and Fertility in Tropical Asia." Prentice-Hall of India Private Ltd., New Delhi, 1970.

Thorne, D. Wynne and Marlowe D. Thorne. "Soil, Water, and Crop Production." Avi Pub. Co., Westport, Connecticut, 1979.

CHAPTER 9

Irrigation and Drainage

9: 1 INTRODUCTION

Irrigation is necessary on arid soils for growing most of the world's useful crops. It is startling to most people to learn that according to one source, one-third of the soils of the world are classified as arid (Heady, 1980). Another reference lists the percentage of arid soils as 18.8 percent (Soil Conservation Service, 1972). The discrepancy is understandable because of variations in criteria for determining aridity. Most semiarid soils also need irrigation water to make them more productive. Crops suffer a great deal in many parts of India for want of timely rainfall and adequate irrigation.

In preparation for establishing new irrigation facilities, the command area must be studied scientifically. A standard soil survey is one of the first assessments to be made. Many questions are required to be answered before venturing on an irrigation project.

Are the soils sufficiently level to use row or flood irrigation? Are the soils fertile? Will deep percolation be excessive? Is drainage adequate? Is soil and water salinity and/or sodicity normal or excessive? Is the catchment area large enough and rainfall adequate to fill the reservoir and to supply the needed hectare-meters of water? *Average* rainfall may be sufficient but what about its variation from year to year? In arid and semiarid regions, climatic variability increases with aridity.

Do the farmers understand irrigation techniques? Are access roads adequate? Is a consolidation of farmers' holdings necessary to achieve efficiency of irrigation? Will cropping systems become sufficiently more intensive to pay for the increased cost of the new irrigation water? Is there a market for the new or increased amount of crops?

9: 2 SOURCES OF IRRIGATION WATER

Water is the most important single requirement in the growth of plants and rainfall is the main source of water.

Water resources of India have been assessed from time to time right from the beginning of the century. Rough approximation was attempted by the first Irrigation Commission (1901-1903) in the beginning of the century and the latest estimate is by the National Commission on Agriculture, 1976. According to this estimation the country receives about 400 million hectare meters of rain water annually and 75 percent of it during the four monsoon months from June to September. About 125 million hectare meters of this is directly transpired by the vegetation. It is estimated that out of the remaining 275 million hectare meters about 77 million hectare meters would become available for irrigation and 28 million hectare meters for other uses. It is also estimated that it would be possible to bring about 84 and 110 million hectare area under irrigation out of the expected 200 and 210 million hectares of gross cultivated area by A.D. 2000 and A.D. 2025 respectively.

9:3 IRRIGATION WATER QUALITY

Irrigation water is needed in largest quantities in arid and semiarid regions where its quality is most likely to be inferior. Total soluble salts have degraded more irrigation water than any other contaminant; followed by the proportion of sodium to calcium and magnesium; and probably then by excessive boron, bicarbonate, chlorides, lithium, and selenium.

Surface irrigation water is also usually degraded by suspended sediments such as sands, silts, clays, and organic matter. Such sediments fill reservoirs and water channels and thus reduce their capacity and useful life. Filters and settling basins can be used to reduce the amount of sediment once it is suspended in water. However, the best practice is to reduce erosion and sedimentation by practicing soil and water conservation (See Chapter 8, Soil and Water Conservation).

The relative salinity hazard and the relative sodium hazard of irrigation waters can be evaluated by using Fig. 9.1. To help in interpreting this figure, "medium salinity hazard" lies between 250 and 750 micromhos/cm of electrical conductivity, as measured on a Wheatstone Bridge; and "medium sodium hazard" lies between a sodium adsorption ratio (SAR) of 10 and 18.

Underground water is tapped for irrigation all over the world. About one-third of the total irrigated area in the country depends on ground water at present. It is estimated that a gross area of about 40 million hectares could be irrigated with groundwater in A.D. 2025. The quality of groundwater varies from region to region and saline water with E.C. up to 10,000 micromhos have been used for raising some crops (Bhumbla, 1972).

A wise use of the poor quality water is possible by developing and adopting appropriate land layout and crop growing techniques and also by choosing and growing suitable crops.

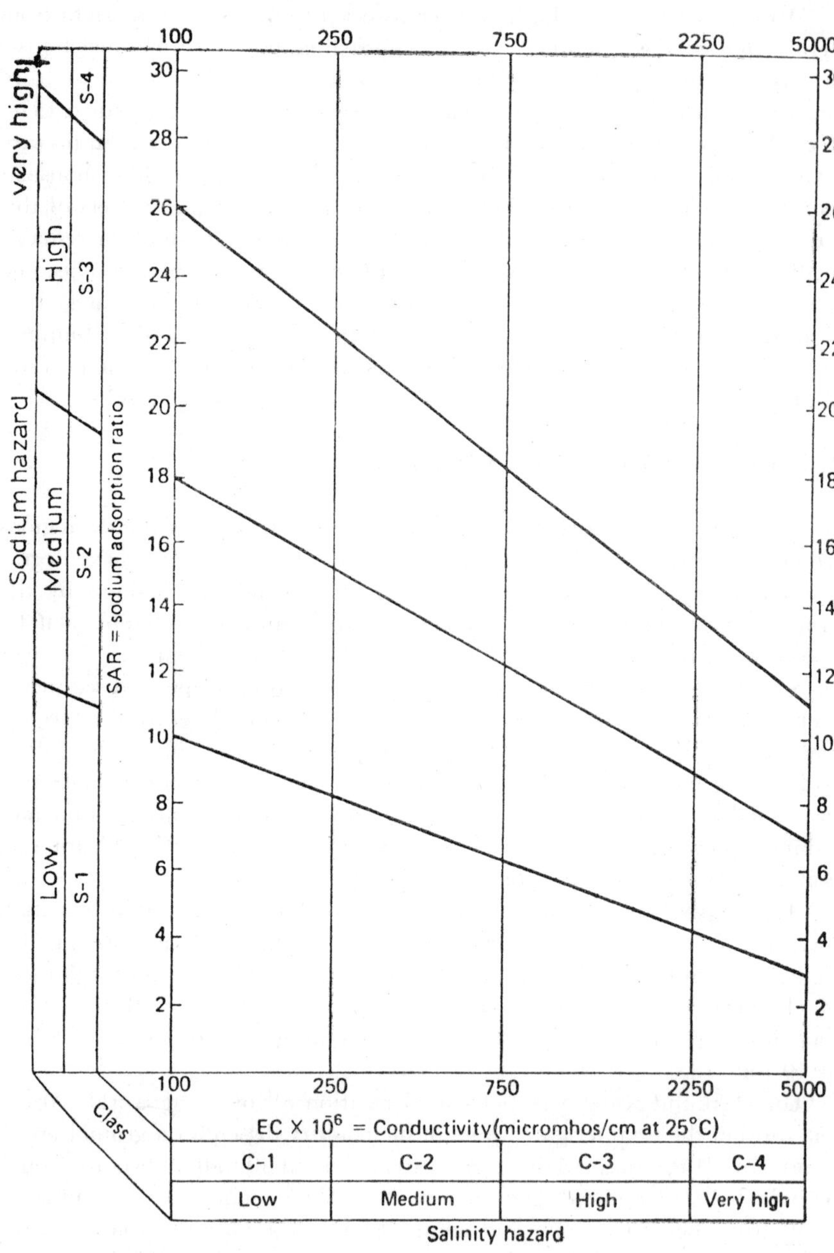

Fig. 9.1. USDA classes of salinity and sodium hazard for irrigation water. (*Source: Diagnosis and Improvement of Saline and Alkali Soils*, USDA Agr. Handbook 60,1954.)

9: 4 SEWAGE WATER FOR IRRIGATION

In most villages throughout India, house-drains end in one or more banana or papaya plants and a patch of green vegetables. In Agra, Bangalore, Gwalior, and Pune, open city drains are lined with vegetable or grass plots irrigated by a diversion ditch which taps the city drainage channels. Also in Pune as well as in Delhi, city sewage effluent is mixed with water in irrigation canals. This enriched mixture is used to irrigate vegetables, grapes, sugarcane, lawns, and other horticultural crops. Sewage effluents from Hyderabad have been used for irrigating field crops such as maize. Similarly paragrass is commonly grown with effluent water around Bangalore. However, precautions must be taken to reduce the hazard of spread of intestinal parasites and diseases. One technique to reduce this hazard is to allow the soil surface to dry between subsequent irrigations. Another is to use the sewage water for field crops and not for vegetables to be eaten raw.

A project for scientific utilization of sewage was started in India in 1896, with the establishment of the first sewage farm near Ahmedabad. At present about 220 urban centers are covered. Potential availability is estimated to be of the order of 1,000 million gallons per day which is sufficient to cover an area of about 0.25 million hectare (Sorkar, 1981).

9: 5 IRRIGATION METHODS

The principal methods of irrigation in India are those involving surface flow and those using special techniques. Surface flow methods include wild flooding, furrow, border, and basin. Other methods include pot, trickle, and sprinkler techniques. Each method will be evaluated on the basis of its adaptations, advantages, and disadvantages (Arakeri, et al., 1962 and Donahue, Miller, Shickluna, 1983).

9: 5.1 Wild Flooding

Wild flooding is one of the oldest, most primitive, and most inefficient of irrigation methods. It is adapted in areas where water for irrigation is plentiful and available at the highest elevation in each field. The technique consists of releasing a flow of water at the highest point in a field and with a shovel "teasing" the water over the surface of the field.

Advantages include a very low level of expertise, low cost, usefulness on all medium- to fine-textured soils, it cannot be damaged by livestock, and it does not interfere with tillage.

Disadvantages of the wild flooding technique are: inefficient use of water, nonuniform distribution of water and therefore irregular crop response, excessive soil erosion on steeper slopes and some areas may require artificial drainage to reduce ponding.

9: 5.2 Furrow Irrigation

Around the world some kinds of furrow irrigation are used more than any other method. The technique usually consists of conducting water through an open ditch and then into furrows, either straight or on the contour, that are established on a grade of 0.25 to 2 percent. Crops are usually planted on top or sides of the ridges or even in furrows: sometimes the ridges are broad enough to plant two or three rows. For most uniform water application, ridges and furrows should be no longer than 70 m on sandy soils and 200 m on clay soils.

The irrigator should aim to release water down each furrow as fast as possible without causing erosion. In this way, the soil will be more uniformly wetted along the furrow. Another general aim is to determine the time it takes water to flow to the end of the row, then continue adding water for an equal length of time.

Furrow irrigation is adapted to a variable water supply, slopes as steep as six percent (if on the contour), medium-to-slowly-permeable soils and farms where the furrows can be laid out with a level.

Advantages of furrow irrigation are that the method results in relatively high water efficiency, is relatively cheap to install and to maintain, and with contouring can be adapted to flat slopes up to six percent.

Disadvantages of furrow irrigation are that it requires a person skilled in the use of a level to establish, serious erosion is a hazard; conveyance ditches may interfere with field traffic; sediment must be removed periodically from water channels and furrows; and adequate drainage must be provided at the lower ends of the rows.

9: 5.3 Border and Basin Irrigation

Border and basin irrigation methods consist of establishing a small bund (ridge) around an area to be flooded and flooding each confined area in sequence with a predetermined amount of water.

To establish border irrigation, parallel bunds are made from 5 to 15 m apart, leveled from bund to bund but sloping the length of each strip from one to two percent. Strips may vary in length from 30 meters for sandy loam soils to 150 meters for clay soils. On sloping land the border strips should be established on the contour. Each bordered strip is then irrigated by flooding (Fig. 9.2).

Basin irrigation is established in a similar way to border irrigation except that the former encloses a smaller area, say around one or more orchard

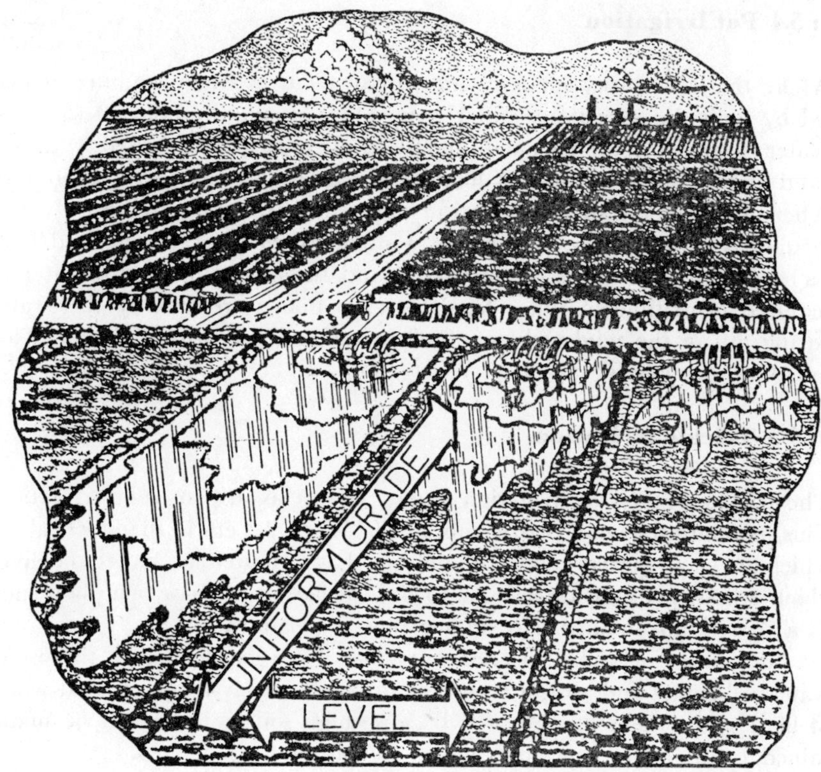

Fig. 9.2. The field has been prepared for border irrigation by building small levees around each leveled area. Then the areas are flooded in rotation to irrigate them (*Courtesy:* USDA).

trees or a field of wetland (paddy) rice. For efficient irrigation each basin must be level. However, level basins can be established on the contour on sloping lands.

The border and basin methods of irrigation are adapted to most soil textures, most gentle slopes, high-value-crops, but are restricted to areas where an expert with a level can lay out and build the bunds (levees).

Advantages of the border and basin methods are that water is used efficiently, water is applied uniformly when the strip or basin are properly established, labor requirement is small, there is a low maintenance cost, and the method is rapid.

Disadvantages of these methods are that the initial cost is fairly high, a large supply of water is needed, deep and uniform soils are required, expert leveling and construction are necessary, specialized land-leveling equipment must be used, and drainage must be provided.

9: 5.4 Pot Irrigation

Where there is nearby surface water, small fields in India are often irrigated by individuals carrying water pots. The pots usually hold 10-15 liters. Water is carried in the pots and poured on the crop to be irrigated, with one hand at the mouth of the pot helping to scatter the water as it is poured. Where labor is cheap and plentiful and the water source close by, this method is cost-effective. Burying of a small earthen pot is suggested near each plant when crop is broad spaced and the pot is filled with water as required from time to time. Needs of crop plants are met by this water oozing out of the unglazed pot. Such a method has proved practical for tomatoes, brinjals (eggplant) etc.

9: 5.5 Trickle Irrigation

The trickle method of irrigation is also known as drip or tube irrigation. This method uses small plastic tubes from 1.5 to 2.5 cm in diameter, along which are small outlets known as emitters. Each emitter can be set to deliver about 3 liters per hour directly on the soil surface at the base of a plant such as a tree in an orchard. No surface flow is permitted.

Advantages of trickle irrigation are that it is very efficient in the use of water, all slopes and all soil textures can be effectively irrigated, and water of high salt content can be used because high soil moisture can be maintained to dilute the concentration of salt around plant roots.

Disadvantages include its nonadaptation to close-growing crops, the emitters often plug up, and the tubes may interfere with cultivation. Also wild animals and roaming cattle may disturb the system.

Studies carried out in India show that it is possible to increase productivity substantially and double water use efficiency by adopting drip irrigation method as against surface irrigation systems (AICSRWMSS, 1975). It is shown in Tamil Nadu (Sivanappan and Padma Kumari) that the area under irrigation can be increased three-fold by adopting drip irrigation method and also increase employment opportunities and returns.

9: 5.6 Sprinkler Irrigation

The sprinkler method of irrigation consists of pumping water through a large pipe at high pressure and releasing the water by rotating sprinkler heads (nozzles) in a manner similar to rainfall.

Advantages of sprinkler irrigation include adaptation to any slope and any soil texture, uniform water application if set properly and there are no high winds, labor costs are low, and certain fertilizers and insecticides may be mixed with the irrigation water.

Disadvantages include a very high initial investment, an assured source of surface or underground water supply must be available, and the nozzles may become plugged if the water is not carefully screened.

The sprinkler irrigation method is proving popular in some parts of India where the water source is limited. However, studies carried out in the Central Arid Zone Research Institute, Jodhpur show that when the soils are a loamy sand and the climate hot and arid the sprinkler system proves to be less efficient as compared to the drip irrigation method for vegetable crops (Singh and Singh, 1978).

9: 6 SCIENTIFIC AND PRACTICAL IRRIGATION

Scientists use instruments to determine for each soil type and crop when to start to irrigate and when to stop. Wise farmers use as much science as they understand plus wisdom gained from experience. A blend of science and wisdom assures success.

9: 6.1 Scientific Methods

Plants extract water from soils when it is held in the root zone with a suction between one-third bar (at field capacity) and 15 bars (at the wilting percentage). It is time to start irrigating when the soil moisture is about half way between the field capacity and the wilting point, and to apply adequate quantity of water to bring the soil moisture to field capacity (Figs. 9.3 and 9.4). To interpret a reading from these field instruments into, "When

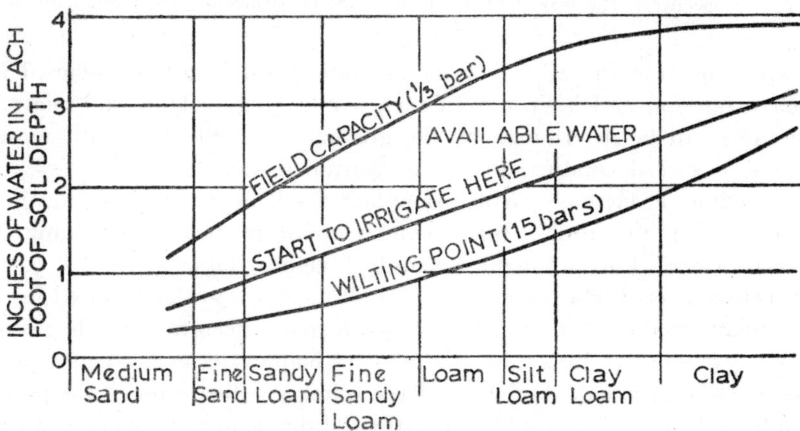

Fig. 9.3. The amount and frequency of irrigation are determined partly by soil texture. A clay loam soil has the largest available water capacity and, therefore, should require irrigation water less frequently than a sand (inches × 2.54 = cm.) (*Source: Water: The Yearbook of Agriculture,* USDA, 1955.)

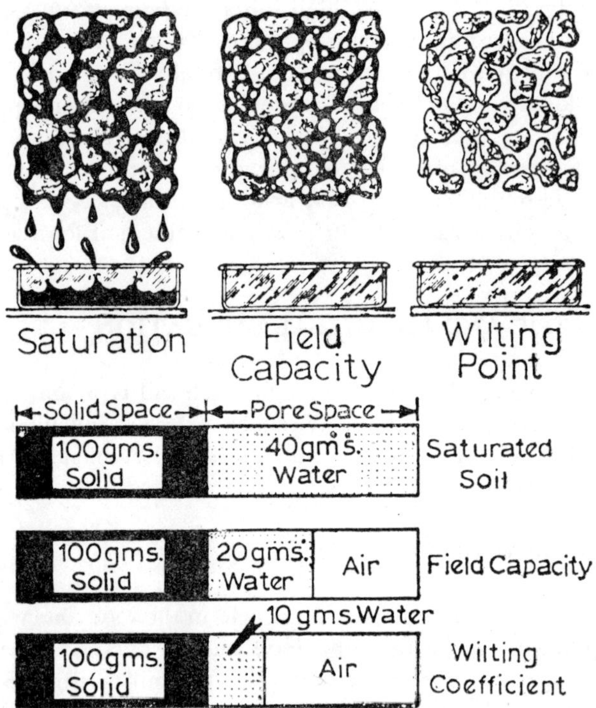

Fig. 9.4. Diagram showing the solids-water-air relationships in a well-granulated silt loam soil when the water volumes are at *saturation, field capacity,* and *wilting point* (wilting coefficient), respectively. (*Courtesy:* USDA and the U.S. Department of the Interior.)

to start and stop irrigating," prior laboratory data must be obtained for each major soil and interpreted for each major crop. These soil moisture constants can be determined by the gravimetric method or with tensiometers, electrical conductivity, or a neutron probe.

Gravimetric methods involve sampling a soil in the field, drying it in an oven at 105°C until it loses no more moisture, then determining the percent water. (Loss in weight ÷ oven-dry weight × 100).

Tensiometers use a porous clay cup filled with water and buried in the soil usually at the depth of maximum plant root concentration. The porous clay cup is attached by a tube to a mercury manometer or a vacuum gauge that measures suction. As the soil dries, water is pulled through the porous cup by soil water suction. The drier the soil the greater the suction as read on the mercury manometer. The range of measurement of tensiometers is from 0 to 0.85 bars. For this reason, tensiometers are more useful in sandy soils and for crops requiring a low water tension (high water requirement) such as Irish potatoes, sugarcane, turfgrass production, and nurseries.

Electrical conductivity techniques are used extensively to determine moisture from the field capacity to the wilting point. The original technique used a gypsum block inside of which were two bare wires set a fixed distance apart. These wires had leads fastened at a convenient height above ground, with the gypsum block buried usually at a soil depth of maximum root concentration. Moisture would move from the soil and permeate the gypsum block. The more water in the soil the wetter the gypsum block and the more readily a current of electricity would pass from one embedded bare wire to another. Readings are taken by attaching the above-ground wires to a Wheatstone Bridge (a resistance box). The most modern resistance blocks are made from more durable nylon.

Neutron probes are the latest and most sophisticated technique for determining the amount of water in a soil. The probes contain radioactive materials that emit rapidly moving neutrons. Hydrogen in water slows the velocity of the neutrons and deflect some of them back to the probe where a counter records them. Only slowed neutrons are counted; meaning that the more the soil water the more the slowed neutrons.

Yet another scientific approach is to predict irrigation needs based on the quantum of evaporation of water during a certain period as measured from an evaporimeter. Rate of evaporation from free water surface as also the evapo-transpiration losses from vegetation are essentially controlled by climatic factors. It has been shown that there is a close relationship between the rate of consumptive use by crops and the rate of evaporation as estimated with the aid of an appropriately placed evaporimeter.

The standard U.S. Weather Bureau class A pan is a common equipment used all over the world to measure the rate of evaporation. It is a 25 cm deep pan of 120 cm diameter made of 20 gauge galvanized iron sheet. It is painted white and placed on a wooden frame. It is filled with water to a depth of 20 cm and level is measured by means of a hook gauge in stilling well. The differences in the levels indicate the extent of evaporation during the intervening period and the same is converted into standard rain gauge measurement units for convenience by using an appropriate formula.

The sunken screen pan evaporimeter is suggested to be used in place of open pan evaporimeter by Sharma and Dastane (1968). It is claimed to be a simpler device and gives fairly accurate estimation of consumptive use. It also has an evaporation pan but half in size, independent stilling well connected by a tube to the main pan and a water level measuring device in the well. It works on the same principle as the larger one.

Use of a small tin can evaporimeter has been developed and suggested by Dastane (1969) for scheduling irrigation for different crops. It is a simple 1 kg capacity can with a pointer inside at 1.5 cm below the brim to facilitate recording of water levels. When the accumulated evaporation attains a certain value the crop should be irrigated.

Indian Meteorological Department has designed an experimental tank which is placed in the center of a large field on a platform balance of two ton capacity (Gangopadhyaya et al.). This tank is placed inside a container of a size slightly bigger than the experimental tank and buried in the field with its rim 6 cm above ground. The experimental vessel is filled with soil of the same field and the crop plants are grown in it in the same manner as in the surrounding field. The soil mass in the inner tank is raised to field capacity whenever the field is irrigated. Daily readings of the weight of the tank give the evaporation loss. This equipment being complex is more useful for experimental work rather than for predicting irrigation needs.

The Piche evaporimeter consisting of a graduating tube 1.5 cm in diameter and 30 cm long with one end open can also be used for estimating the rate of evaporation. Open end is covered with paper and the tube is turned upside down. Water evaporates from paper and level in the tube indicates the loss at fixed intervals.

Irrigation water is recommended to be applied in quantities required to make good the evaporation losses that occur during the period between two turns of irrigation.

All the instruments are required to be properly calibrated according to local soil, crop and climatic conditions to get the desired results. Calibrations are required to be related to the instrument readings with soil moisture loss and evapo-transpiration.

9: 6.2 Practical Methods

For centuries, farmers have used conventional wisdom to determine when to start and when to stop irrigating. Some of these techniques are explained here.

o When the largest leaves on plants wilt at midafternoon, it is time to start irrigating.

o When irrigation water is scarce or difficult to obtain, only "survival" amounts are applied in the hopes that rain will come soon. Also, during water shortage, the best-paying crops receive the most water.

o When irrigation water is plentiful and is not sold by volume, an excess of water is usually applied because there may not be any more later.

o When there is no prediction of rain, sandy soils may be watered once a week and clay soils every 10 days.

o It is time to start irrigating when a handful of soil from the zone of greatest root concentration is manipulated in the hand in an attempt to make a mud ball, and it has these characteristics, depending on soil texture, as follows:

Sandy loam—will not form a mud ball but will turn lighter in color upon drying and cracking—start irrigating.

Loam—will form a mud ball but the ball easily crumbles when tossed in the air one foot high and is caught in the hand—start irrigating.

Clay—will form a ball that cracks open when pressure is applied with the thumb—start irrigating.

o It is time to stop irrigating when you can easily push a blunt stick to about a one-foot (30 cm) depth. The stick pushes easily in wet soil but with difficulty in dry soil. Several probes over the field are required to obtain an average depth of water penetration.

o It is time to start irrigating when crop plants turn darker green than normal.

9: 7 IRRIGATION AND WATER USE EFFICIENCY

Irrigation water is an expensive input. Efficiency of water use, therefore, becomes a critical factor in determining cost of production of various crops. It is to encourage the efficient use of water that in some countries water is sold on a volumetric (measured) basis instead of charging a flat rate per unit crop per season as is the practice in India.

9: 7.1 Irrigation Efficiency

There are many factors that affect irrigation requirements of crops. This requirement is expressed in terms of total amount of water applied in addition to the rain water that becomes available through soil profile to meet its needs for optimum growth. The total quantity applied through the entire season can be measured by means of a suitable measuring device like flumes, notches, orifice and water meters. Net irrigation requirement is the sum total of water applied at each turn of irrigation during the life time of a crop to bring the soil moisture content in the root zone to about field capacity each time.

Water is required to be conveyed from where it is stored and applied to the fields where crops are grown. Considerable losses occur in this process. These losses are termed as conveyance and application losses respectively. In addition some losses also occur due to evaporation and infiltration from the soil in the field after application. The gross irrigation requirement includes net irrigation requirement plus the losses. Overall irrigation efficiency is, therefore, measured in terms of percentage of water actually transpired by crop plants out of the total quantity of water stored and conveyed from the source to the field.

As indicated earlier water resources in India that are expected to be available for agricultural use have been estimated to be 77 million hectare meters (National Commission on Agriculture, 1976). At present on an average, 0.8 million hectare meters of water is used to raise a crop on one hectare area. There is scope and need for improving the irrigation efficiency and bring down the rate per hectare to 0.7, then only can it be possible to irrigate an envisaged 110 million hectare area out of 210 million hectare of gross cultivated area by A.D. 2025.

In India at present, about half of all irrigation water is used on rice and 15 percent on wheat. These are the facts, even though irrigation water is scarce and very expensive and rice uses water less efficiently than wheat. Table 9.1 indicates that rice uses water only one-third as efficiently as wheat, and less than half as efficiently as maize, sorghum, and *bajra*.

Table 9.1. Water use efficiency of selected crops (National Commission on Agriculture, 1976)

Crop	Annual water requirement (mm)	Average yield (kg/ha)	Water use efficiency (kg yield/ha mm)
Rice	1,200	4,500	3.8
Maize (corn)	625	5,000	8.0
Sorghum	500	4,500	9.0
Bajra	500	4,500	9.0
Wheat	400	5,000	12.5

The principal reason for the low efficiency of water use in rice is the loss by deep percolation on sandy soils. Research in India has revealed that on loamy soils loss of water by percolation was two-thirds of that applied. To reduce water loss by deep percolation it is therefore recommended that irrigated rice should not be planted on soils with a daily percolation rate higher than 5 mm.

9: 7.2 Water Use Efficiency

There are two aspects involved in water use efficiency. One concerns input that is application of irrigation water with least losses of various kinds and the other concerns the output that is the crop yield. The losses in storage, conveyance and application depend upon the engineering structures and regulation of delivery and application. The output depends on the one hand on the season, crop and variety and on the other hand on various agronomic practices adopted for raising the crops. Water use efficiency is expressed in different ways. Crop water use efficiency is the ratio of crop yield and the amount of water used for evapo-transpiration. Field water use efficiency is a ratio of crop yield and the total amount of water applied to a field.

The crop grown during warmer and drier period of the year would require large quantity of water than the one grown under cooler and humid period. Climatic parameters like solar radiation, day length, temperature, rainfall, relative humidity etc., interact and affect the physiological process and thus the final crop yield. It is, therefore, necessary to understand the requirement of each crop and variety and adjust the growing season to suit the same to get best agronomic as well as economic results.

Plant species differ from one another to a very great extent in their efficiency of dry matter production per unit of water. Similarly, varieties of the same species also differ from one another in this respect. Hence there is a need for wise choice of crop species as well as variety in order to get maximum returns. Plant physiologists and agronomists are studying all over the world to understand the relationship between the water use and ultimate dry matter production with special emphasis on economic production. Similarly, plant breeders are attempting to develop varieties which are more efficient in water use.

Yields of crops vary from plot to plot depending upon the way the crop is managed although quantity of water used for raising the same may not differ much. Crop management includes all aspects starting with seed bed preparation, seed selection and sowing through harvesting. Timely sowing of crop is of very great importance all over the country. Delayed planting of many crops are shown to result in lowering of yields to a considerable extent despite other management practices remaining the same. Careful attention is required to be paid to soil management in general and fertility management in particular to ensure higher yields. Special attention is required to be paid to timely irrigation. Timely irrigation does not mean supply at regular intervals but supply according to the needs of crops. Some crops like sorghum, wheat, millets etc., give better performance as far as grain yield is concerned when irrigation is restricted well before flag leaf stage to check vegetative growth. It may be difficult to implement this suggestion fully when there is no control over water supply.

The synergistic effects were seen on yields of grain sorghum when grown on an Alfisol with a "package" of improved practices as compared with the sum of single practices. The improved practices included one 5 cm application of irrigation water to the grain sorghum stubble to stimulate a ratoon crop and a second 5 cm application at the flowering stage of the ratoon crop (Fig. 9.5) (ICRISAT Annual Report, 1976-1977).

9: 7.3 Reduction of Evapo-transpiration

In recent years attempts have been made to control evapo-transpiration of crop plants through the use of antitranspirants. Some chemicals when applied to crops are shown to retard or suppress transpiration through a physiological

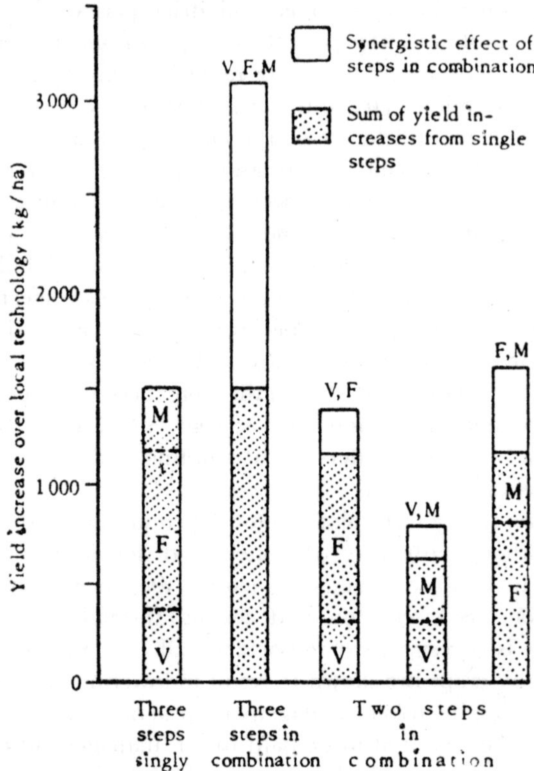

Fig. 9.5. A package of improved practices applied to grain sorghum in central India resulted in yields nearly twice as great as the sum of the increases when the practices were applied singly or two at a time. The application variables were improved variety (V), fertilization (F), and improved soil and crop management (M) which included 2–5 cm applications of irrigation water (ICRISAT Annual Report, 1976-1977).

process. Plants lose water to the atmosphere mostly through stomatal pores of leaves. Losses can be reduced by lowering the vapour pressure gradient between the water vapour in the stomatal cavity and the outside atmosphere and/or by increasing the stomatal resistance to water vapour diffusion.

Use of growth retardants has also been suggested to check vegetative growth which may result in increasing the yield of economic products in certain crops and thus influence crop water use efficiency. Increase in yield is attributed to less lodging, prolific growth of root system and increase in number and size of grains etc. It is, however, not clearly understood as to whether transpiration is reduced or not (Singh, N.P. and S.K. Sinha, 1977). Use of straw, plastic or polyethylene sheet mulching to reduce evaporation from soil surface is also shown to be advantageous under certain situations.

Even live plants as shelter belts or physical barriers have been useful in this respect under specific conditions.

9: 8 CROPPING SYSTEMS AND IRRIGATION

Temperature conditions over most of India are such that it is possible to grow crops throughout the year provided water is available for irrigation. Suitable cropping systems are adopted according to the duration and amount of water available. Water for irrigation may become available round the year or for a short period only depending upon the source of supply.

According to the duration of supply of water the irrigation systems are known as perennial or seasonal. When supply is perennial it is possible to plan for annual harvest of one crop like sugarcane or two harvests—one of cotton and another of groundnut or three harvests of short-duration crops. In some parts in the south where temperature conditions are mild even in winter, three crops of paddy are harvested in succession during a year. Sugar cane is commonly grown in rotation in these parts.

Mixed cropping has been practiced in India since time immemorial. In recent years scientific studies have been carried out and very large number of recommendations have emerged. It has been shown that it is possible to grow different kinds of vegetables, pulses, oil seeds etc. as intercrops in broadly spaced crops like sugar cane, cotton, maize, sorghum etc. Intercropping involves growing of crops simultaneously in the same field and in the same season. Crops chosen, however, should differ in growth habits and agronomic requirements. It is preferable if they differ in height, canopy, growth rates and nutritional requirements; they should not compete with each other but share the resources. The total production and returns should be more than what is obtained from possible sole cropping systems.

It has been shown that it is possible to grow lucerne as an intercrop in sugarcane planted in October-November months (Arakeri et al., 1956). Growing of wheat in October sown crop of sugarcane is feasible in northern India. New technology of intercropping of pulses has been developed and recommended by the Indian Agricultural Research Institute, New Delhi (1980).

A large variety of multiple and intercropping systems suited to different situations have become available for adoption by farmers in different parts of the country. One such system applicable to Bihar State of India is shown in Table 9.2.

9: 9 DRAINAGE

A loam soil in good physical condition for growing upland plants, on a volume basis, must have about half solids and half pore spaces. And the

Table 9.2. Proposed cropping systems for various regions in Bihar State, India, irrigated and non-irrigated (National Commission on Agriculture, 1976, Part VI)

Region	Irrigated areas	Non-irrigated areas	Flood affected/low land areas
1	2	3	4
(i) north Bihar plain (a) terai area (comprising parts of Champaran, Muzaffarpur, Darbhanga and Purnea districts)	paddy-potato-jute paddy-rabi maize-jute paddy-wheat-jute paddy-wheat-paddy paddy-berseem paddy-sugarcane	paddy-paira (for low land) jowar +*meth*-oats+peas *marua* (Ragi) barley *aus* paddy-sweet potato	for flood affected areas of north Bihar plain flood resistant paddy-barley (FR 13A & FR 43B) summer maize + *moong* + barley flood resistant paddy-summer maize for low lands of north Bihar
(b) non-calcareous non-saline (districts of Saharsa, part of Purnea, Darbhanga, Muzaffarpur, Champaran, and northern parts of Monghyr and Bhagalpur)	paddy-wheat-paddy paddy-potato-paddy paddy *rabi* maize-paddy paddy-wheat-*cheena* paddy-wheat-jute paddy-potato-jute paddy-potato-summer maize paddy-mustard-*moong* paddy-berseem-paddy paddy-wheat-*moong*	*aus* paddy-barley+pea *aus* paddy-*sarson* paddy-paira (gram, linseed or *khesari)* jute-sweet potato groundnut-barley *marua*-barley+pea Jute-paddy	plain deep water paddy (BR 14) sown in April *moong*+*cheena*+paddy deep water paddy-sugarcane (B.O.3)
(c) calcareous soil (major part of Saran, southern Darbhanga, Champaran and Muzaffarpur)	paddy-wheat-jute paddy-potato-jute paddy-wheat-paddy paddy-potato-paddy maize-wheat-*moong*	maize+turmeric+*arhar* turmeric+*arhar* maize+*arhar*-castor-*arhar*+castor maize-chillies maize-tobacco	

	maize-sugarcane+mustard maize-early potato-*moong* maize-*tori*-wheat-*moong* maize-berseem maize-potato-*cheena*	maize-sweet potato maize-*kajai*-wheat early paddy-wheat or barley *marua*-barley+pea
(ii) south Bihar plain (comprising Patna, Gaya, Shahabad, major parts of Monghyr and Bhagalpur districts)	for light soils of upland-maize-wheat maize-potato-*cheena* maize-early potato-late potato-summer vegetable-maize-early potato-wheat-*moong* maize-*tori*-wheat-*moong*	for light soils of upland maize-barley or gram maize+*kalai*-wheat (NP 852, K. Sona) Groundnut-wheat (NP 852, K. Sona) jowar+*meth*-linseed *marua*-wheat (NP 852, K. Sona) maize-linseed (T 397)
	for heavy soils of low land— paddy-wheat-paddy aus paddy-potato-onion paddy-sugarcane *aus* paddy-wheat-summer vegetable carly-paddy-potato-*cheena* *aus* paddy-winter maize paddy-berseem-*moong*	for heavy soils of low land— paddy-*paira* (gram, lentil, linseed, *tori*) paddy-wheat paddy-barley
(iii) Plateau region (comprising Ranchi, Palamau, Hazaribagh,	for *tanr* lands (uplands)— maize-*kalai*-wheat	for *tanr* lands (uplands)— groundnut-linseed

(*Contd.*)

Table 9.2 (*Contd.*)

Region	Irrigated areas	Non-irrigated areas	Flood affected/low land areas
1	2	3	4
Dhanbad, Singhbhum and Santhal Pargana districts)	maize+cowpea—wheat jowar-*kalai*-wheat or potato bajra+*kalai*-wheat or potato maize-potato-wheat maize-potato-wheat-*moong* for medium uplands– paddy (IR 8 or Jaya)-wheat paddy (IR 8 or Jaya)-potato paddy (Jaya)-wheat (sonalika)-paddy (Padma)— paddy (IR 8)-winter maize jute for seed-wheat paddy-wheat-*moong* for *don* lands (low lands)— early *aman* paddy (BR 34)- wheat-late aman paddy (BR 8, T 141)- rabi vegetables or wheat jute for seed-potato-vegetables	maize+*arhar-arhar* rainy season potato-linseed *marua*-linseed jowar-ratoon *jowar* maize-*kalai*-sweet potato cotton+groundnut-cotton *gora* paddy-linseed maize-cowpea-linseed for medium uplands— *aus*-or early *aman* paddy-linseed (T 397) direct sown paddy (Padma)-linseed (T 397) for *don* lands (low lands)— early paddy-linseed (T 397) late *aman* paddy-*paira* paddy-gram	

pore spaces must be about half filled with water and half with air. When the pore volume is more than half water, artificial drainage is indicated. Sandy soils can have more water than air and still be a good medium for growing upland plants, but clay soils must have more air than water. The reason for this difference is that in sands, the pores are larger and oxygen can diffuse through them faster than through smaller pores in clays. The principal exception to these generalizations is rice which can grow as an upland crop, such as wheat but is more productive when grown as an aquatic plant, such as water lilies or cattails.

Wet soils that require artificial drainage are usually the most fertile and *potentially* productive of any on a farm; draining them will make them the most productive. The reason is because nutrients have been moved into them from fertile productive soils on the watershed and organic residues have been preserved due to low oxygen caused by wetness. Drainage hastens microbial decomposition of the accumulated organic matter and the more rapid release of nutrients.

9: 9.1 Soils Requiring Artificial Drainage

Soils that must be drained artifically for optimum production of upland crops include:

1) Parts of fields that are irrigated such as around dams, along seepy canals, and at the lower ends of fields with wild flooding, border, and furrow irrigation.

2) Soils with high suspended or true water tables.

3) Soils in depressions that stay wet because of inflow or seepage from surrounding watersheds.

4) Soils in tidal flats that are inundated by periodic high tides.

5) Soils with excessively high salt content. Artificial drainage is a means of flushing the salt from the root zone (rhizosphere) to enhance plant growth.

9: 9.2 Soil Surveys—An Assessment of Drainage Needs

Because flowing water does not recognize land ownership boundaries, drainage systems must be established on an area basis. For this reason, drainage assessment must be for entire drainage basins. The only practical way to assess potential drainage schemes is to conduct a standard soil survey (Donahue, Follett, and Tulloch, 1983).

Standard soil surveys are usually modifications of the system used in the United States since 1899. In this system there are seven natural (internal) soil-drainage classes. This refers to the frequency and duration of present soil saturation or partial saturation and including the years the soil was being developed in nature. These seven drainage classes, recognized in the field by color and thickness of specific subsurface horizons, are as follows:

Excessively drained soils are very porous and freely permeable to great depths. No mottling occurs in any horizon, indicating that no artificial drainage is needed.

Somewhat excessively drained soils are ones through which water and air move freely in all horizons but slower than in excessively drained soils. No artificial drainage is needed.

Well-drained soils are usually loams and are almost free of mottling. These soils do not need artificial drainage for any crop.

Moderately well-drained soils have slower internal drainage as indicated by a mottled layer between the B and C horizons. These soils seldom need artificial drainage except for such deep-rooted crops as alfalfa.

Somewhat poorly drained soils have mottling in the B horizon and are usually wet on the surface for several weeks in a year during the monsoon. Artificial drainage is required for some deep-rooted crops.

Poorly drained soils are mottled in the A horizon and are wet at the surface for several months in the year. Maize (corn) and cotton on these soils require artificial drainage.

Very poorly drained soils have water standing on them throughout the rainy season. They are mottled in the A horizon and uniformly gray in the B horizon. Almost all crops on these soils will grow best when the soil is artificially drained. However, such soils may lie in such depressions that gravity-drainage is not possible.

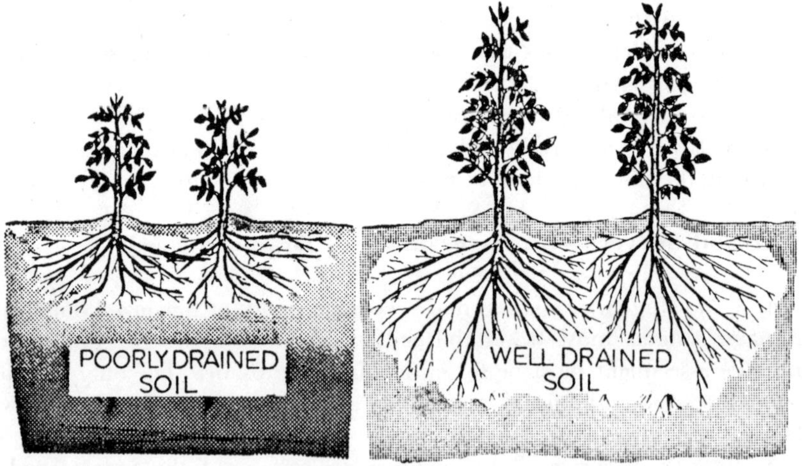

Fig. 9.6. Most plants need large amounts of oxygen supplied from the air to their roots. In a poorly drained soil, the surplus water prevents such rapid movement. When wet soils are drained, oxygen can move faster to the roots, plants grow better, and crop yields are higher. (*Courtesy:* Texas Vocational Services for Agricultural Education.)

9: 9.3 Results from Drainage

Artificial drainage of wet soils increases the oxygen supply to plant roots, decreases loss of soil nitrogen by denitrification, increases root proliferation (Fig. 9.6), decreases root rots, permits all cultural operations to be implemented with greater timeliness and precision, and increases yields.

9: 9.4 Types of Drainage Systems

Most drainage systems throughout India and the world are open ditches. The cross-section is designed to be adequate to carry the anticipated volume of water and the gradient steep enough for the designed volume to be discharged with a non-erosive velocity. Suggested maximum drainage channel grades for sandy loam soils is 0.2 percent and for clay soils about 1 percent. A trial-and-error technique for determining the necessary cross-sectional area and grade of drainage channels is to accept the criteria that all standing water should be removed within a 12-hour period. Water standing for longer periods will be likely to affect upland crops. A more scientific approach is to use the calculated maximum volume to be discharged from ten-year storms. Engineers usually have such tables available. Types of drainage patterns are shown in Fig. 9.7.

More expensive drainage systems include tile drainage, tube drainage, drainage-by-beds, sump-and-pump drainage, and vertical drainage (Donahue, Follett, and Tulloch, 1976).

9: 10 SUMMARY

Up to one-third of the world's soils are arid and require irrigation water to make them most productive.

Establishing new water supplies for irrigation is so expensive that an exhaustive assessment must be done, including the making of a detailed standard soil survey.

Scientists and wise farmers with experience in applying irrigation water can learn much from each other on when to start irrigation, how much to apply, and when to stop applying it.

Water used for irrigation in India comes from surface and underground sources. In India, the scope for development of irrigation varies from state to state The quality of the water may be inferior because of the high incidence of soluble salts, sodium, boron, bicarbonate, chlorides, lithium, selenium, or sediment.

Sewage water is used successfully in India and throughout most of the world. To reduce the hazard of spreading pathogens, sewage water should not be used on vegetable crops that are eaten raw. Cooking and desiccation destroy most pathogens.

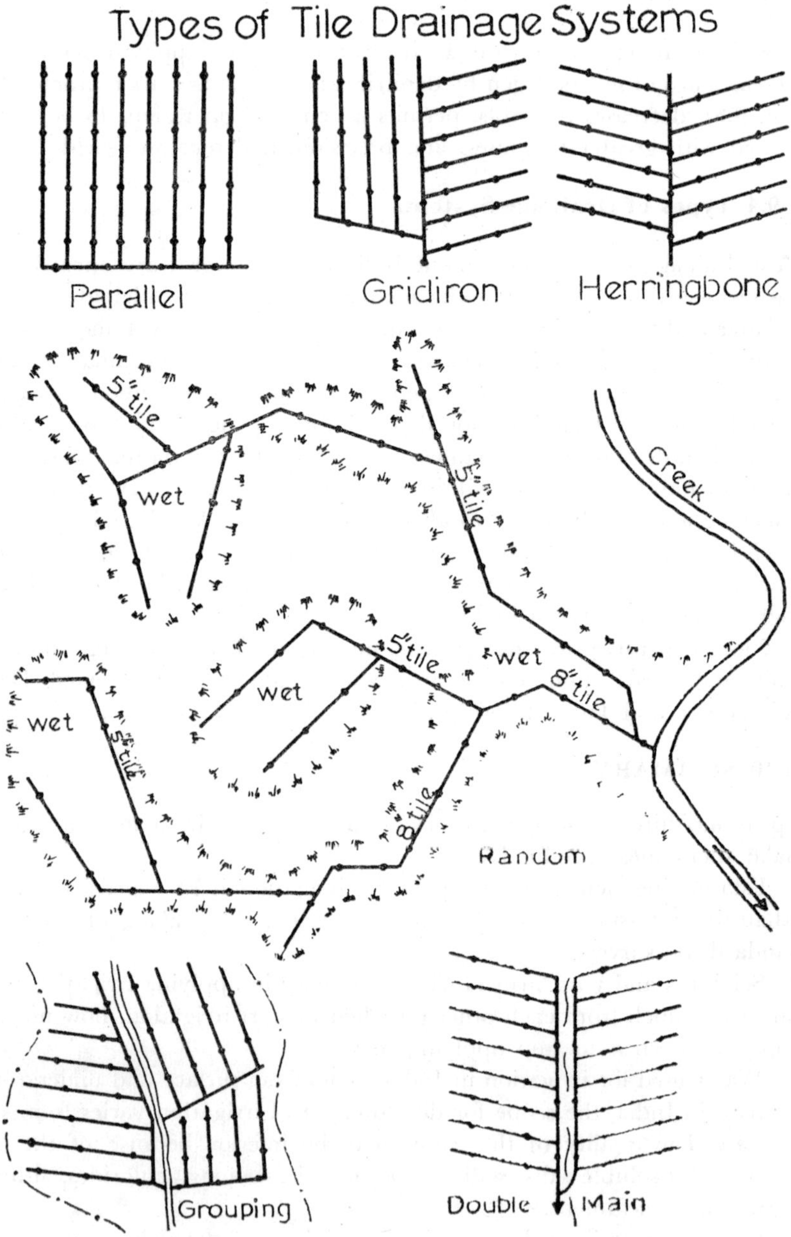

Fig. 9.7. Types of drainage patterns. (*Courtesy:* U.S. Department of Agriculture.)

The principal irrigation methods include wild flooding, furrow, border, basin, pot, trickle, and sprinkler techniques.

Efficiency of water use by crops in India is greatest with wheat, followed by bajra, sorghum, maize, and rice. There are many factors that affect irrigation and water use efficiency. There are also various ways of improving the same. A synergistic effect of about 100 percent is shown by applying a package of practices to grain sorghum.

In India it is possible to cultivate crops for most part of the year because of favorable temperature conditions. A variety of multiple and mixed cropping systems have been evolved through research and advocated for use to suit different situations depending upon the duration for which water is available.

Drainage is required on many soils with a high water table, on low-lying soils receiving an inflow of water, and on many sites where new irrigation water supplies have been established. Just as a soil survey is a necessary part of assessment of the feasibility of a new irrigation scheme, so also is a soil survey necessary before establishing a new drainage system.

CITED REFERENCES

All India Coordinated Scheme for Research on Water Management and Soil Salinity (AICSRWMSS). Annual Progress Report. (Mimeograph) 1973-75 ICAR, New Delhi, 1975.

Anonymous. "Intercropping of Pulses—A New Technology." Research Bull. No. 18, Ind. Agri. Res. Inst., New Delhi. 1980.

Arakeri, H.R., R.S. Patil. and S.V. Patil. "Mixed Cropping in Sugarcane in Deccan Canal Tract." Proc. Deccan Sug. Tech. Assn. 13th Convention. 1956, pages 103–110.

Arakeri, H.R., G.V. Chalam, P. Satyanarayana, and R.L. Donahue. "Soil Management in India", 2nd Edition, 1962. Asia Publishing House, London.

Bhumbla, D.R. "Water Quality and Use of Saline Waters for Crop Production." Symposium on Soil and Water Management, Hissar, 1969. ICAR, New Delhi, India, 1972, pages 87–108.

Dastane, N.G. "New Concepts, Practices and Techniques in the Field of Water Use and Management." Symposium on Soil and Water Management, Hissar, 1969. I.C.A.R., New Delhi 1972, pages 109–133.

Donahue, R.L., R.H. Follett, and Rodney W. Tulloch. "Our Soils and Their Management." The Interstate, Danville, Illinois, 1983.

Donahue, R.L., Raymond W. Miller, and John. C. Shickluna. "Soils: An Introduction to Soils and Plant Growth." 5th Edition, 1983. Prentice-Hall, Inc., Englewood Cliffs, New Jersey, 07632.

Gangopadhyaya, M., S. Venkataraman and V. Krishnamurthy. "The Role of the Mesh Covered 'Class A' Pan in the Extrapolation of Evapo-transpiration Estimates" Symposium on Soil and Water Management, Hissar, 1969. I.C.A.R., New Delhi, 1972, pages 40–49.

Heady, Harold F. "Arid Land Characteristics, Resources and Uses—An Overview." *In* "Arid Land Resource Inventories: Developing Cost-Effective Methods." USDA—Forest Service, General Technical Report WO 28, 1980, pages 5–7.

ICRISAT Annual Report, 1976–1977. International Crops Research Institute for the Semi-Arid Tropics, Hyderabad, India, page 169–171.

National Commission on Agriculture, Part V, Resource Development, New Delhi, India, 1976.

National Commission on Agriculture, 1976, Part VI, pages 39, 40, New Delhi, India.

Sharma, R.G. and N.G. Dastane. "Use of Screened Evaporimeters in Evapo-transpirometry." Proc. Water Management Symposium, Udaipur (1966), Ind. Soc. Agron., New Delhi, 1968, pages 66–67.

Sivanappam, R.K. and O. Padma Kumari "Drip Irrigation" Tamil Nadu Agricultural University, Coimbatore, India, 1980, 57 pages.

Singh, S.D. and Punjab Singh. "Value of Drip Irrigation Compared with Conventional Irrigation for Vegetable Production in a Hot Arid Climate". Agron. Jour. Vol. 70, 1978, pages. 945–947.

Singh N.P. and S.K. Sinha, "Water Use Efficiency in Crop Production." Monograph No. 4. "Water Requirement and Irrigation Management of Crops in India." IARI, 1977, pages 286–335.

Soil Conservation Service, U.S.D.A., "Area of Soils Measured From Soil Map of the World, 1: 50,000,000." 1972.

Sorkar, A.N. "Prospects of Sewage Waste Utilisation in India." Jour. Sci. Ind. Res. Vol 40. 1981, pages 287–294.

ADDITIONAL REFERENCES

Arakeri, H.R. "Indian Agriculture." Oxford and IBH Publishing Co., New Delhi, 1982.

DeDatta, Surajit K. "Principles and Practices of Rice Production." John Wiley & Sons, New York, 1981.

Schwab, Glenn O., Richard Frevert, Kenneth K. Barnes, and Talcott W. Edminster. "Soil and Water Conservation Engineering" 3rd Edition, John Wiley & Sons, New York, 1981.

Troeh, Frederick R., J. Arthur Hobbs, and R.L. Donahue. "Soil and Water Conservation for Productivity and Environmental Protection." Prentice-Hall, Inc., 1980.

U.S. Department of Agriculture, "Climate and Man: The Yearbook of Agriculture, 1941." Wash. D.C.

U.S. Department of Agriculture, "Soils: The Yearbook of Agriculture, 1957." Wash. D.C.

U.S. Department of Agriculture. "Water: The Yearbook of Agriculture, 1955." Wash. D.C.

Symposium, "Soil and Water Management", Hissar, 1969. ICAR, New Delhi, India, 1972.

Monograph No. 4, "Water Requirement and Irrigation Management of Crops in India." IARI. New Delhi, 1977.

Proc. Water Management Symposium. Udaipur (1966), Ind. Soc. Agron., New Delhi, 1968.

Proc. Multiple Cropping Symposium. Hissar, 1972, Ind. Soc. Agron., New Delhi, India, 1973.

CHAPTER 10

Reclamation of Saline and Sodic Soils

10: 1 INTRODUCTION

Salts restrict the growth of plants of the world more than any other naturally occurring substance. World-wide estimates of salt-affected soils vary from 20 million hectares (Follett, Murphy, Donahue, 1981) to 268 million hectares (Dudal, 1977). Estimates vary so widely because most soils of the world have not been surveyed and researched.

Most of the saline and sodic soils occur within the 2.4 billion hectares of low-rainfall areas of the world. However, smaller areas of saline and sodic soils exist in humid areas adjacent to oceans where salty sea sprays or seepage of seawater makes and keeps them salty and sodium saturated. Smaller but agriculturally-important salt-affected soils occur in such humid countries as the Netherlands where about 250,000 hectares of soils under shallow seas have been reclaimed for agricultural use.

In India about 7 million hectares of land is estimated to be afflicted by the problem of soil salinity/alkalinity mostly in the irrigated tracts of the Indo-Gangetic plain, arid areas of Rajasthan and Gujarat, black cotton soil region in central India and in coastal tracts (Yadav, 1981).

Salts present in saline and sodic soils are mostly chlorides, sulfates, bicarbonates, and sometimes nitrates of sodium, calcium, magnesium, and occasionally potassium. These salts sometimes originate from local geologic deposits but more often they accumulate as residues from local groundwaters, incoming irrigation water and/or from runoff waters on adjoining catchment areas. Drainage basins in arid and semiarid areas with no outlet to permanent streams, such as the Great Salt Lake in Utah, U.S.A., are prone to the development of saline and sodic soils. Soils of low permeability become salt-affected more quickly than those with high permeability.

Table 10.1. Salt-affected soil classification

Classification	Conductivity (mmhos/cm at 25°C)	Soil pH	Exchangeable sodium percentage	Other features	Former names	Indian local names
Saline Soil	>4.0	<8.5	<15	Chief anions are chlorides and sulphates with little bicarbonates; Physical condition satisfactory.	White alkali, *solonchak*	*Reh*, *Thur*, *Uppu*, *Lona*
Sodic soil	<4.0	>8.5	>15	Chief anions are carbonates with Na; physical condition very poor	Alkali, black alkali, *solonetz*	Bara, Rakkar
Saline-sodic soil	>4.0	<8.5	>15	Chief anions are carbonate with some chlorides and sulphates; physical condition satisfactory outwardly but poor inwardly	Saline-alkali	*Usar*, *Kallar*, *Bari*, *Khar*, *Chopan*, *Karl*

Sources: (1) United States Salinity Laboratory Staff, Diagnosis and Improvement of Saline and Alkali Soils: USDA Hand Book 60, 1969.
(2) Yadav, J. S. P.: Saline, Alkaline and Acid Soils in India and their Management Fertilizer News, Fertilizer Association of India, 1976.

10: 2 CLASSIFICATION AND CHARACTERISTICS OF SALT- AND SODIUM-AFFECTED SOILS

Salt-affected soils are classified into *saline, sodic,* and *saline-sodic.* Three criteria are used to differentiate among them: electrical conductivity of a saturated soil paste in millimos per centimeter (mmhos/cm) at 25°C, soil pH, and exchangeable sodium percentage. The threshold level of 4 mmhos/cm was adopted because the yield of most crop plants is reduced at this point. A pH of 8.5 was chosen to differentiate the three categories of salt-affected soils because this is approximately the pH of a calcium-saturated soil under field conditions. Nitrogen, magnesium, copper, iron, zinc, and manganese have a very low availability to most plants at a soil pH above 8.5. An exchangeable sodium percentage of 15 was selected to differentiate among the three kinds of salt-affected soils because that is the value above which most crop yields are reduced. Saline, sodic, and saline-sodic soils are differentiated as follows:

Saline soils have a conductivity of *more than 4* mmhos/cm, a pH of *less than 8.5,* and an exchangeable sodium percentage of *less than 15. Sodic soils* are characterized by a conductivity of *less than 4* mmhos/cm, a pH *more than 8.5,* and an exchangeable sodium percentage of *more than 15.* Saline-sodic soils possess a conductivity of *more than 4* mmhos/cm, a pH *less than 8.5,* and an exchangeable sodium percentage *more than 15* (Table 10.1).

10: 3 PLANT STRESSES OF SALT AND SODIUM

Salts in the soil solution increase the osmotic pressure and thereby reduce the ability of plant roots to absorb water (Fig. 10.1).

Plants sensitive to excess salt may be stunted in growth with blue-green, waxy-appearing leaves with "scorched" edges that wilt prematurely even though the soil appears to have enough water. Some plants tolerant of salt have special salt glands where salt accumulates and is released to the ambient environment by wind or water.

High exchangeable sodium percentage may stress plants in two ways: (1) Physiologically, by reducing the absorption of exchangeable and available cations such as calcium, magnesium, potassium, ammonium, copper, zinc, iron, and manganese; and (2) Physically, by dispersing the clay and humus and thereby making the soil a less favorable medium for plant growth.

10: 4 MANAGING SALT- AND SODIUM-AFFECTED SOILS

Salt-affected soils are usually managed by applying two unrelated techniques: (1) Selecting tolerant plants and, (2) soil reclamation to reduce the concentration of salt and sodium.

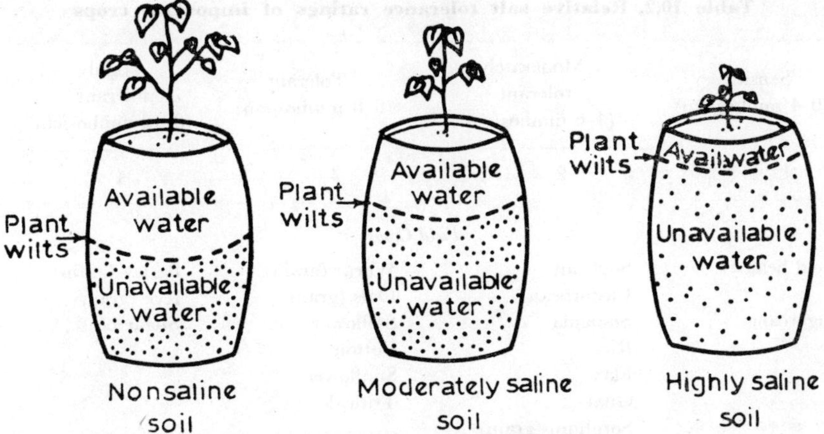

Fig. 10.1. Diagrammatic representation of the fact that with an otherwise identical soil, the greater the salinity the less the available water. (*Courtesy:* U.S. Dept. of Agriculture, Agricultural Research Service.)

10:4.1 Selecting Salt-tolerant Plants

Plants differ widely in their tolerance to total soluble salts, as measured by electrical conductivity in mmhos/cm at 25°C. Most sensitive are beans, most clovers, carrots, all citrus crops, and blackberries. Most tolerant of salts are barley, bermudagrass, asparagus, date palm, and saltcedar (Table 10.2). Plants listed in the Table can be grown at salt concentrations lower but not higher than those indicated. Plants also vary in tolerance to total soluble salts between the time of germination and when well established. Crops more tolerant of salt when germinating are barley, rye, and corn. Conversely, crops more salt-tolerant when well established are alfalfa and sugar beets (Milne and Rapp, 1968).

10:4.2 Selecting Sodium-tolerant Plants

Plants vary widely in their tolerance to the physiological environment of, and soil physical conditions induced by, soils high in sodium. Physiologically, in soils with more than 15 percent of the total exchange capacity occupied by sodium, plant absorption of nutrients may be restricted because of ion competition and antagonism. Also, the soil pH may be between 8.5 and 10 resulting in further reduction in available nutrients because of their low solubility.

However, the adverse physical condition caused by a high-sodium soil may be a more serious plant-growth-limiting factor. Sodic soils are characterized by dispersed clay and humus that are black and are tightly packed.

Table 10.2. Relative salt tolerance ratings of important crops

Sensitive (0–4 mmhos/cm)	Moderately tolerant (4–6 mmhos/cm)	Tolerant (6–8 mmhos/cm)	Highly tolerant (8–12 mmhos/cm)
1	2	3	4
		Field Crops	
Field bean	Soybean	Wheat (grain)	Barley (grain)
	Castorbean	Oats (grain)	Rye (grain)
Sugarcane	Sesbania	Safflower	Sugar beet
	Rice	Cotton	
	Flax	Sunflower	
	Guar	Triticale	
	Sorghum (grain)		
	Corn (field)		
		Forage Crops	
White clover	Reed canarygrass	Hardinggrass	Bermudagrass
Dutch clover	Oats (hay)	Kleingrass	Crested wheatgrass
Alsike clover	Orchardgrass	Alfalfa	Barley (hay)
Red clover	Bromegrass	Birdsfoot trefoil	Rye (hay)
Ladino clover	Big trefoil	Hubam clover	Panicgrass
Crimson clover	Gramagrass	Dallisgrass	Alkali sacaton
Meadow foxtail	Sour clover	Tall fescuegrass	Rhodesgrass
	Milkvetch	White sweetclover	Saltgrass
	Timothy	Yellow sweetclover	Zoysiagrass
	Sudan-sorghum hybrids	Perennial ryegrass	
	Sorghum (forage)	Wheat (hay)	
	Corn (forage)	Johnsongrass	
		Vegetable Crops	
Carrot	Lettuce	Tomato	Asparagus
English pea	Corn (sweet)	Beet	
Radish	Potato	Kale	
Celery	Squash	Spinach	
Green bean	Onion	Broccoli	
Lima bean	Sweet potato	Cabbage	
Kidney bean	Bell pepper	Cauliflower	
Cucumber	Blackeyed pea	Watermelon	
Rhubarb	Muskmelon	Pineapple	
		Sunflower	
		Fruit, Nut, and Vine Crops[a]	
Grapefruit	Pecan	Pomegranate	Date palm
Orange	Peach	Fig	Coconut
Lemon	Apricot	Olive	
Avocado	Grape	Macadamia nut	
Pear	Quince	Mango	

Table 10.2 (*Contd.*)

1	2	3	4
Apple			
Cherry			
Plum			
Walnut			
Blackberry			
Raspberry			
Strawberry			
Boysenberry			
Banana			
Celery			
Papaya			
		Ornamental Shrubs	
	Spreading juniper	Oleander	Purple sage
	Arborvitae	Bottlebrush	Saltcedar
	Lantana	Most flowering plants	
Viburnum	Pyracantha	Most ornamental plants	
	Privet		
	Japonica		

[a]Ratings may vary somewhat depending on the particular rootstock used for propagation.
Primary Sources: Publications of the U.S. Salinity Laboratory, Riverside, Calif.

Pore spaces are few, bulk density may be about 1.8 gm/cc, and permeability may be nearly zero. Very little growth is possible of even a tolerant plant when the exchangeable sodium percentage exceeds 60 percent.

Plant tolerance to exchangeable sodium varies from the very sensitive deciduous fruits such as apples, pears, and plums; to rice and clovers; to rhodesgrass that tolerates 60 percent or more exchangeable sodium. The plants listed in Table 10.3 are in the approximate rank from extremely sensitive to most tolerant of sodium.

Studies in India (Yadav, 1981) show that some varieties of rice, barley and wheat are quite tolerant of sodium. Efforts are being made to identify and breed varieties of various crop plants which are even more tolerant than the existing ones and which are shown to be suited to such adverse conditions. Forage grasses such as paragrass and bermudagrass and trees like eucalyptus hybrid and Acacia and *Prosopis* (mesquite) species have proved to be salt-tolerant and can be grown without or with the addition of small amounts of soil amendments (Yadav, 1976, 1980, 1981).

10: 4.3 Selecting Plants Tolerant to both Salt and Sodium

Saline-sodic soils have a conductivity of more than 4 mmhos, an exchangeable sodium percentage more than 15, and a pH below 8.5. Because of a lower pH, the physiological conditions for plants absorbing nutrients are greater than in a sodic soil. However, the high salt content would restrict

Table 10.3. Relative tolerance of important crops to exchangeable sodium percentage (ESP)

Crop	Tolerance to ESP and range at which affected	Growth response under field conditions
Deciduous fruits Nuts Citrus Avocado	Extremely sensitive (ESP=2–10)	Sodium toxicity symptoms even at low ESP value
Beans	Sensitive (ESP=10–20)	Stunted growth at low ESP values even though the physical condition of soil is good
Clover Oats Tall fescuegrasses Rice Dallisgrass	Moderately tolerant (ESP=20–40)	Stunted growth due to both nutritional factors and adverse soil physical conditions
Wheat Cotton Alfalfa Barley Tomato Beets	Tolerant (ESP=40–60)	Stunted growth usually due to adverse soil physical conditions
Crested wheatgrass Tall wheatgrass Rhodesgrass	Most tolerant (ESP=more than 60)	Stunted growth usually due to adverse soil physical conditions

Source: George A. Pearson, 1960.

water absorption by plant roots. Furthermore, the high salt content keeps the clay and humus flocculated and as a result, the soil is in a good physical condition for plant growth.

Table 10.4 lists plants with relative tolerance to *both* total soluble salts and exchangeable sodium. This table has been developed from Tables 10.2 and 10.3 In general, crops have a similar tolerance for total soluble salts and exchangeable sodium percentage. The principal exceptions are beans, clovers, and rice.

10: 5 RECLAIMING SALINE SOILS

Economical reclamation of saline soils requires a detailed study of the physical parameters. A study should be made of the soil and water. These questions should be answered satisfactorily before proceeding further.

Table 10.4. Relative tolerance of important crops to total soluble salt and exchangeable sodium percentage (ESP)

Crop	Sensitive		Moderately tolerant		Tolerant		Highly tolerant	
	0–4 mmhos/cm	2–10 ESP	4–6 mmhos/cm	10–20 ESP	6–8 mmhos/cm	20–40 ESP	8–12 mmhos/cm	>40 ESP
Deciduous fruits	×	×						
Nuts	×	×						
Citrus	×	×						
Avocado	×	×						
Beans	×			×				
Clovers	×					×		
Oats					×	×		
Tall fescuegrasses					×	×		
Rice			×			×		
Dallisgrass					×	×		
Wheat					×			×
Cotton					×			×
Alfalfa					×			×
Barley							×	×
Tomato					×			×
Beet					×			×
Crested wheatgrass							×	×
Rhodesgrass							×	×

1) Is the hectarage large enough to be economical when reclaimed?

2) Is the soil deep, friable, and potentially fertile? A soil surveyor can determine this.

3) Is the natural drainage adequate to discharge surplus water? Is it possible to lower the free water table if any?

4) Is there adequate low-ion, low-sediment water to leach the salts below the plant-root zone? Assuming a root-zone of one meter depth of soil, it is estimated that one meter depth of water used for leaching will move about 80 percent of the soluble salts below one meter depth in the soil. This is often adequate (Rhodes, 1974).

5) What is the percentage and kinds of total soluble salts in the soil?

6) Is the irrigation water low enough in salts? Does it contain toxic boron or bicarbonates?

When it has been determined that all physical and economic factors are satisfactory, reclamation consists of building a bund (levee) around the area and flooding. Several partial floodings, with drying in between, are more effective than one even though the total amount of water used is the same.

Successful reclamation is possible only by adopting a package of practices suited to the specific situation. In general, essential components comprise the following (Yadav, 1981 and Dargan, K.S. 1979):

1) Proper bunding and land leveling.

2) Application of suitable amendment in right quantity and right manner.

3) Adequate application of fertilizers and manures.

4) Choice of proper crops and varieties and cropping sequences.

5) Use of appropriate cultural and agronomic practices.

6) Proper water management including requisite drainage.

10: 6 RECLAIMING SODIC AND SALINE-SODIC SOILS

Reclaiming sodic soils cannot be done by leaching alone because the sodium adsorbed on the surfaces of clay and humus particles are not leachable. By mass action, another cation must be added to replace adsorbed sodium before the sodium can be leached below root depth. Because it is relatively low in cost and because it flocculates clay and humus, calcium sulfate (gypsum, $CaSO_4 \cdot 2H_2O$) is the most common source of soluble calcium. The reaction may be written like this :

$$\text{Na-clay} + \underset{\text{(in soil solution)}}{Ca^{2+}} \longrightarrow \text{Ca-clay} + \underset{\text{(in soil solution)}}{Na^{+}}$$

The calcium-clay (calcium-saturated clay) is in a desirable physical state for good air-water relations and for enhanced plant growth.

If the sodic soil contains a large amount of calcium carbonate, the soluble calcium may come from adding powdered sulfur or sulfuric acid and producing gypsum. Sulfur must first be oxidized to sulfuric acid by a special group of sulfur bacteria, *Thiobacillus thiooxidans*. The reaction can be written in this way:

$$CaCO_3 + H_2SO_4 + H_2O_4 \rightarrow CaSO_4 \cdot 2H_2O + CO_2$$

Other chemicals sometimes used are ferric sulfate, lime-sulfur, calcium chloride, and calcium nitrate. Rates to use are presented in Table 10·5 (Follett, Murphy, Donahue, 1981).

Table 10.5. Amendments for water and soil and their relative effectiveness in supplying calcium

Amendment	Tons equivalent to 1 ton of 100% gypsum[a]
Gypsum ($C_aSO_4 \cdot 2H_2O$)[b]	1.00
Sulfur (S)[c]	0.19
Sulfuric acid (H_2SO_4)[b]	0.61
Ferric sulfate [$Fe_2(SO_4)_3 \cdot 9H_2O$][c]	1.09
Lime sulfur (9% Ca+24% S)[b]	0.78
Calcium chloride ($CaCl_2 \cdot 2H_2O$)[b]	0.86
Calcium nitrate [$Ca(NO_3)_2 \cdot 2H_2O$][b]	1.06

[a]These are based on 100% pure materials. If not 100%, make the following calculation to find tons (X) equivalent to 100% material:

$$X = \frac{100 \times \text{tons}}{\%\ \text{purity}}$$

Example: If gypsum is 80% pure,

$$X = \frac{100 \times 1.00}{80} = 1.25 \text{ tons}$$

Answer: 1.25 tons of 80% gypsum is equivalent to 1 ton of 100% gypsum.

[b]Suitable for use as a water or soil amendment.

[c]Suitable only for soil application.

(*Source:* M. Fireman and R.L. Brauson, 1965)

In the process of reclaiming saline-sodic soils with low-ion irrigation water, salts are first leached downward. As a result, the sodium left in the surface soil hydrolyzes into sodium hydroxide. This increases soil pH and clay and humus are dispersed—producing a sodic soil. When leaching with low-ion water is accompanied by the simultaneous addition of excess soluble calcium, the calcium replaces much of the sodium and soluble sodium salts move downward with soluble calcium salts, along with total soluble salts. This is a more desirable reclamation technique for saline-sodic soils (U. S. Salinity Laboratory Staff, 1969).

The reclamation process as developed and advocated by the Central Soil Salinity Research Institute, Karnal, India consists of:

1) Chemical measures consisting of adding gypsum as required according to soil type and mixing the same in surface 10 cm soil depth. Effectiveness of gypsum is enhanced if applied along with farmyard manure.

2) Agronomic and cultural practices such as inclusion of rice crop in the rotation with high density of crop plants, light and frequent irrigation, growing of *dhaincha* in summer as green manure crop, adoption of rice-wheat-*dhaincha* for sodic soil, applying nitrogenous fertilizers in the form of ammonium sulfate in two split doses and application of zinc sulfate.

3) Biological methods including green manuring, addition of organic matter like paddy straw and press mud and continuous growing of crops.

4) Hydro-technical aspects including drainage and proper management of rain water.

10: 7 CROPPING SALINE SOILS

Soils fairly high in total soluble salts can be cropped to *avoid* maximum salt accumulation. Salts always rise from lower soil layers and accumulate in the *center* of raised beds. The technique of avoiding maximum salt accumulation is to plant on one or both sides of raised beds, as detailed in Fig. 10.2.

Field experiments conducted by the Central Soil Salinity Research Institute at Karnal, India (Yadav, 1980) have shown that few species of trees can be grown successfully in alkali soil by treating the soil in the pit with small quantities of gypsum, farmyard manure and fertilizer mixture consisting of 400 gram of ammonium sulphate in two equal spilts, 700 gram of single supersulphate in one dose per plant pit of 90 cm^3.

Growing of some types of forage grasses has also been demonstrated with success by adopting the fertilizer application technique developed by the Institute.

10: 8 SUMMARY

Total soluble salts restrict growth of plants around the world more than any other natural cause. Sodium, calcium, and magnesium chlorides, sulfates, and bicarbonates are the principal salts.

Salt- and sodium-affected soils are classified into saline, sodic, and saline-sodic soils. The criteria for classification are conductivity, pH, and exchangeable sodium percentage.

These three classes of soils can be managed to increase their productivity by: (1) Selecting plants tolerant of salt and/or sodium, and (2) by reclaiming the soils. Plants most tolerant of *both* salt and sodium are barley, crested wheatgrass, and rhodesgrass.

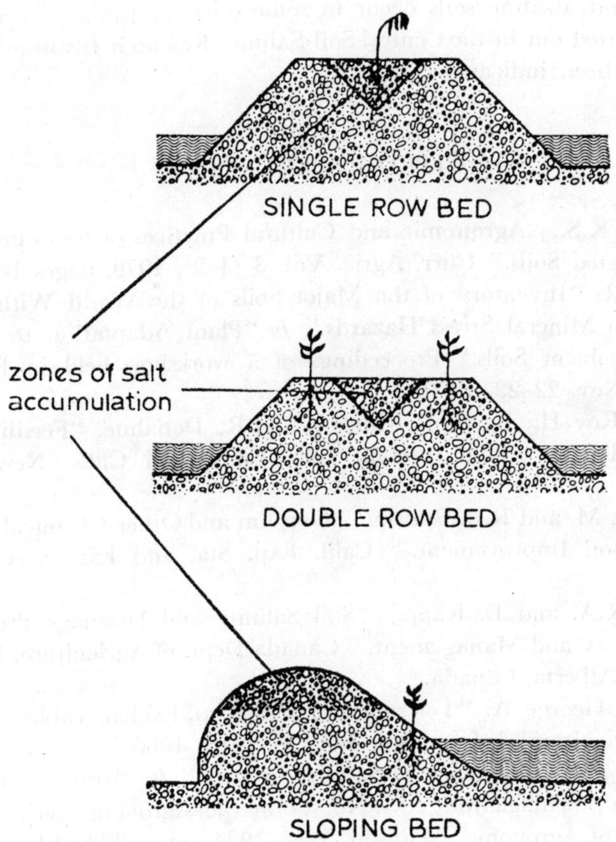

Fig. 10.2. Maximum salt concentration can be avoided by planting crops on one or both sides of raised beds. (*Courtesy:* Texas Vocational Instructional Services for Agricultural Education.)

Saline soil reclamation is relatively simple if the soil is permeable to at least one meter, there is adequate low-ion and low-sediment water, and surface drainage is feasible. The technique consists of ponding to leach salts below the root zone.

Sodic soil reclamation is more difficult because the sodium on the surface exchange complex of clay and humus is not leachable. The sodium ion must be replaced by another cation, usually calcium from gypsum, before it can be leached out of the root zone. Saline-sodic soils require replacement of the adsorbed sodium as well as leaching of the total soluble salts.

Much salt injury can be avoided by planting crops on the sides of raised beds, as salts always accumulate in greater concentration in the *center* of the beds.

Saline and alkaline soils occur in some parts of India. The results of research carried out in the Central Soil Salinity Research Institute, Karnal, India have been indicated.

CITED REFERENCES

Dragon, K.S., "Agronomic and Cultural Practices of Crop Production in Salt Affected Soils." Curr. Agric. Vol. 3 (1–2), 1979, pages 1–20.

Dudal, R. "Inventory of the Major Soils of the World With Special Reference to Mineral Stress Hazards." *In* "Plant Adaptation to Mineral Stress in Problem Soils." Proceedings of a workshop held in Beltsville, Maryland, Nov. 22–23, 1976.

Follett, Roy H., Larry S. Murphy, and R. Donahue. "Fertilizers and Soil Amendments." Prentice-Hall, Inc., Englewood Cliffs, New Jersey, 1981.

Fireman, M. and R.L. Brauson. "Gypsum and Other Chemical Amendments for Soil Improvement." Calif. Exp. Sta. and Ext. Serv. Leaflet 149, 1965.

Milne, R.A. and E. Rapp. "Soil Salinity and Drainage Problems—Causes, Effects, and Management." Canada Dept. of Agriculture, Pub. No. 1314, 1968, Alberta, Canada.

Pearson, George A. "Tolerance of Crops to Exchangeable Sodium." USDA, Agricultural Information Bul. No. 216, 1960.

Rhodes, J.D. "Drainage for Salinity Control." *In* "Drainage for Agriculture," J.V. Schilfgaarde (ed.), No. 17 in the Agronomy series. American Society of Agronomy, Madison, Wis., 1974, pages 433–461.

United States Salinity Staff, Agriculture Handbook No. 60, 1969, U.S. Dept. of Agriculture, Washington, D.C.

Yadav, J.S.P. "Saline, Alkaline and Acid Soils in India and Their Management". Fertilizer News, Vol. 15, No. 9, 1976, pages 15–23.

Yadav, J.S.P. "Efficiency of Fertilizers used in Saline and Alkali Soils for Crop Production." Fertilizer News, Vol. 25, No. 9, Fertilizer Association of India, New Delhi, 1980, pages 19–27.

Yadav, J.S.P. "Reclamation and Crop Production in Alkali Soils." Current Science, Vol. 50, No. 9, 1981, pages 387–393.

ADDITIONAL REFERENCES

Ayers, R.S. and D.W. Westcot. "Water Quality for Agriculture." Irrigation and Drainage Paper No. 29, Food and Agriculture Organization, Rome, Italy, 1976.

Bernstein, Leon. "Effects of Salinity and Sodicity on Plant Growth." Annual Review of Phytopathology, Vol. 13, pages 295–312, 1975.

Bernstein, Leon. "Salt Tolerance of Field Crops." USDA Agriculture Information Bulletin 217, 1960.

Bernstein, Leon. "Salt Tolerance of Grasses and Forage Legumes." USDA Agriculture Information Bulletin 194, 1958.

Bernstein, Leon. "Salt Tolerance of Vegetable Crops in the West." USDA Agriculture Information Bulletin 205, 1959.

Epstein, Emanuel. "Mineral Nutrition of Plants, Principles and Perspectives." John Wiley & Sons, Inc., New York, 1971.

Food and Agriculture Organization. "Prognosis of Salinity and Alkalinity." FAO Soils Bulletin 31, 1976, Rome, Italy.

Index